In Trust for the Nation

# HMS Belfast

1939—1971

by John Wingate, D.S.C.

*With illustrations by*
JAMES GOULDING

Profile Publications Limited
Windsor, Berkshire, England

Other Profile Books

1. Modern US Armored Support Vehicles
2. British and Commonwealth Armoured Formation 1919–1946
3. 79th Armoured Division—Hobos Funnies

Other Famous Profile Bound Volume Series

Warships in Profile: Volume 1
Armoured Fighting Vehicles of the World: Volumes 1–3
Aircraft in Profile: Volumes 1–10
Locomotives in Profile: Volume 1

Warship Profile No. 33: KM *Scharnhorst*

© Copyright John Wingate, D.S.C.
   1972

SBN 85383 083 5

First published in 1972 by
Profile Publications Ltd
Windsor, Berkshire, England

Printed in England by Mears Caldwell Hacker Ltd., London, England

# Contents

# FOREWORD

**by Admiral Sir Frederick Parham, G.B.E., K.C.B., D.S.O.,** *Captain of HMS* Belfast *from 1942–1944.*

I am honoured to be asked to contribute a brief foreword to this book.

I had the immensely good fortune to command HMS *Belfast* during her second commission, in what were, I suppose, the most exacting two years (1942–44) of her long active life, spent largely in the Arctic.

Her designers, builders and re-builders had made her the fine ship that she was (and still is). The officers and men who served in her, and were so proud to do so, made her the efficient and happy ship that she was throughout her successive commissions. In this connection it should, I think, be remembered that during her service in the Second World War a considerable number of her officers and men were not professional sailors: they were R.N.V.R. and 'hostilities only'. It was always amazing to me how quickly they became efficient and reliable and absorbed the spirit of the ship from the Active Service nucleus.

I am sure that this book will be a great success: not only as a careful and accurate account of the ship and her doings, but also in conveying to its readers the pride and love which all who served in HMS *Belfast* felt for her, and their gratitude that she has been preserved for future generations.

FREDERICK PARHAM

**Battle Honours**

| | |
|---|---|
| North Cape 1943 | Normandy 1944 |
| Arctic 1943 | Korea 1950–1953 |

*Off Korea, 23 August 1951. The Union flag is clearly visible on 'A' turret. Note the wind scoops in the scuttles and the Bofors on 'B' turret* (MOD)

# HMS Belfast

by John Wingate, D.S.C.

### LAST of the Dreadnought ERA

*PRO TANTO QUID RETRIBUAMUS* is carved into the wooden scroll beneath the ship's badge of HMS *Belfast*. In the language of the sailor, *"We give as good as we get"*, was a strangely prophetic motto for one of the largest cruisers of the Royal Navy. She suffered grievously but contributed through her experience to far-reaching improvements in Warship design under battle conditions and, when recovered from her wounds, fulfilled her promise with ruthless efficiency.

"Why," visitors to this surviving cruiser from World War II must ask, "Why have we, an island people, chosen this particular ship to be preserved as a memorial of our heritage?"

The answer lies in the list of "firsts" achieved by HMS *Belfast* during her long life of 32 years.

She was:

One of the largest cruisers in the Royal Navy of World War II.

The last big ship to be built of steel withpeace-time specifications.

One of the first ships to capture German prizes in World War II.

The first large warship to be immobilised by Hitler's secret weapon, the magnetic mine.

To act as Flagship longer than most other cruisers.

One of the most heavily damaged ships to survive and fight again.

To undergo one of the longest and most comprehensive refits of any ship during World War II.

One of the last cruisers in the Royal Navy to retain a catapult aircraft.

*HANDSOME FOREBEARS.* Ajax *entering Grand Harbour Valetta, 2.4.46.*  (Naval Photograph Club)

*Leaving Valetta 8.10.45, HMS* Orion. *In the background is that most famous of all merchant ships of World War II: the sunken tanker* Ohio *still lies on the bottom.*
(Naval Photograph Club)

Achilles, *February 1939, leaving Portsmouth. The Nyon Patrol markings on "B" and "X" turrets are easily identified and her catapult is trained on the starboard bow, her Walrus ready for launching.* (Naval Photograph Club)

Manchester, *August 1938, in her Far East colouring.*  (Naval Photograph Club)

To take part in the last capital ship action in the history of the Royal Navy.

Engaged in the first and the last radar-controlled gun action fought by the Royal Navy between big ships.

The Headquarters ship and Flagship off the Normandy beaches, when she spearheaded the attack on D-day.

The first Flagship of the Royal Navy to serve in a World Peace-Keeping Force.

To provide the power of a "fleet-in-being" from Hong Kong during the *Amethyst* incident.

The first warship since HMS *Victory* to be preserved by the nation.

## Cruiser Policy in the Thirties: Re-appraisal

Though the Treaty of Versailles in 1918 had dealt decisively with the vanquished, there were world powers other than Germany jostling for naval supremacy during the post-war years. As a consequence, the exhausted nations of the Great War were resolved to enforce, through the first world organisation of the League of Nations, armament limitations upon the naval powers.

The complexities and evasions that evolved from the various naval treaties and conferences, Washington (1921), Geneva Conference (1927), First London Treaty (1930), resulted finally in the farce of the Second London Treaty of 1936. By this ultimate absurdity, the Royal Navy was fettered by its politicians, whilst Japan, on December 31, 1936, jettisoned all agreements and proceeded to re-arm her navy under a cloak of secrecy.

The 8 in. gun cruiser of the twenties (*Kent, London, Norfolk* and *York* classes) was designed under the restrictions of the naval treaties but these ships were built primarily for the protection of our far-flung sealanes and for troop-carrying. Though these County-class cruisers were of high freeboard and constituted considerable targets, they were armed with the most efficient gun of the day—the high muzzle-velocity 8 in. gun—in twin turrets. Though the machinery was complex and often unreliable, the fire control and long range of the projectile, made the 8 in. gunned cruiser a formidable fighting unit.

The advent of Fascism in the early thirties spawned the Nazism of Hitler's Germany and the aggressive Japanese military machine. So, when Japan contemptuously turned its back upon armament limitations, Royal Naval officers considered carefully their probable adversaries of the future—and, in cruiser strength, particularly the most revolutionary and modern of the Japanese secret building programme: the $15 \times 6$ in.-gunned *Mogami*-class cruiser.

## The Japanese Cruiser Challenge

After modification in 1937, the characteristics of the *Mogami*-class cruiser were:

| | |
|---|---|
| Displacement: | 11,200 tons |
| L.O.A.: | 661½ ft. |
| Beam: | 19¼ ft. |
| Armament, main: | 15 × 6·1 in. guns in triple turrets |
| H.A.: | 4 × 25 mm. twin mountings |
| Torpedoes: | 12 × 24 in. (4 triple tubes) |
| Speed: | 35·6 knots |
| Protection: | |
|   Armour: | 2 in.—inclined and tapered |
|   Bulges: | one each side (1937), two each side (1939/40) |

The British Naval Architects reacted to the challenge of the *Mogami*-class, which, by artificial treaty limitations, constituted a new concept in cruiser thinking. Inevitably, the US Navy reacted immediately also and produced the *Brooklyn*-class (10,000 ton; $15 \times 6$ in.; 32 knots).

## The British Reply

Instead of standing off at extreme range and deliberately picking off the enemy with the 8 in. gun, the proposition was that a fast cruiser, heavily armoured against 8 in. hits, should be able rapidly to close an opponent and smother him with a hurricane of smaller but highly penetrative shells.

The original proposal was for sixteen 6 in. guns in four quadruple turrets and, the politicians being nudged by the spectacle of Hitler across the Channel, included the building of 4 *Southampton* cruisers in the 1933 estimates. No longer was the Royal Navy to be hamstrung by treaty limitations.

## The *Southampton*-class Cruiser

By a Board decision (MFO 192/36), triple turrets were substituted instead of quadruple to compensate for the weight of an increase in the thickness of the deck armour on the same displacement.

The following changes were made to the original *Southampton* design to allow for this extra deck protection:

1. By substituting triple turrets instead of quadruple, it was possible to shorten the 6 in. magazines accordingly.
2. Reducing the length of the magazines made possible the shortening of the ship by 10 ft.
3. The 3-4 in. armoured belt and the deck were shortened at the fore-ends, and the forward 6 in. magazines and shell rooms were protected by internal box armour. The more important control positions were placed under the protection of the armoured belt and in the deck extension forward of the machinery.
4. Protection of the decks, machinery spaces and the forward belt extension was increased from 1½ in. D plating to 2 in. NC plating.
5. The thickness of the deck over the 6 in. shell rooms was increased from 2 in. NC to 3 in. NC plating.
6. The siting of the 4 in. HA mountings was rearranged to avoid blast interference between mountings.
7. The mutiple pom-poms (2-pdrs.) were moved forward to a position clear of blast from the after 6 in. turrets, but the pom-pom would inevitably be exposed to blast from the midship 4 in. HA guns at high angles of elevation.

The *Southampton* was a natural development of the 6,980 ton *Amphion* (twin turrets) and it is interesting to compare characteristics:

| | Amphion | Southampton |
|---|---|---|
| Displacement: | 6,980 tons | 9,100 tons |
| Dimensions: | 530 × 56¾ × 15¾ ft. | 558 × 61¾ × 17 ft. |
| SHP and speed: | 72,000 = 32¼ kt. | 75,000 = 32 kt. |
| Oil Fuel: | 1,800 tons | 1,970 tons |
| Armament: | 4 × twin 6 in. | 4 × triple 6 in. |
| Complement: | 550 | 700 |

## Staff Requirements

1. 9,000 tons.
2. Armoured to withstand a direct hit by 8 in. gunfire.
3. High speed—32 knots.
4. Rapid smothering fire with twelve 6 in. guns.

5. To be able, by intensive air reconnaissance, to cover wide areas of the world's trade routes.
6. A realistic, close range anti-aircraft defence, made possible by the success of the 8-barrelled pom-pom which had been installed in the *Nelson* and *Rodney* since 1927. (The 4-barrelled pom-pom was developed later for cruisers and destroyers).

## The Design Problems
To achieve these requirements, the position of the main machinery, boiler rooms, and the main and secondary armaments were similar to that in the *Amphion*-class:

Boiler room, engine room: boiler room, engine room.

Two turrets forward.

Two turrets aft.

6 in. Director Control Tower—one, above the after end of the bridge.

Catapult and crane—as in *Amphion*.

The air reconnaissance requirement produced the conception of three Walrus amphibians, two to be housed in hangars built into each side of the after bridge structure, and one on an athwartship fixed catapult. It was this innovation which produced the powerful but revolutionary profile of these beautiful ships.

Because of the height of the hangars, an extra deck was added to the bridge island. Funnel fumes had been a severe handicap to the efficiency of bridge personnel and to the fire control team in the main Director Control Tower (DCT), so the foremost funnel was heightened and raked.

The mutiple pom-poms were mounted on top of the hangars but, if a traditional pole mast had been fitted, the attendant stays and shrouds would have "wooded" the guns and seriously restricted the arcs of fire. The solution was the tripod mast, to be seen for the first time in a British cruiser.

Other differences in design from the *Amphion* were that the centre-line HA Director Tower (HADT) was replaced by one in each wing of the lower bridge; and two cranes were sited abreast the after funnel to handle the three Walruses.

## The Three Groups
The *Southampton* class cruisers were divided into three groups, the first two ships of the first group originally being named *Polyphemus* and *Minotaur* after mythological monsters. Happily, these impressive ships, whose unique lines seemed so starkly different, finally adopted the names of the nation's towns and cities, so that the bond was strengthened between the people and their Navy.

**Southampton Class**

| | | |
|---|---|---|
| **1st Group**<br>9,100 tons | 1933 Estimates | *Southampton (ex Polyphemus)*<br>*Newcastle (ex Minotaur)* |
| | 1934 Estimates | *Birmingham*<br>*Glasgow*<br>*Sheffield* |
| **2nd Group**<br>9,400 tons | 1935 Estimates | *Liverpool*<br>*Manchester* |
| | 1936 Estimates | *Gloucester* |

**Edinburgh Class**

| | | |
|---|---|---|
| **3rd Group**<br>10,000 tons | 1937 Estimates | *Belfast*<br>*Edinburgh* |

The common features between all groups were the

*Three great men: Rear-Admiral Burnett, Mr. A. V. Alexander and Admiral Tovey (left to right).* (IWM)

main armament of twelve 6 in. guns in four triple turrets, the torpedo armament of six 21 in. torpedoes in two triple tubes and the four 3-pdr. saluting guns.

The Second Group was slightly larger than the first, having a standard displacement of 9,400 tons:

| | Group I | Group II |
|---|---|---|
| LOA: | 591½ ft. | 591½ ft. |
| Beam: | 61¾ ft | 62¼ ft. |
| Draught: | 17 ft. | 17½ ft. |
| SHP: | 75,000 | 82,500 |
| Speed: | 32 knots | 32½ knots |
| Armour: | Belt 3-4 in. | Belt 3-4 in. |
| | Deck 2 in. | Deck 2 in. |

Improvements included:
(i) shelters for the 4 in. HA guns' crews between the mountings.
(ii) the curve of the forward surface of the bridge structure became semi-circular instead of the flat curve of Group I: estimates of inclination and angle-on-the-bow thereby became more difficult for enemy gunnery officers and U-boat captains.
(iii) a second LA DCT was sited aft on the centre-line.

## The Third Group: *Edinburgh* and *Belfast*
The third group consisted of *Edinburgh* and *Belfast*, the class being named after the former.

Their Lordships' opinion of these two ships is best reflected in a letter from the Naval Constructive Department of January 2, 1940 (six weeks after *Belfast*'s Firth of Forth disaster) to Harland & Wolff who were informed that it was proposed to build repeat *Belfast*s with an extra 2 ft. 6 in. beam on a standard displacement of 10,885 tons. The ships were to be more heavily protected with a deck armour of 4 in. No more was heard of this proposal and it can be presumed that the disasters of the war at sea were soon to overtake the warship building programme.

## Design Stage and Building Programme
| | |
|---|---|
| April 1936 | 6 in. triple gun turrets, Mk. XXIII ordered for 6 in. Mk. XXIII guns (XXII *Southampton*). |
| May 29, 1936 | Design of *Edinburgh*-class approved by Admiralty Board. Both ships to be fitted out as flagships. |
| June 30, 1936 | Hull and machinery tenders invited from John Brown, Fairfield, Scotts, Harland & Wolff, Swan Hunter, Alexander Stevens. |

| September 21, 1936 | Contracts placed: |
| | *Edinburgh*: Swan Hunter. |
| | *Belfast*: Harland & Wolff; |
| | estimated building time, $2\frac{3}{4}$ years. |
| September 1936 | Torpedo tubes ordered. |
| October 16, 1936 | Controller permits increase of 135 tons standard displacement in order to fit a complete $4\frac{1}{2}$ in. armoured belt and a $2\frac{1}{2}$ in. armoured deck between the for'd end of the forward magazine and the after end of the after magazine: Mean draught increased by 21 in.; cost increased by £10,000 per ship. |
| October 26, 1936 | Names, *Edinburgh* and *Belfast*, approved. |
| December 10, 1936 | HMS *Belfast*: keel laid. |
| December 30, 1936 | HMS *Edinburgh*: keel laid. |

## HMS *Belfast* building at Harland & Wolff

Supervision by a ship's officer of the actual construction of a ship is vital for the future efficiency and happiness of a warship's life. It was fortunate for *Belfast*, who was now growing visibly day by day on the slip of the greatest shipbuilder in Ulster, that a man of the calibre of her first Senior Engineer (the "Senior"), Lieutenant (E) Stuart Ferguson RN, was appointed to stand by her.

When Ferguson joined her in October 1937, the ship was on the slip and well advanced: the drums of the boilers were being drilled, the boilers tubed and the turbines bladed. The castings for the main machinery had just arrived from Clyde Alloys and soon the weapons, the main gearing, the diesel generators (she was a DC ship), the catapult (ordered in February 1938) and the many auxiliaries were being accepted from the sub-contractors.

During this spell, Ferguson had forged a very happy relationship with the Yard and the city authorities. By 1939, a sports Olympiad had been held between Harland & Wolff and the ship's stand-by crew; Orange medal ribbons were awarded to selected officers and men, and a beautiful silver ship's bell had been ordered and paid for by public subscription. So valuable was this gift that it was deemed imprudent to go to war with it on board.

## The Ship's Crest

Commander Stuart Ferguson, R.N. (Ret'd) F.I.Mech. E., records how the original design was conceived:

"I recall that the ship was without a crest before the launch, being the first *Belfast* ever (Job No. 1000), and that, having the skeleton of a seahorse I picked up on the shores of Lake Avernus (shades of Agrippa), this idea of a crest was born; particularly as the seahorse appears also in the crest of the City of Belfast.

My drawing was passed from the Admiralty to the College of Heralds who arranged the 'red gorged crown' for the seahorse and presumably had it redrawn; I had a letter back from the Admiralty informing me that the design was accepted with this minor modification. On Trafalgar Day, 1971, I had the seahorse with me and gave it to the Admiral."

(Note: the original seahorse is now in the possession of HMS *Belfast* Trust.)

*Part of the Olympiad against Harland & Wolff, 1939: the cricket match. Sitting: (l. to r.) Lt. Cdr. R. Tosswill, Navigating Officer; Lt.(E.) Stuart Ferguson, Senior Engineer; Lt. Cdr. W. Smith, Torpedo Officer; Captain Cole, H. and W.; The Captain's Secretary; Mr. W. Underwood, H. and W.; Mr. W. Strachan, H. and W.; Commander James Roper, O.B.E., The Executive Officer; Standing: (l. to r.) Paymaster Commander H. G. E. Pertwee, C.B.E.; Commander (E.) F. S. Lister; Lt. (E.) Noel Hunter.*
*(Courtesy Commander S. Ferguson R.N. (Ret'd.))*

## The Launch

*"May God bless her and all who sail in her . . ."* With these hallowed words appropriately pronounced on St. Patrick's Day, March 17, 1938, Mrs Neville Chamberlain, wife of the Prime Minister, sent HMS *Belfast* sliding safely down the ways.

The ceremony was a memorable one, Mrs Chamberlain being presented with a beautiful brooch by the Yard; also at the launching was Lieutenant-Commander Woodroffe, affectionately notorious for his "The Fleet's lit up" broadcast at the Spithead Jubilee Review four years earlier.

## Fitting out and Trials: March 17 to August 3, 1939

The trials proceeded satisfactorily, each department undergoing thoroughly every conceivable test to a standard not again insisted upon during the years of war.

After the guns and gunhouses had been embarked on March 8, basic trials for testing the ship's stability were carried out four days later on March 23, 1939.

On May 23, 1939, the visibility was good, the sea smooth, and the light breeze was north-westerly. At 0915 the ship sailed from Belfast and, after checking her gyro compasses, carried out anchor trials at 1145.

Proceeding to the measured mile range off Greenock, the first full power trial began at 1600: average power for the hour was 78,785 SHP and the mean revolutions 293·5. At 1830 the ship stopped for one and a half hours, having lost oil fuel suction.

During trials the displacement was only 10,410 tons because the 4 in. guns and 6 in. directors had not yet been embarked.

Commissioning ceremony. The Red Ensign is reluctant to be hauled down. (IWM)

Captain G. A. Scott, D.S.O., R.N., her first Captain. The speed flag sockets can be seen on the port guard rails. (IWM)

The four boilers waiting to be installed.

One of the four LP and Astern turbines before assembly.

LP and Astern turbine, bottom half and rotor, port outer.

Cruiser turbine before assembly.

Cruiser turbine with rotor assembled.

HP turbine, bottom half casing.

(All photos. on this page courtesy Commander S. Ferguson, R.N. (Ret'd.))

| Date | Displacement | Trial (revs) | Duration (hrs) | SHP | Speed (knots) |
|------|-------------|--------------|----------------|-----|---------------|
| May 23 | 10410 | 293·5 (full) | 1 | 78785 | 32·1 |
| May 25 | 10170 | 197·1 | 6 | 20090 | 23·36 |
| later date | 10600 | ? | 12 | 63685 | 31·27 |
| May 31 | 10415 | 293·6 (full) | 8 | 81140 | 32·98 |

Finally, the tedious months of painstaking measurements and observations were over; the trials were completed on August 3, the only outstanding main items being the incompleted catapult and trouble with the AITON bends of the boiler room piping.

## Commissioning Day: August 5, 1939

On behalf of the Lords Commissioners of the Admiralty, Captain G. A. Scott, D.S.O., RN, accepted from her builders HMS *Belfast*, who lay at anchor in Belfast Lough. The Commissioning Service was conducted by her chaplain and, after a technical hitch over lowering the Red Ensign, the White Ensign was hoisted for the first time. The Ship's Company of 761 officers and men, who were assembled on the quarterdeck, had taken over a well-built and splendid ship.

### HMS *BELFAST* SPECIFICATIONS

| | |
|---|---|
| Standard displacement: | 11,550 tons |
| Seagoing displacement (deep load): | 13,175 tons |
| With tanks full and all fuel on board, Deep load draught: | 14,325 tons |
| With tanks full and half fuel: | 13,200 tons |
| Length between perpendiculars: | 578 ft. 11⅜ in. |
| Length overall: | 613 ft. 6$\frac{7}{16}$ in. |
| Beam, extreme: | 66 ft. |
| Draught of Water— at standard displacement: | |
| Forward: | 18 ft. 3 in. |
| Aft: | 19 ft. 9 in. |
| Deep load: Forward: | 22 ft. 3¾ in. |
| Aft: | 22 ft. 5¾ in. |
| Number of tons necessary to increase draught by 1 in. in standard condition: | 67·6 tons |
| Moment in tons-feet to change Trim by 1 in. in standard condition: | 2,279 (between draught marks) |
| Oil fuel carried: | 2,256 tons (including diesel oil) |
| Authorised stowage of fresh water for boilers: | 150 tons |
| SHP—full power: | 80,000 |
| Corresponding speed: | 32 knots |
| Type of engines: | Parsons Geared Turbines |
| Makers: | Messrs Harland & Wolff Ltd. Belfast |
| Type of boiler: | Three drum, small tube type superheaters and preheaters |
| Aircraft—number carried: | 2 (designed for 3—one on catapult) |
| Type: | Walrus |
| Catapults: | 1 in No. DIH type; 55·5 knots |
| Makers: | Messrs. Brown Bros. Edinburgh |
| Searchlight Projectors: | 6 |
| | *Height above standard WL* |
| 2 in No. 20 in. | 52 ft. |
| 44 in. after pair | 45 ft. 6 in. (ACP) |
| 44 in. fore pair | 48 ft. (Hangar top) |
| Where built: | Messrs Harland & Wolff Ltd. Belfast |
| Date when: guns ordered: | April 1936 |
| laid down: | December 10, 1936 |
| launched: | March 17, 1938 |
| completed: | August 3, 1939 |
| Protection: | Main belt: 3-4 in |
| | Decks—over magazine: 3 in. |
| | —over machinery, upper and lower decks: 2 in. |
| Armament: | 12 × 6 in. (4 × 3) |
| | 12 × 4 in HA (6 × 2) |
| | 16 × 2-pdr. AA (2 ×8) pom-poms |
| | 8 × ·5 in. AA (2 × 4) |
| | 6 × 21 in. (2 ×3) TT. |
| | 3 aircraft |
| Complement: | 761 |

## The Hull Structure

It was possible to improve *Belfast*'s armoured protection because of the absence of treaty limitations. The longer 4½ in. belt and the additional 2½ in. armoured deck spread across her magazines, added £10,000 to her cost; the improvements required a larger hull—22 ft. longer (bp) and 4 ft. beamier than her predecessors in Group I. In order to restrict the enlargement within bounds, the safety training arcs of the main armament were only 140° on each relative bearing (145° in *Southampton*) so that distances between turrets could be reduced.

There was one other significant difference in design between the first group and *Belfast* which was to have far-reaching results:

In *Southampton* the 4 in. HA magazines were below the guns and were therefore tucked in abaft the after boiler room and engine room.

In *Belfast*, the 4 in. HA magazines, bomb room and small arms magazines were sited below the catapult and between the forward boiler room and the bridge structure. Above the magazines and below the armoured belt were the Transmitting Station (TS) and the fore High Angle Calculating Position (HACP).

Considering the length of the hull, therefore, there was, forward, the combined weights of A and B turrets and the massive bridge structure; aft, the combined weights of the boiler rooms and machinery spaces (total weight 1,507 tons) plus X and Y turrets. These two masses were "hinged" together at the space between the for'd funnel and the aircraft hangar, approximately at section 119.

## Machinery

The original design called for a Shaft Horse Power of 82,500 but in May 1936 the Controller found that propulsion was more efficient at 300 revolutions instead of 330, so the SHP was reduced to 80,000.

*The Propelling Machinery.* The propulsion was of four independent units arranged in two Engine Rooms: outer shafts, for'd ER; inner shafts, after ER.

Each unit consisted of one High Pressure (HP) turbine working in series with a Low Pressure (LP) turbine, each driving through a flexible coupling a pinion which geared to a common wheel coupled to the propeller shafting.

The Astern Turbine was incorporated in the LP turbine.

For economical speeds (20,000 SHP and below), a cruising turbine could be clutched down on the HP turbine by means of a fluid flywheel device.

The main engines were Parsons Geared Turbines, built in April 1938 and designed to operate at maximum working pressure of 300 lb./sq. in. at 250° (superheat).

*Designed Turbine Revolutions.* The main turbines were designed for 3,500 and 2,400 revolutions per minute for the HPs and LPs respectively, at full power of 80,000 SHP total for the four shafts, when the propellers were turning at 300 revs./min.

The cruising turbines were designed for 6,400 revs./min. for the maximum cruising power of 20,000 SHP on all four shafts.

*The Boilers.* In April 1938, four Admiralty Type Three Drum, Water Tube Boilers, built by Harland & Wolff and fitted with superheaters and air preheaters, were installed in A and B boiler rooms.

With a safety load of 350 lb/sq. in., each boiler produced 20,000 SHP: each boiler room, 40,000 SHP. Total SHP, 80,000.

*Consumption, Speeds and Endurance.* In November 1939, the ship carried 2,008 tons of oil fuel. Her fuel expenditure in tons per hour was:

| Speed (Knots) | Cruising Turbine | Main Turbine | Speed (Knots) | Cruising Turbine | Main Turbine |
|---|---|---|---|---|---|
| 8 | 1·95 | – | 21 | 7·3 | 8·2 |
| 9 | 2·05 | – | 22 | 8·2 | 9·1 |
| 10 | 2·2 | – | 23 | – | 10·1 |
| 11 | 2·4 | – | 24 | – | 11·2 |
| 12 | 2·65 | 3·5 | 25 | – | 12·4 |
| 13 | 2·95 | 3·8 | 26 | – | 13·7 |
| 14 | 3·3 | 4·15 | 27 | – | 15·1 |
| 15 | 3·7 | 4·55 | 28 | – | 16·7 |
| 16 | 4·1 | 5·0 | 29 | No data available | |
| 17 | 4·6 | 5·5 | 30 | No data available | |
| 18 | 5·15 | 6·05 | 31 | No data available | |
| 19 | 5·75 | 6·7 | 32 | No data available | |
| 20 | 6·5 | 7·4 | 32·5 | No data available | |

This consumption resulted in the following ranges and speeds:

| | |
|---|---|
| *Maximum speed* (Trials): | 32 knots |
| *Economical speed:* | 13 knots |
| (6 months out of dock, maximum draught, temperate water at 3·8 tons/hr. (106 revs)): | 8664 miles |
| *Maximum speed* with cruising turbines: | |
| Clean bottom: 23 knots at 7·5 tons/hr. = | 6141 miles |
| 6 months out of dock = 22 knots at 8·2 tons/hr. = | 4890 miles |

It is interesting to compare her endurance some twenty years later in 1962, after such an eventful life and after such considerable alteration and rebuilding:

| | |
|---|---|
| *Maximum speed:* | 28 knots |
| *Economical speed* (2 shafts): | |
| 10 knots at 3·0 tons/hr. (104 revs) = | 7350 miles |
| At 13 knots: 5·3 tons/hr. (112 revs) = | 5420 miles |
| *Maximum speed* with cruising turbines: | |
| 6 months out of dock: 20·5 knots at 10·1 ton/hr. = | 4695 miles |

## The Armament

**Main:** 6 in. breech loading, Mark XXIII on Triple Mark XXIII Mounting. Total weight, 615 tons, plus 28 tons for the hoist.

### The Revolving Structure:

Four 6 in. Triple Mark XXIII mountings were fitted in *Edinburgh* and *Belfast* and in ships of the *Fiji* and repeat-*Fiji* classes.

The design of the mounting was very similar to that fitted in *Southampton* except that the turret trunk and magazines stretched down to the double bottom in the hold deck; and that cordite and shell hoists were fitted, on the revolving structure, from the cordite handing room and the shell room, one to each gun in the gun house.

In *Belfast* and *Edinburgh*, the magazine and cordite handing room were on the hold deck; the shell room was on the platform deck level.

The gunhouses were armoured as follows:

| | |
|---|---|
| Gunhouse floor: | 1½ in. D quality plate |
| Shield, side, rear and roof: | 2 in. in NC plate |
| Shield, front: | 4 in. NC plate |

The turret was powered hydraulically from the power pump using special mineral oil.

The trunnions of the centre gun were set back 2 ft. 6 in. abaft the trunnions of the wing guns:

(i) to prevent adjacent guns' crews hindering each other
(ii) to balance better the revolving mass
(iii) to allow the wing projectiles to travel through the air ahead of the centre shell.

This last advantage was fortuitous because it was not until trials were carried out in HMS *Newcastle* at Shoeburyness on October 14 and 15, 1937, that the wild shooting of the triple 6 in. turrets was remedied. Spreads of 700 yd. had been experienced and it was thought that the air currents set up by the wing shells were affecting the centre shell.

Professor Hay, in charge of the trials, thought this cause only partly to blame. He postulated the theory that, because the cordite charge lay in the bottom of the chamber, the resulting explosion tended to exert its force against the top of the chamber, more than upon the bottom and sides. This produced uneven vibrations along the whole gun barrel and sometimes the vibration curve would coincide with the instant that the shell left the muzzle.

Cameras were mounted in the turrets and, by magnetising the shell, the shutters of the cameras were operated as the tube was fired until the projectile left the muzzle.

Results proved that some shells were definitely canted on leaving the muzzle. The solution was to delay by a fraction the firing of the centre gun; this was effected by introducing a slight time delay in the electrical firing circuits.

## The Fixed Structure

There was one shell room, magazine and cordite handing room to each turret.

Shell in the shell room was transferred by hand from the shell bins to the power operated revolving shell ring which accepted two shells, one on each side of the ring and fed by hand into the hoists.

Cordite was passed by hand from the magazine, through the revolving flashlight scuttles to the cordite handing room where it was fed by hand into the cordite hoists.

## Turret Capabilities: Triple Mark 23 Turrets

| | |
|---|---|
| Elevation: | 45°, elevating power or hand. |
| Extreme range: | at 44°—24,800 yd. with 112lb. shell. |
| Training arcs: | 120° on either side of the fore and aft line. |
| Rate of training: | 5°/second (both training engines) 7°/second (one training engine only). Hand training available. |
| Rate of fire: | 8 rounds per gun per minute. |
| Rate of supply: | 10 rounds of shell and 10 of cordite charges per minute. |
| Ramming: | by hand. |
| Breech mechanism: | hand-worked. |

*The Gunhouse.* The turntable floor was three feet below the gunhouse deck. On the underside of the turntable floor was the upper roller path resting on the rollers of the live roller ring.

The local director sight was sited in the fore end of the turret, between the left and centre guns. Alongside were the training receiver and the training control handwheel.

*Auxiliary supply (by hand):*

| | |
|---|---|
| auxiliary cordite: | to the rear and to the left of the centre shell hoists. |
| auxiliary shell hoist: | on the right hand side to the rear of the right hand shell hoist. |

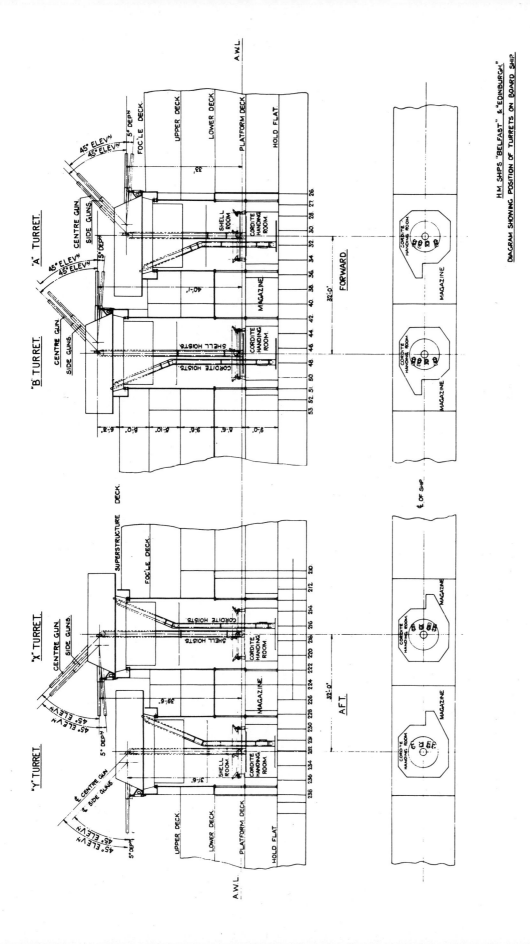

"A" TURRET.

"B" TURRET.

45° ELEV<sup>N</sup>
45° ELEV<sup>N</sup>
5° DEP<sup>N</sup>

CENTRE GUN
SIDE GUNS

FOC'LE DECK.
UPPER DECK
LOWER DECK
PLATFORM DECK
HOLD FLAT

SHELL ROOM
CORDITE HANDING ROOM.
MAGAZINE

SHELL HOISTS.
CORDITE HOISTS.
CORDITE HANDING ROOM.

FORWARD

32'-0"
40'-1"
33'

26 27 28 30 32 34 36 38 40 42 44 46 48 50 51 52 53

5'-2" 8'-0" 8'-10" 9'-6" 6'-6" 9'-0"

A.W.L

CORDITE HANDING ROOM
MAGAZINE

CORDITE HANDING ROOM
MAGAZINE

"X" TURRET.
"Y" TURRET.

CENTRE GUN
SIDE GUNS
₵ CENTRE GUN
₵ SIDE GUNS

45° ELEV<sup>N</sup>
45° ELEV<sup>N</sup>
5° DEP<sup>N</sup>

SUPERSTRUCTURE DECK.
FOC'LE DECK.
UPPER DECK
LOWER DECK
PLATFORM DECK
HOLD FLAT

CORDITE HOISTS
SHELL HOISTS
CORDITE HANDING ROOM.
MAGAZINE.

SHELL ROOM.
CORDITE HANDING ROOM.

AFT

32'-0"
39'-6"
31'-6"

210 212 214 216 218 220 222 224 226 228 230 232 234 236 238

A.W.L

₵ OF SHIP

CORDITE HANDING ROOM
MAGAZINE

MAGAZINE

CORDITE HANDING ROOM
MAGAZINE

H.M. SHIPS "BELFAST" & "EDINBURGH"
DIAGRAM SHOWING POSITION OF TURRETS ON BOARD SHIP

(Courtesy MOD)

13

The Control Officer's turret bearing indicator
(*Author's collection*)

*Left gun of 'A' turret. Note the recoil cylinder below the breech block, and shell loading tray. (Author's Collection)*

Breech mechanism of left gun. Note gun-ready lamps, recoil cylinder, loading tray and cordite supply delivery tubes. *(Author's collection)*

Centre gun, breech mechanism from left hand side, showing loading tray. *(Author's collection)*

View of the centre gun of 'A' turret. The guns' crews adopted their own mascots. The upper end of the cordite hoists and the hoist pedals are visible *(Author's collection)*

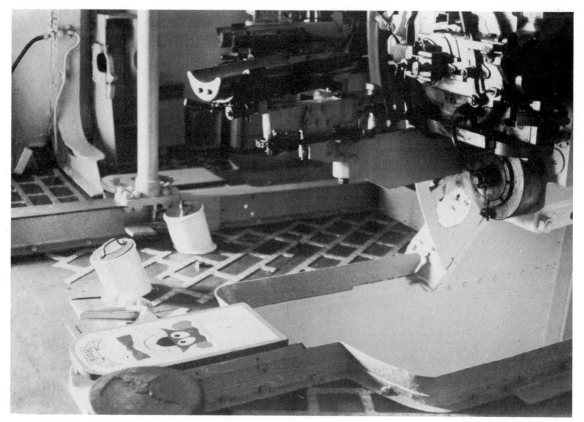

gun wash-out tank:    25 gal. of fresh water at rear of each gun-well.

disposal of cordite containers: through chutes in the rear of the turret.

Officer's Look Out (OLO)

Platform and periscope:    rear of gunhouse.

### The Guns

Twelve 6 in. breech loading, Mark XXIII, of the all-steel type.

weight of projectile:   112 lb.
weight of charge:     30 lb.
elevation:          45°
loading angle:     between 5° depression and $12\frac{1}{2}°$ elevation.

### Elevating

The Layers sat at their local director sights, to the rear of the trunnions, and faced towards the breeches, opposite their director elevation receivers. The guns were elevated by the elevation control levers which operated the elevating motors, the levers returning automatically to neutral if released. Alongside the Layer's foot was the power clutch pedal for engaging power elevating.

### Turret Crew

The turret's crew consisted of 46 men:

| | |
|---|---|
| Captain of Turret | CT |
| Local Sight Layer | LSL |
| Turret Trainer | TT |
| Sightsetter | SS |
| Telephone Operator | TO |
| Three Guns' crews of 7 men each: | |
| Shell Room crew | 9 men |
| The Cordite Handing Room crew | 3 men |
| The Magazine crew | 8 men |

In addition, 1 OA and 2 EMs were allowed per pair of turrets.

*Loading Procedure.* As soon as the gun has fired:

  (i) Layer lays the gun to a loading angle between $12\frac{1}{2}°$ elevation and 5° depression.

  (ii) Breech worker:   opens the breech, inserts fresh tube, masks the vent.

  (iii) Trayworker (No. 5): slides back the guard, swings the gun loading tray into the breech and partly enters the shell into the chamber.

  (iv) Rammers (Nos. 3 and 4):   ram home the shell.

  (v) Cordite Member: (No. 6)   tips the charge from its cardboard case which he is holding on his shoulder into the hands of No. 5.

  (vi) No. 5:   loads the charge through the tray and into the gun; withdraws the tray.

  (vii) No. 2:   closes the breech.

  (viii)   Layer re-lays the gun by director.

  (ix)   as the loading tray is withdrawn, the intermediate tray, which should already be loaded, is released; as it comes down and trues up with the gun loading tray, the shell will slide into it.

*Anti-flash precautions.* Each cordite charge remained in its cardboard container inside an anti-flash metal case, from the magazine to the gunhouse. The whole complex of the shell and cordite supply was flashtight.

The gunwells were watertight to a depth of 12 in.

*Sighting Arrangement.* A local director sight was fitted in a forward compartment between the left and centre guns, watertight sighting ports being provided in the front plate of the gunshield.

In this sighting compartment was the change-over switch from Director to Local Control, the gun-ready lamp indicators, the fire gong, the cease fire bell and the firing pistol.

*Sub-calibre.* A sub-calibre gun was fitted in each gunhouse against the left hand side shield. Sub-calibres were shipped for practice firings to save wear and tear on the guns.

*Spraying and Flooding arrangements.* Spraying of cases in the magazine was through the fire main system, the spraying being operated by rod gearing from inside the magazines, from the handing room and from the flooding cabinet on the upper deck.

Flooding could be achieved through a 7 in. pipe direct from the sea, by opening a flood and a sea valve which could be operated by rod gearing from the magazine handing room, from the lower deck or from the upper deck flooding cabinet.

## HA Armament: 1939

Twelve 4 in. Quick firing Mark XVI* guns on HA Twin Mark XIX mountings.

The HA and close range armament was concentrated aft, where arcs were restricted. This concentration made the ship very vulnerable to hits in this position.

*The Mountings.* Three twin mountings of the extended shield type ($\frac{1}{4}$ in. armour plate) were sited on each side between the for'd funnel and the foremost end of the after superstructure. Blast screens were sited between the mountings.

The guns were mounted in a common cradle; they therefore elevated together but each had its own recoil and run-out arrangements.

*The Guns.* The guns were quick-firing, with breech blocks which moved downward to open: this arrangement allowed for the guns to be placed close together in the cradle, but a large and strong spring was required to close the breech in semi-automatic firing.

*Safety firing gear:* a series of levers actuated by a cam rail fixed to the deck ensured that the firing circuit was broken when the mounting was bearing on a danger arc.

*The Sights* for LA only, but barrage sights fitted at Layer's and Trainer's positions for local barrage fire up to 70° elevation.

*Fuse setting:* fuses were set by the Mark I to III fuse setting machines which were mounted on the outboard side of each gun. Two men worked each machine:

1. followed the fuse setting pointer from the HACP.
2. operated the fuse-cone setting.

Starshell fuses were set by means of a hand fuse-setting key.

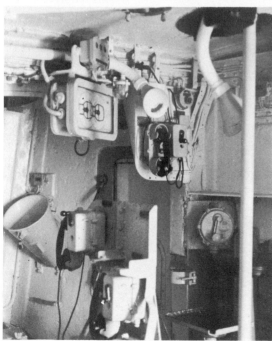

**Top**
*Royal Marine 4 in. guns' crew closed up: the loading numbers are wearing action anti-flash protective headgear and gloves. The breech blocks are open and both loading numbers are in the act of loading the shells. At the left, the next shell for left gun is about to be fused in the fuse-setting machine.* (Belfast Trust)

**Centre**
*Rear view of a 4 in. Seamen's guns' crew. The loading number facing the camera has just grabbed his next shell from the Ready-Use locker.* (Belfast Trust)

**Left**
*The Turret Officer's Control Position.* (Author's collection)

**Below**
*A and B turrets.* (Courtesy Graham Haskell, Esq.)

*The Fo'c'sle Division: Petty Officer Parker   Sub-Lieut. Morrison   Lieut. A. E. Bugle, Divisional Officer   Midshipman R. N. Garnons-Williams   Petty Officer Day*

*Firing arrangements.* Ammunition was fitted with combined electric and percussion primers. The guns were normally fired electrically from the HA Director's Control position or locally by the gun layer's trigger.

## The Close-Range Weapons 1939
1. Two ·5 in. quadruple mountings, one on each side of the hangar top.
2. Two 8-barrelled 2-pdr. quick firing Mark VIII pom-poms on Mark VIA mountings, with cosine sights, sited at superstructure level abreast the mainmast. These mountings had originally been designed to be sited further aft but, by the Board's decision of MFO 192/36, in order to clear the blast from the 6 in., the pom-poms were removed to this new position which would inevitably be exposed to blast from the 4 in. HA at high elevations.
3. Two Vickers GO (Gas Operated) machine-guns.
   For landing parties: $10 \times$ ·303 Lewis for seamen, $6 \times$ ·303 Bren for Royal Marines.

## Main Armament Fire Control
*The Director Control Towers (DCTs).* The 6 in. triple turrets were controlled from the two armoured Director Control Towers, one above the upper bridge, the other on the after superstructure.

A 22 ft. Rangefinder was mounted in the for'd DCT. (In a minute dated January 12, 1940, provision was made for Type 281 RDF+HF/DF equipment to be fitted as soon as precise details, particularly of weights, were known.)

The DCTs could be trained through 190° on either side, both power-operated and in hand.

The DCT consisted of two compartments, the front and rear, the front being below the rear. The following instruments were sited as follows:

*Front Compartment:*
Gyro Sight for Layer and Trainer
Director Setting Unit
Director Training Unit
Cross Levelling Unit
TIC Unit (Time Interval Compensating)
Evershed Target Bearing Indicator
Dial Sight Unit
Voice Pipes to Control Officer.

The following personnel manned the front compartment:
Director Layer, Director Trainer, Cross Levelling Operator, Auxiliary Trainer.

*Rear Compartment:*
Control, Rate and Spotting Officers' binoculars
Rangefinder unit, with air-disturbing, desiccating and window-cleaning units
Range indicators from TS
Deflection indicators from TS
Fire gong
Spotting Lamp Box
Voice pipes to Director, Layer, Trainer, and to Bridge
Telephone to Bridge Plotting Room.

The rear compartment was manned by:
The Control Officer (a Lieutenant-Commander)
The Rate Officer
The Spotting Officer
The Inclinometer operator

The W/T operator
The Rangetaker.
*Note:*
The Action Station of the Principal Control Officer was with the Captain on the bridge, whence the PCO directed the ship's gunnery armament.

For bombardment purposes, he transferred his position to the Action Plot.

## The Transmitting Station (TS)
The Main Armament Transmitting Station was sited immediately above the 4 in. HA magazine and was therefore protected by the main armoured belt and by the armoured deck.

In this compartment was the calculating machine—The Admiralty Fire Control Table—which converted the range and bearing received from the Director Control Towers into gun elevation and gun training. These two components were then transmitted electrically direct to the guns and turrets.

The Gunlayers, as soon as their own pointers and those of the Turret Trainers were following the pointers of their Director receivers, made their interceptor switches. As soon as the gun-ready lamps from two turrets glowed in the DCT, the Director Gunlayer squeezed his trigger and *Belfast's* broadside fired.

At Action Stations, the TS was manned by the Royal Marines, the TS Officer being in charge of this vital compartment which, apart from the drill of crisp orders and reports, was notable for its silence.

## The Admiralty Fire Control Table (AFCT)
Centrally in the TS stood the Admiralty Fire Control Table Mark VI, No. 18, a mechanical calculating machine.

Fed with data from the Fore DCT and the After DCT, the main function of the table was to produce continuous gun elevation and gun training and to transmit these readings to the turrets. The main armament could therefore be controlled from either DCT; divided control was also possible, the Fore DCT controlling the forward turrets; the After DCT, the after turrets.

To achieve this object, the table carried out the following:
(i) Applied the range and deflection corrections: dip, height of target, cross levelling and convergence
(ii) Calculated: gun range
gun deflection
(iii) Converted: range into gun elevation through the Range-to-Elevation Unit
(iv) Included arrangements for indirect fire and concentration of fire
(v) Through Magslip power transmission, transmitted gun elevation and gun training direct to the receivers in the turrets.

## Admiralty Fire Control Clock (AFCC)
Off this main TS compartment was an adjacent annexe which contained the *Admiralty Fire Control Clock (Mark VI).* Also manned by the Royal Marines, it was a smaller edition of the AFCT and transmitted gun elevation and gun training to only the after turrets. Fed with information from the after DCT, but unlike the forward DCT, the AFCC could not be used for indirect fire or for concentration of fire.

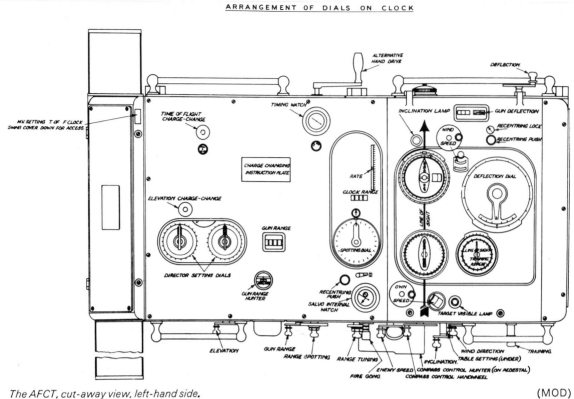

*The AFCT, cut-away view, left-hand side.*

(MOD)

*The AFCT, cut-away view, right-hand side.*

(MOD)

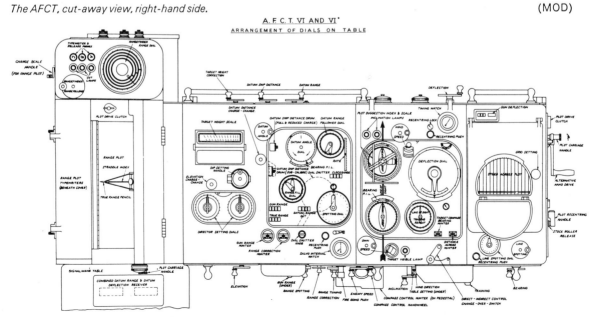

## A.F.C.T. VI AND VI*
### ARRANGEMENT OF DIALS ON TABLE

*Bombardment:* The Bombardment Director was in the TS and was associated with the AFCC.

*The Main Armament Blind-Fire Barrage Directors:* Four Barrage Directors which served the 6 in. turrets were sited, two each side of the lower bridge, and two abreast the after superstructure. They covered all sectors of arc from 0°-360°.

## High Angle Control System (HACS)

The 4 in. HA armament was controlled by the High Angle Control System, Mark IV.

The HACS comprised:

Two sided-HA Director Towers (HADT) on the lower bridge, forward.

One centreline HA Director Tower on the after superstructure.

One HA Calculating Position (HACP) forward, next to and for'd of the TS, and protected by the armoured belt.

One HA Calculating Position, port side aft, abaft the after Engine Room and protected by the armoured belt.

*The HA Calculating Positions (HACPs).* Either the Starboard Battery, S1, S2, S3, or the Port Battery, P1, P2, P3, could be controlled though the Fore HACP by the port and starboard HADTs.

Either battery could also be controlled through the After HACP by the After HA Director.

*The HA Director Towers (HADTs).* All three HADTs were fitted with 15 ft. UD4 height finders on MR7 anti-vibration mountings. The HA Directors could be cross-connected through a system of change-over switches.

*Starshell and Bombardment.* The 4 in. armament was used to fire starshell in order to illuminate a surface target for the main armament.

The 4 in. armament had no Surface Fire Control Clock, so the HACS had to be used. During the Korean War direct bombardments were carried out with the 4 in. armament using the HACS, but the results were not very accurate:

Port HACT (lower bridge) Mountings P1, P2.

After HACT (after superstructure) Mountings S1, S2.

through the respective HACPs (TSs) port and starboard (not aft).

*Pom-Pom Fire Control.* The Pom-pom directors were sited on each side of the after superstructure, forward of the after HACT and on shielded platforms at a level above the 44 in. searchlight projectors. Each director controlled its own multiple pom-pom, training and elevating receivers being fitted at the mounting which could be worked either in power (hydraulic by VSG pump) or in hand.

*Enemy Bearing Indicator (The Captain's Sight).* Mounted on a pedestal on each side of the bridge. The Captain's binocular position was linked to the 6 in. and 4 in. Director Towers and so to the Fire Control Systems.

## Ammunition Supply: Main Armament

*6 in. shell per gun:*

| | |
|---|---|
| HE, AP or SAP | 200 |
| Practice, low angle | 34 |
| high angle | 2·5 |

*Stowage:* shell — Turret shell rooms

Cordite (flashless) — Turret magazines

*Supply:* mechanical hoists in turret trunks.

## Secondary Armament

*4 in. HA shell per gun*

| | |
|---|---|
| fused shell | 250 |
| Practice HA | 65 |
| Practice LA | 4 |
| Target smoke | 4 |

*Note:* 200 4 in. Starshell (flashless cordite) *per ship* was the total illumination outfit, i.e. 12·5 rounds per gun.

*Stowage:* 4 in. magazines forward of A Boiler Room. Ready Use (RU) lockers at mountings on the upper deck.

*Supply:* From 4 in. HA magazines up the two Duplex hoists to the two anti-flash hatches on the catapult deck just aft of where the Walruses were ready for launching. Then, via the rails of the "Scenic Railway" as it was irreverently termed, to Ready Use lockers at the rear of each mounting: this arrangement was a failure and a grave disadvantage in battle conditions, for the ammunition was very exposed along the upper deck.

## Close Range Weapons (AA)

*Pom-poms:* 2,500 rounds per barrel—40,000 rounds total.

*Stowed:*

(i) in pom-pom and ·5 in. magazine, sited beneath the main central store, below the armoured deck and next to "B" 6 in. magazine.

(ii) belted ammunition in ready-use lockers between the mainmast tripod legs on the pom-pom gun deck.

*·5 in. machine-guns:* 2,500 rounds per barrel—20,000 rounds total.

*Stowed:*

(i) in pom-pom and ·5 in. magazines.

(ii) in RU lockers at the guns.

*Vickers Gas Operated (GO) ·303 in.:* 5,000 rounds in pans and in Small Arms Magazine below armoured deck and forward of the bomb room which was adjacent to the 4 in. magazine.

*Lewis and Brens:* variable amount of ·303 in. in portable boxes in small arms magazine.

*Saluting guns:* landed on outbreak of hostilities.

*Sub-Calibre:* 140 rounds per parent gun, plus 1,680 fused for practice.

*Note:* The 4 in. magazine, the Bomb Room, Small Arms, pom-pom and ·5 in. magazines were all able to be flooded from various positions, including from flooding cabinets on the upper deck.

## Torpedo Department

*Torpedoes:* 6- 21 in. Mark IV torpedoes were carried in the triple TR 21 in. Mark IV* torpedo tubes mounted on the upper deck in the waist on each side. No spare torpedoes were carried.

Torpedo Warhead Room: Stb'd side, platform deck, abreast "X" barbette. Torpedo control sights were mounted, one on each side of upper bridge.

*Searchlights:* 44 in. Four stabilised Mark VII searchlights, two on after control deck, two in wings of hangar top, controlled from stabilised sights at the four searchlight control positions on the upper bridge. Six

Belfast *fires her torpedoes during exercises.*
*(Courtesy: Cdr. S. Ferguson RN (Ret'd))*

*Recovery of practice torpedo by second whaler. Note the calcium flare burning in the practice head.*
(Courtesy of B. H. Palk, R.M. Retired)

air look-out sights, three each side, were abreast the S/L control positions.

*20 in:* Signalling Projectors—four, two on top of for'd 40 in. S/Ls, two on lower bridge.

*Paravanes:* Four paravanes "S", Mark I, were stowed, two on each side of the forward superstructure deck. In wartime, the PV clump and bow chains were to be permanently rigged on the fitting at the forefoot. The 3 ton PV derricks were sited between each paravane and the towing wire was 100 fathom of special eight-yarned, three-stranded, cable laid, serrated wire rope which had a life of 100 towing hours. "G"-type cutters were used for severing the mine mooring wire.

*Depth Charges:* 6 in rails; spares on port quarter of quarterdeck.

### Navigational Department: 1939

*Equipment:* Pitometer log in compartment between small arms and pom-pom magazine; one Walker log for emergency use.

Type 758N Echo-sounder—Chart House D/F Set (FCI) in D/F Office. 60 Khz.-20 Mhz. Designed 1928/ 31.

*Radar:* Nil.

*Compasses:* Two Pattern 1015 Admiralty Gyro Compasses and an AGTU for smoothing the outputs from the Master Compass to the Fire Control Systems. One Brown B Gyro Compass, with no repeats, in Wheelhouse as stand-by steering compass.

No magnetic compass, but it is interesting to note that a requirement for a portable magnetic compass was requested in 1947, but not approved.

*Action Plot:* ARL table in Bridge Plotting Office on lower bridge. Ship's speed and true compass headings were fed automatically into the Table.

*Ship Handling:* With considerable power and with her four propellers, *Belfast* handled excellently. Being heavy, she took some stopping and, having a quick roll, tended to be wet. There was a noticeable difference in acceleration when four boilers were connected, in contrast to two and, when manoeuvring, she was slow to turn. She made little leeway and was beautifully balanced, never yawing at anchor. Six revs. were added to maintain speed when paravanes were streamed.

*Propellers:* Outboard turning when proceeding ahead. 11 ft. 3 in. dia., pitch 13 ft. 9 in. Made by J. Stone & Co. Ltd. Weight: 6·82 tons.

*Rudder:* Single, balanced, of 207 sq. ft. surface.

### Communications Department: 1939

*V/S:* The primary means of inter-ship communication was Visual (V/S): by flag hoists (blue masthead light at night) or by 20 in. Signalling Projectors.

*W/T:* W/T silence was the norm but for transmitting and receiving the W/T aerials were as shown in 1939 rigging diagrams.

*Transmitters:* Were of bulky design and inefficient in terms of power and frequency stability. All communication was in Morse: setting the frequency was a laborious procedure. The main use was long distance ship-to-shore.

*Receivers:* Straight receivers and only one LF/MF Superhet receiver fitted. Frequency stability was poor and constant attention to controls was essential.

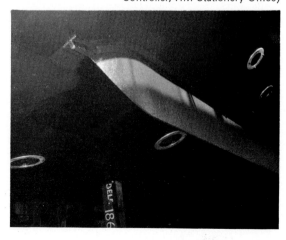

Top left
Her port propellers before scrubbing and anti-fouling. The "A" brackets have already been painted. A post-war photograph, August 1969.
(Crown copyright, reproduced by permission of the Controller, HM Stationery Office)

Top right
Her four propellers looking forward. Note the two men beneath the port propellers for size comparison, August 1969.
(Crown copyright, reproduced by permission of the Controller, HM Stationery Office)

Centre left
From her bottom looking upwards at the ship's side. An unusual view of the bulge and armour, August 1969.
(Crown copyright, reproduced by permission of the Controller, HM Stationery Office)

Bottom right
Starboard bilge keel and hull openings, August 1969.
(Crown copyright, reproduced by permission of the Controller, HM Stationery Office)

Centre right
In dry dock; her balanced rudder.
(Crown copyright, reproduced by permission of the Controller, HM Stationery Office)

This profile line drawing depicts H.M.S. Belfast in her as-built configuration. Note that the only close-range weapons carried were quadruple ·5 inch mountings on each lower bridge wing and the 2 eight-barrelled Pom-poms each side on the Pom-pom deck, abreast the mainmast.

In appearance her rig is clean, carrying only signal halyards, yard braces and W/T aerials.

*(Courtesy Alan Raven, Esq.)*

*Remote Control Office:* The radio circuits could be controlled from the RCO which contained no equipment and which was sited on the lower bridge, abaft the Plotting Office.

*Internal Communication:* Pneumatic tube between offices, voice pipes, sound powered telephones, "S" Buzzer line (morse key, telephone earpieces and oscillation linked all signal offices; communication was brief and swift).

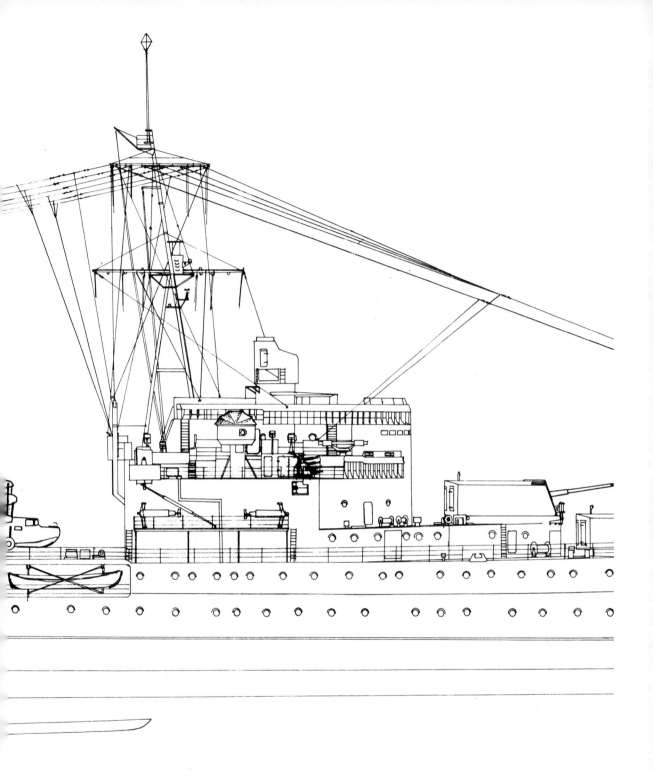

*Aerials:* These were the responsibility of the W/T Staff.

*Rigging:* The Ship's rigging throughout her life is listed on p.112.

All transmitting aerials were of wire construction terminating in deck insulator groups. *Transmitting aerials:* via appropriate trunking to transmitter rooms.

*Receiving aerials:* to aerial exchange board ED. *(ED—*

catered for 10 aerials, 12 receiving bays providing flexibility in aerial selection.)

The W/T staff were responsible for the maintenance of the new equipment, Type Wa/T 405, which was designed:

(a) to transmit an alarm note

(b) to transmit speech, bugle calls etc.

(c) to transmit local signals, by means of radio gramophone etc; no preliminary call was fitted. It was intended that the pipe "d'ye hear there?" should be used in lieu.

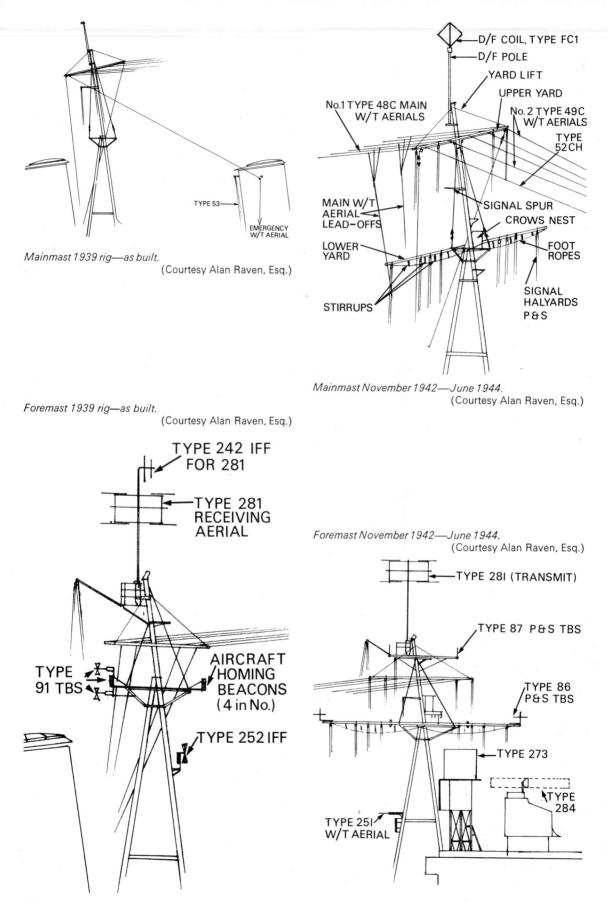

Mainmast 1939 rig—as built.
(Courtesy Alan Raven, Esq.)

No.1 TYPE 48C MAIN
W/T AERIALS

TYPE 53

EMERGENCY
W/T AERIAL

D/F COIL, TYPE FC1

D/F POLE

YARD LIFT

UPPER YARD

No. 2 TYPE 49C
W/T AERIALS

TYPE
52 CH

SIGNAL SPUR

CROWS NEST

MAIN W/T
AERIAL
LEAD–OFFS

LOWER
YARD

FOOT
ROPES

STIRRUPS

SIGNAL
HALYARDS
P & S

Mainmast November 1942—June 1944.
(Courtesy Alan Raven, Esq.)

Foremast 1939 rig—as built.
(Courtesy Alan Raven, Esq.)

TYPE 242 IFF
FOR 281

TYPE 281
RECEIVING
AERIAL

Foremast November 1942—June 1944.
(Courtesy Alan Raven, Esq.)

TYPE 281 (TRANSMIT)

TYPE 87 P&S TBS

TYPE
91 TBS

AIRCRAFT
HOMING
BEACONS
( 4 in No.)

TYPE 86
P&S TBS

TYPE 252 IFF

TYPE 273

TYPE
284

TYPE 251
W/T AERIAL

26

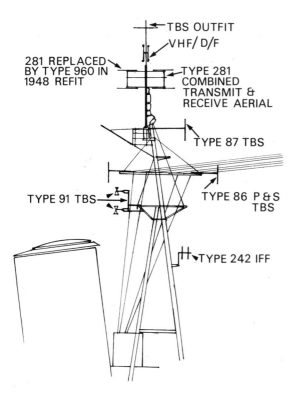

TBS OUTFIT

VHF/ D/F

281 REPLACED
BY TYPE 960 IN
1948 REFIT

TYPE 281
COMBINED
TRANSMIT &
RECEIVE AERIAL

TYPE 87 TBS

TYPE 91 TBS

TYPE 86 P & S
TBS

TYPE 242 IFF

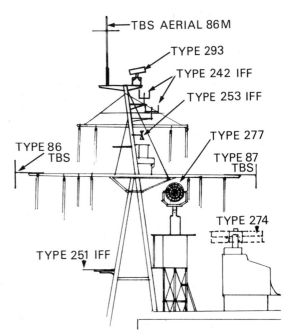

TBS AERIAL 86 M

TYPE 293

TYPE 242 IFF

TYPE 253 IFF

TYPE 86
TBS

TYPE 277

TYPE 87
TBS

TYPE 274

TYPE 251 IFF

*Mainmast post 1945 period.* (Courtesy Alan Raven, Esq.)

*Foremast post 1945 period.* (Courtesy Alan Raven, Esq.)

*Centre left*
*Her foremast, 1971.*
(Crown copyright, reproduced by permission of the
Controller, HM Stationery Office)
*Bottom left*
*274 Radar aerial on after DCT.*
(Courtesy Graham Haskell, Esq.)
*Bottom right*
*The mainmast, 1971, showing radar, D/F, TBS and IFF.*
(Author's collection)

Starboard hawse-pipe, safety strop in position.
(Courtesy Graham Haskell, Esq.)

Port cable-holder: note sockets for capstan bars.
(Courtesy Graham Haskell, Esq.)

*Anchors and Cables.* Three stockless anchors, two bower and one sheet, and each weighing 110 cwt., were originally carried. In June 1943, the sheet anchor was landed to reduce weight and its hawse-pipe blanked over. There were 425 fathoms of cable of $2\frac{1}{8}$ in. dia. Forged Steel Admiralty Quality to each anchor.

One stocked kedge anchor, weighing 16 cwt. was also carried.

*The Ship's Boats: 1939.* The ship's boat complement changed throughout her life, as did her Carley Float outfit which, combined with the boats, were capable of accommodating her war complement, when she carried 30 floats.

| No. | Length | Type | Engine H.P. | Capacity |
|-----|--------|------|-------------|----------|
| 1 | 35 ft. | Admiral's Barge fast MB Vosper | 65/100 | 46 |
| 1 | 35 ft. | Fast MB Vosper | 65/100 | 46 |
| 1 | 36 ft. | Motor and pulling pinnace | 20 | 76 |
| 1 | 25 ft. | Fast MB | 65/100 | 30 |
| 1 | 32 ft. | Cutter | | 59 |
| 2 | 27 ft. | Whaler | | 54 |
| 1 | 16 ft. | Motor dinghy (skimming dish) | 24/48 | 12 |
| 1 | 14 ft. | RNSA dinghy | | 10 |

## The Asdic Compartment: 1939

The Asdic compartment was adjacent to the armoured belt on the port side of the platform deck, for'd of "A" turret. A Type 132 set was installed initially, the Asdic officer (later TAS) and operator working in the Asdic office on the hangar top, next to the chart house.

## Lower Bridge Rangefinders

One 12 ft. U.K. 1 Rangefinder on a Type MS 21 anti-vibration Bridge Mounting was fitted on each side of the lower bridge. These instruments were for tactical and general uses; rubber face-pieces were fitted for use when wearing anti-gas respirators.

## The Flying Department: 1939

The original allocation of aircraft was one Swordfish and two Blackburn Roc fighters, but on November 30, 1938, the Controller stipulated that two Walrus* amphibians were to be carried, one in each hangar.

The catapult was type D1H costing £18,475, and mounted athwartships.

Two cranes were mounted abreast the for'd funnel for recovery of aircraft and loading torpedoes.

The aircraft were loaded on to the catapult by means of a turn-table trolley which ran on a rail leading from each hangar to the catapult.

The hangars were fitted with overhead sprayers for fire-fighting.

Aviation spirit for the two Walruses was stowed in the petrol compartment between both the Asdic compartment and the cable locker.

## The Ship's Complement: 1939

The ship was designed as a flagship and, on commissioning, the authorised war complement was as follows:

| | Flagship | Supernumerary Accommodation available | Private ship |
|---|----------|----------------------------------------|--------------|
| Wardroom | 37 | 13 | 24 |
| Gunroom | 7 | – | 7 |
| Warrant Officers | 13 | 3 | 10 |
| Messmen | 2 | 2 | – |
| CPOs and Men in enclosed messes | 188 | – | 160 |
| Ratings in broadside messes | 634 | – | 580 |
| Total | 881 | 18 | 781 |

It is interesting to note the numbers in later years:

| | | |
|---|---|---|
| **1953** | 974 | 930 |
| **1961** | 886 | 862 |
| **1962** Peace complement | 582 | 542 |

---

*See Aircraft *Profile No. 224*.

*The HMS* Belfast *Flight, 700 Squadron. The Flight Commander, Lt.-Cdr. Tom Sargent RNR, is seated in the centre.*
(Courtesy Lt.-Cdr. T. Sargent)

*The flight deck, HMS* Belfast. *In the foreground is the trolley in position on the catapult. A Walrus, wings folded, is visible in the starboard hangar.*
(Courtesy Lt.-Cdr. T. Sargent)

(a)

Right, centre and bottom                                    (d)
Catapult trials, Scapa Flow, January 1943.
(i)   The Launch: *The hydraulically-operated extension of the catapult can be seen in the extended position. Note the covered single Oerlikon.*
(ii)  Hooking on. *The bearing-off spar is held at the ready.*
(Courtesy Lt.-Cdr. T. Sargent)

*An Accident to the Walrus because the tripping lever was left engaged: May 1943. The trolley is clearly visible.*
(a)   Immediately after the mishap.
(b)   The trolley mechanism.
(c)   The damage.
(d)   Manhandling the aircraft.

(Courtesy Lt.-Cdr. T. Sargent)

(b)

(i)

(c)

(ii)

*Walrus cockpit.*　　　　　(Courtesy Lt.-Cdr. T. Sargent)　　*Walrus W/T Set.*　　　　　(Courtesy Lt.-Cdr. T. Sargent)

*The Walrus nearly airborne in Hvalfjord.*　　　　　(Courtesy Captain Parham)

*The Warrant Officers.* (Courtesy Captain Parham)

*S.E. of Iceland, 1943.* (Courtesy Captain Parham)

*Bottom left*
*The fo'c'sle and bridge in arctic conditions: note the concentration of instruments inside the bridge.*
(Courtesy Captain Parham)

*The Fleet Mail Office, Scapa Flow, January 1943. Belfast's bin shows at far right.* (IWM)

## A Fine Ship: August 3, 1939

This, then, was the ship, the final accomplishment after 3½ years of teamwork from the Naval Staff, the Naval architects, the Constructive Department and Harland & Wolff, the builders.

Now there were a few weeks of working up, gunnery, torpedo and flying exercises. The ship was shaking down and was beginning to sense her identity when, at long last, she joined the Fleet; on August 3, 1939 she left Belfast and sailed for Portsmouth where, two days later, she began her useful life by proceeding to Portsmouth and joining the Second Cruiser Squadron, Home Fleet *(Southampton* and *Glasgow)*, whose base was shortly to be at the Humber.

Work had still to be completed on the catapult but, just as the missing parts were due to arrive, the ship was ordered to sail on August 14 to take part in an exercise, Operation *Hipper.*

*Belfast* represented a German cruiser *(Hipper)* whose rôle was to break out as a commerce raider into the Atlantic off Iceland. The ship proceeded to a point off Heligoland where the exercise began (a German aircraft photographed her) under conditions of W/T silence.

*Belfast* proceeded to a position on an imaginary latitude half-way up Scotland when Admiralty simulated a report to the Home Fleet of an escaping German raider.

With considerable skill, Captain Scott took his ship under cover of darkness through the dangerous waters of the Pentland Firth, thereby escaping the search of the Home Fleet and succeeding in achieving his object. This success had considerable effect on the morale of the ship's company and helped quickly to weld *Belfast* into an efficient and happy unit.

On passage back to Portsmouth to complete the catapult, the ship was abreast East Anglia when the drums of war began to rumble across the North Sea. *Belfast* was ordered to reverse course and to proceed to Invergordon where, during that fateful Sunday forenoon, the voice of the Prime Minister, Mr. Neville Chamberlain, quietly informed messdecks and Wardrooms that the nation was at war.

**"MOST IMMEDIATE"**

To: All concerned Home and Abroad
From: Admiralty

Commence Hostilities at once with Germany

|  |  |  |  | 1117/3 |
|---|---|---|---|---|
| W/T | CTC | Ci | TOR 1140 | 3/9/39 |

## September 3, 1939: War. Northern Patrol

On August 31, 1939, *Belfast* had transferred to the 18th Cruiser Squadron which comprised *Aurora*, flying the flag of Rear-Admiral (Destroyers), *Sheffield* and *Edinburgh*, the squadron operating from the Home Fleet base at Scapa Flow in the Orkneys.

From this bleak and cheerless anchorage—the notoriety of which still cast nostalgic gloom in the minds of those officers who recalled the Grand Fleet and its long sojourn in Scapa—the Home Fleet and its attendant Cruiser Squadrons and Destroyer Flotillas began to exercise its power. The Fleet was at sea when war was declared, its ships having taken up their war stations on August 31, 1939.

Immediate patrols were set up to institute the blockade of Germany and *Belfast,* after picking up at Scapa Flow the missing parts for her catapult (the ship's staff were later to complete the difficult work in Loch Ewe), carried on with the routine chore of a patrolling cruiser in wartime.

On September 8, 1939, in company with *Hood, Renown* and *Edinburgh*, she formed part of the patrol line between Iceland and the Faroes, the object being to destroy enemy raiders trying to break out into the Atlantic and to control contraband by seizing enemy shipping attempting to slip back to Germany. After refuelling and storing at Sullom Voe in the Shetlands on November 15, she returned three days later to patrol, returning to Scapa on September 20.

HM Submarine *Spearfish* was badly damaged off the Horn Reef and on September 24 signalled that she could not dive. Commander-in-Chief Home Fleet, Admiral Sir Charles Forbes, sent the 2nd Cruiser Squadron *Southampton, Glasgow, Sheffield* and *Aurora*, with six destroyers of the 7th Destroyer Flotilla, to protect her and escort her back to Rosyth. The 18th Cruiser Squadron covered this successful operation, this event providing *Belfast* with her first taste of high level bombing from 12,000 ft.

*Norfolk, Newcastle* and *Suffolk* augmented the 18th Cruiser Squadron on September 6 and 15 and replaced *Edinburgh* who was sent to join the 2nd Cruiser Squadron at the Humber.

## Prize Capture

On October 1, 1939, *Belfast* had again left Scapa for the Northern Patrol where, on October 9 at teatime she intercepted in misty weather, 50 miles north-west of the Faroes, the German liner *Cap Norte* (13,615 tons) of the Hamburg Sud-America line. She was disguised as a Swede and was carrying a false name, SS *Ancona;* she had sailed from Pernambuco with German reservists on September 21 and was bound for Germany. Under the protection of her guns, *Belfast's* boarding party pulled swiftly over in the cutter, thereby successfuly preventing *Cap Norte's* engine room crew from opening her sea-cocks. The Boarding Officer, a bearded Lieutenant-Commander named Seal, mounted the bridge formally to capture the ship from her captain. Seal was slightly nonplussed, however, when the German Master offered him a razor. From then onwards, all the Wardroom in *Belfast* grew beards, the last two officers finally to succumb to the craze being her Commander, Commander John Roper, and Lieutenant (E) Stuart Ferguson, her Senior Engineer from her earliest days.

Two other ships were captured that day and, under charge of *Belfast's* prize crews, were steamed independently for Scapa whence *Belfast* also proceeded, having been somewhat depleted of her ship's company.

**FROM THE LOG**
**HMS** *Belfast*—**October 9, 1939—at sea**

| | |
|---|---|
| 0800 | Latitude 63° 51′N   Longitude 07° 35′W |
| | *Wind: ESE Force 4* |
| | *Weather and visibility: blue skies, seven miles* |
| 0800 | A/C to MLA (Mean Line of Advance) 263° Std 4 in. Defence Watch closed up |
| 0854 | Sighted steamship bearing 278° Co SE |
| 0900 | Courses and speeds as requisite for closing ship |
| 0915 | Ordered SS *Tai Yin* to stop |
| 0946 | Armed guard boarded |
| 1102 | SS *Tai Yin* ordered to Kirkwall |

1104  Sighted liner bearing 300°. Closed as requisite. Ordered SS *Ancona* (Swedish) to stop. Ship was found to be SS *Cap Norte* (German)
1210  Strong armed guard boards
1313  2nd armed guard left ship and boarded
1347  *Cap Norte* proceeded
1354  Proceeded. Course 105° 15 knots.

A quick visit to Glasgow for treatment to her main inlet and outlet water pipes, which were suffering from a peculiar wastage of copper, and *Belfast* returned to the Home Fleet Base at Scapa Flow.

## Loss of *Royal Oak*: October 14, 1939

The dithering of peace-time politicians, in spite of constant naval pressure to safeguard Home Fleet bases, was the direct cause of the disaster which occurred during the night of October 14, 1939. Korvettenkapitän Prien in *U-47* proved conclusively that Scapa was insecure: he skilfully slipped through the barrage of sunken ships in Kirk Sound and entered the main anchorage of Scapa. He torpedoed and sunk with terrible loss of life the battleship *Royal Oak* and then proceeded calmly to return the way he had come. Also in Scapa that night was *Belfast* and the 18th Cruiser Squadron.

The next morning, the Commander-in-Chief moved the Home Fleet to Port A, the fleet anchorage at Ault Bea, so hurriedly and recently prepared in Loch Ewe. The lack of success of German air attacks on the Home Fleet bases, however, had caused the Home Fleet to use also Rosyth in the well defended Firth of Forth.

From October 16 until 21, *Belfast* accompanied *Nelson*, *Rodney*, *Hood*, *Furious*, *Aurora* and ten destroyers to the Northern Patrol in order to cover our armed Merchant Cruisers. Further patrolling continued from Port A until October 24 when *Belfast* visited the Clyde for docking and repairs until November 6.

The ship was then taken off the Northern Patrol to join on November 10 the 2nd Cruiser Squadron consisting of *Southampton* (Flagship) *Glasgow* and *Aurora* and her ten destroyers (including Tribals): these powerful ships, with the light cruiser *Enterprise*, were to form an independent striking force based on Rosyth. On November 21, the Striking Force proceeded out of the Firth of Forth on its first sortie. *Belfast* was to exercise gunnery practice firings with *Southampton* and two destroyers before clearing the A/S boom.

**FROM THE LOG**
**Tuesday, November 21, 1939: At Rosyth**
(Leave granted to ship's company: Nil)
0800  *Wind: SW Force 3*
*Weather and visibility: blue skies, seven miles*
*Sea and swell: 7*
*Barometer: 1032.2 (rising)*
0917  Weighed and proceeded. Course and speed as requisite for leaving harbour and carrying out firings in company with *Southampton*
0947  Passed through A/S boom. 1005 out paravanes
1030  a/c to 025°   1037 295°   1042 115°   1049 060°
1058  Violent explosion felt in *Belfast*. Extensive damage
1140  Taken in tow by tug *Krooman*
1314  Prepared to abandon ship

At the time of the explosion, the immediate reaction of the Captain and his officers was that *Belfast* had been torpedoed by a U-boat lurking off May Island.

All the W/T sets were out of action. The V/S signals record accurately the scene on that still November afternoon:

To: D Four
From: *Belfast*
Please keep me informed of your condition so that I can inform C in C Rosyth                                              1112
Light PL     TOD 1117                                    21/11/39

To: D Four
From: *Belfast*
Keep Destroyers on the move screening me               1115
Light PL     TOD 1116                                    21/11/39

To: *Belfast*
From: D Four
Do you require towing ?                                 1114
REPLY: Yes certainly                                    1115
Light PL     TOD 1115     TOD 1116                       21/11/39

To: C in C Rosyth (R) C S 2
From: *Belfast*
"A" Boiler and Engine Room out of action. Improbable that steam can be raised. Explosion was abreast "A" Boiler Room
                                                        1116
Light PL     TOD 1119                                    21/11/39

To: *Belfast*
From: *Euryalus*
Can we be of any assistance ? Divers are dressed and all ready
Light PL     TOR 1120                                    21/11/39

To: *Euryalus*
From: *Belfast*
Return to harbour and be ready to help when we return to harbour
                                                        1125
Light PL     TOD 1127                                    21/11/39

To: *Belfast*
From: *Whitley*
Shall I come alongside your starboard side forward to facilitate passing tow
Light PL     TOR 1130                                    21/11/39

To: D Four, *Whitley*
From: *Belfast*
Tug *Krooman* is endeavouring to tow me if he is able to do so, keep *Whitley* screening
                                                        1130
Light PL     TOD 1133                                    21/11/39

To: *Whitley*
From: *Belfast*
Keep on the move                                        1131
Light PL     TOD 1132                                    21/11/39

To: *Krooman*
From: *Belfast*
Come alongside starboard bow, slip your targets
                                                        1133
Light PL     TOD 1155                                    21/11/39

To: *Belfast*
From: *Euryalus*
Shall I take the target from Tug ?
REPLY: Yes tug has slipped target endeavour to get them in tow
                                                        1137
Light PL     TOR 1126     TOD 1138                       21/11/39

To: D Four
From: *Belfast*
Report to Rosyth that Tug *Krooman* is towing, but further assistance is urgently required. Ship will not be able to steam and probably not steer. Approximate casualties Dead NIL Injured 16
                                                        1148
Light PL     TOD 1152                                    21/11/39

To: *Belfast*
From: D Four
Is it certain that it was a torpedo please ?
                                                        1211
REPLY: No I cannot tell as nothing was seen
                                                        1216
Light PL     TOR 1214     TOD 1216                       21/11/39

To: *Belfast* for C D
From A S
Outer caisson of lock is open. Ship can enter lock whenever there is sufficient depth of water to navigate main channel
                                                        1249
Light PL     TOR 1333     TOD 1549                       21/11/39

To: C-in-C Rosyth, CS2, CD
From: *Belfast*
Explosion at about 80 and possibly two other right aft. Ship flooded to waterline from 66 to 93. 4 in. HA magazine flooded. Making water in forward Engine Room and possibly "A" Boiler Room. Steam can-

The German liner Cap Norte *captured by* Belfast, *9 Oct 1939*          (*Courtesy:* Belfast *Trust*)

not be raised except for one dynamo as all Turbo oil fuel pumps out of action. Steering gear in use. Draught increased to two feet forward four inches aft. Oil fuel cannot be pumped out forward. Casualties Dead NIL, 21 injured, some seriously. Hope to arrive for immediate docking 1500, essential to dry dock immediately.

| | | 1259 |
|---|---|---|
| Light PL | TOD 1300 | 21/11/39 |

. . . . . .

To: A S
From: C D
Propose to berth *Belfast* in "Y" berth. Will you please clear berth, rough time of arrival 1630 today Tuesday.

| | | 1303 |
|---|---|---|
| Light PL | TOD 1325 | 21/11/39 |

. . . . . .

To: D Four
From: *Belfast*
Destroyers are to continue screening up to the Gate so far as navigationally possible and to remain in close company till ship enters basin.

| | | 1318 |
|---|---|---|
| Light PL | TOD 1332 | 21/11/39 |

. . . . . .

To: *Belfast*
From: D Four
C in C and R A D think I am hunting. May I take *Gurkha* and *Isis* and search when you have reached Inchkeith.

| | | 1349 |
|---|---|---|
| Light PL | TOD 1349 | 21/11/39 |

. . . . . .

To: D Four
From: *Belfast*
Yes I had no idea that you were supposed to be hunting Many thanks for your screening.

| | | 1351 |
|---|---|---|
| Light PL | TOD 1355 | 21/11/39 |

. . . . . .

To: C D
From: *Belfast*
At 1315 draught was as follows: 23 feet 9 forward
22 feet aft

| Light PL | TOD 1400 | 21/11/39 |
|---|---|---|

### Captain Scott's Report

On November 29, Captain Scott made his final report, a copy of which is reproduced on p. 109. Paragraph 20 describes the subsequent opinion of Captain Scott as to the cause of the explosion which crippled his ship:

"In view of the large alterations of course immediately prior to the explosion, and the fact that nothing was seen although a number of His Majesty's Ships were in the vicinity, I consider it most unlikely that the damage was caused by submarine attack. In my opinion, the *Belfast* struck a mine; possibly more than one, though I do not think this was so."

As later events were to prove, Captain Scott's conjecture was correct, but already the Admiralty's suspicions had been aroused by the possible advent of a new secret weapon (the Navy had experimented before the war with a magnetically operated mine): on September 16, two months earlier, a merchant ship, *The City of Paris*, was seriously damaged in the shallow waters of the East Coast by a mysterious underwater explosion; and in similar waters to those in which *City of Paris* was damaged, and on the same day as *Belfast* was struck, the destroyer *Gipsy* was sunk in unexplained circumstances off Harwich.

**Extract from Paymaster Commander's Report:**
This absence of damage, compared to what was received in the Galley adjacent, seems noteworthy. It may perhaps be due to the presence of ten bags of flour, which were piled on the Bakery deck, and which acted as sandbags.

### The Fight for Life

The target tug, *Krooman*, slipped her targets and at 1140 began to tow the stricken *Belfast* towards Inverkeithing. By 1333 three more tugs arrived from Rosyth; at 1700 *Belfast* was secured in the dockyard alongside the lock where the casualties were put ashore in the waiting ambulances.

At 2230, in the darkness of a wartime night, the ship was safely secured in the dry dock where, on the next day, pumping began for an emergency survey.

*Docking the ship: Rosyth Dockyard. Belfast* had broken her back between the bridge structure and the for'd funnel. There was a step across the upper deck and she would not sit properly on the level keel blocks which showed excessive signs of breaking. Pumping was stopped and when divers were sent down they reported that the keel had a hog extending from Station 42 to 184, with a maximum of three inches at Station 80.

The ship was taking in no further water and so she was undocked to lighten her, by removing the 6 in. guns and turrets. She was then re-docked on soft-wood blocks which were shaped to allow for the hogging.

It was soon apparent from the survey and the Dockyard conferences, that HMS *Belfast* would not for some time, if ever, survive to fight again. The story is recalled that a young Constructor Officer decided her fate by his vehement insistence that she *could* be rebuilt. Though only a six-inch hole was visible in the middle of the ship's bottom beneath "A" Boiler Room, the shock damage was extensive, including the fracturing of the cast iron feet of the HP and LP turbines. In the majority view, Rosyth could not undertake the major rebuilding and it was doubtful if a major Yard could undertake the work now that the menace of the magnetic mine was crippling our ports.

*Beating the Mine.* It was ironic that only two days after the damage to *Belfast*, Lieutenant-Commander Ouvry succeeded in dismantling the first example of Hitler's secret weapon, a magnetic mine which had been located in the mud of Shoeburyness. For his bravery and coolness he was awarded the D.S.O..

*Belfast's* sacrifice was to play a not unimportant part in the final victory: 'de-Gaussing' was the immediate counter to this gruesome and sinister weapon which, had the Germans produced it in sufficient quantities, could have brought Britain to her knees.

*Out of the War.* Rosyth Dockyard decided that it could repair *Belfast* for her passage to Plymouth for major reconstruction but that the temporary repairs would take several months: not only had the main engines to be realigned in dock, but a temporary structure had to be built over the fractured metal and over the hull where it was deformed. Sadly, therefore, it was decided to pay the ship off into Care and Maintenance on January 4, 1940, when the ship was decommissioned. Valuable officers and men were needed elsewhere.

On March 8, 1940, it was decided that she would need at least six months in dock to repair her underwater machinery and electrical damage. On June 28, less than a month after Dunkirk, she sailed secretly from Rosyth; steaming eastabout, she proceeded down the swept channels and arrived safely at Devonport on the last day of June. On July 4 she was reduced to Special Complement under the command of HMS *Drake* in the Plymouth Command.

## Major Reconstruction
## July 4, 1940—October 31, 1942

Over two years of savage and ruthless war were to elapse before *Belfast* was again to play her part at sea. Nevertheless, during this long period in Devonport Dockyard she, too, made her contribution. From her wounds were learnt the lessons in design that were to be incorporated in future ships built to combat the rigours of war.

The reconstruction dragged through the years, mainly because of pressure of work and dislocation of the dockyard by bombing but also because much of *Belfast's* undamaged gear and armament were "cannibalized" to keep fighting ships at sea.

During re-building, vital constructional lessons were learnt:

(i) Due to shock damage, particularly in the castings of the LP turbines, the problem of mountings withstanding shock was thoroughly researched and new designs for shock-proof machinery were produced.

(ii) The policy of accepting the fact that, on explosion, machinery would inevitably break; it would therefore be more prudent to ensure that the part which fractured should be easy and cheap to replace.

(iii) Other magnetic mining also added impetus to research in counter measures.

*Devonport Dockyard: The Docking.* On August 1, 1940 the ship was finally paid off and taken into dockyard hands. Britain was now alone and preparing to repel invasion by the Nazi hordes from across the Channel; the Battle of Britain was but six weeks in the future; and bombs rained down on our cities and particularly upon the Royal Dockyards.

First, the ship was opened up and lightened of stores; then the machinery was extricated from both boiler rooms and the for'd engine room. Because of the deformed keel and the difficulties experienced at Rosyth, soft fir caps, which varied in height, were retained and fitted to the Middle Line blocks and shaped to the deformation of the keel.

The ship was then trimmed as nearly as possible to the declivity of the blocks; she was plumbed upright, her draught readings being: for'd, 12 ft. 2 in.

aft, 14 ft. 6 in.

In this condition she was docked down, careful watch being kept on the fir caps which showed no further signs of strain.

It was essential to measure accurately the deformation of her hull. A straight line of keel was therefore sighted from 11 to 248 stations and fixed bases were rigged at main watertight bulkheads and intermediate stations. From these fixed points, measurements were taken of the heights of the longitudinals and the deck edges. These readings were compared with those obtained from the lines drawn out on the Mould Loft floor, the difference being plotted to show the distortion along the length of the ship at the various longitudinal deck edges.

From these measurements, curves were obtained which revealed that the maximum hog was approximately at station 80; the whole hull, up to the upper deck, followed the same deformation. The remedy therefore lay in dropping the ship as a whole and this was the plan which the Constructive Department followed.

*Straightening the ship.* A series of side blocks were fitted, cap pieces being erected under the main bulkheads from stations 40 to 186, in the wake of the third longitudinal; intermediate blocks were also spaced about 12 ft. apart, the wedges being cleaned and greased so that the height of the blocks could be easily adjusted.

At the same time, internal shoring was installed from the hangars and bridges down to the outer bottom. The lower portions of bulkheads 117, 135 and 158 were cut out; and these bulkheads were then shored to the inner bottom.

Beginning for'd and aft and working to the centre, the soft cappings along the Middle Line blocks were then removed by splitting them or easing them out. At the same time the descent of the hull was controlled by the adjustable side blocks.

*Dockyard Skill.* The evolution of the dropping of the ship took sixteen days, careful measurements from the longitudinals being taken all the while. At the same time as the wedges were being removed, the temporary structure built into the ship by Rosyth was released so that the ship could again take up her original shape.

To assist this movement, the wedges of the breast shores were adjusted, the end shores being kept tight while those in the middle were eased to be only hand tight. All vertical shores between the dock bottom and the ship's side were kept slack.

The last part of the operation was to ease out the wedges of the cradle blocks along the wake of the fractured structure, from 60 to 117 stations, so that the ship could fall as nearly as possible at station 80 while the releasing of the temporary structure proceeded.

When the soft capping had been removed and the temporary structure freed, the keel was touching the blocks from her stem to 66, and from 93 to the stern.

Tanks between 80 and 93, and 93 to 100 were filled with water to deck level in an endeavour to force down

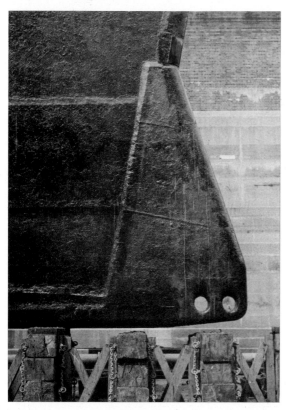

SECTION 96

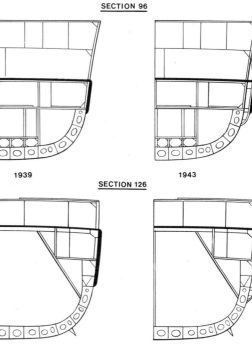

1939                1943

SECTION 126

1939                1943

*Left: Sections 96 and 126 in 1939 before the mining.*
*Right: Sections 96 and 126 after the major reconstruction of 1940-42. The side armour belt was removed and rebuilt outboard of the bulge which was incorporated in the reconstruction.*

*Her underwater shape after the major reconstruction of 1940-42. Note the bulge and, outboard of it, her side armour; her bilge keel runs the length of the ship*

*As she emerged from her major reconstruction in Devonport, 1940-42. Her new radar outfit and Oerlikon armament can be seen. She is now wearing her Admiralty Disruptive Camouflage* (MOD)

The First Lord visits the Fleet, January 18, 1943.    (IWM)

The King visits his Fleet, August 15, 1943, Scapa Flow. Captain Parham welcomes His Majesty. In the background, at left, is another Town-class cruiser.    (IWM)

Kola inlet, Russia, May 1943. A photograph taken from the destroyer Inglefield, showing the covering forces at anchor: left to right, Cumberland, Obdurate, an unidentifiable destroyer and Belfast with a "V & W" destroyer alongside her starboard side. In the background at right lies an oiler and, on the foreshore, Russian administrative buildings.    (IWM)

Rear-Admiral Burnett welcomes His Majesty King George VI.    (IWM)

The King recognises a shipmate.    (IWM)

Belfast cheers the King as the Royal Barge shoves off.    (IWM)

the structure, but to no avail. Because this position was in the wake of the fractured material, it was assumed that the ship had suffered a permanent set.

The structure between 66 and 93 was removed and rebuilt in order to remove the deformation. Any other slight deviation in the keel, it was hoped, would disappear and flatten out as the internal structure was rebuilt. The machinery was then replaced and the superstructure added.

*Strengthening the Hull.* Now that the ship was again straight, the dockyard proceeded to strengthen the hull along this weakened section. As can be seen from the sections of 1939 and 1942, the armour was removed, its thickness increased and replaced outside the strengthening plating which was extended and faired-in along a considerable length of the ship's side. At the same time all the decks were strengthened by bolstering up the thickness of the plating in this section and by constructing longitudinal overlaps at the joints.

It was the considerable enlarging of the armoured belt and the fairing, extending to forward of "B" turret, which changed radically *Belfast*'s appearance and which rendered her unique from 1942 onwards.

In addition to this vast reconstruction, other major alterations were incorporated to strengthen her hull. A new transverse bulkhead was built in at 104 station.

The break in the fo'c'sle was plated in and taken further aft to abaft the foremost funnel. The sea boats (27 ft. whalers) had therefore to be raised a deck and davits fitted on the catapult deck.

The fo'c'sle deck was modified as was the sheer strake to make her drier and to improve her seakeeping qualities; the sheet anchor was removed and its hawsepipe blanked over.

## New Weapons
Many months elapsed before the final decisions were taken as how best to reconstruct *Belfast*. During these crucial days, the heat of battle was forcing upon scientists, architects and constructors the need for counter measures to combat the dreadful weapons in the air, on the sea and underwater.

The most vital development was in the field of radar, a counter weapon which was already revolutionizing war at sea and in the air. It was High Frequency Direction Finding combined with radar, termed initially RDF, that were to be the greatest factor in overcoming the U-boats in the Atlantic; it was radar which was to give *Belfast* those "eyes" which, in the not too distant future, she was to need so acutely.

Developments had also raced ahead in defence against aircraft. New guns and new fire control systems were available, and the weapons were beginning to pour out from the factories where men and women now toiled night and day.

Finally, in *Belfast* the scenic railway was abandoned, to be used only for ammunitioning purposes.

The 4 in. ammunition supply arrangements were modified to supply the fixed ammunition direct to the mountings. Large Ready Use lockers were provided at the guns and protective plating was erected between the mountings for shielding both the crews and the ammunition.

Protective plating was also to be built around the radar offices which were shortly to be constructed as soon as the new, secret equipment arrived.

## The Bulges
These major alterations added many tons of topweight and, to counteract the deterioration in stability, it was decided to add bulges to her underwater shape, not only for stability reasons, but to strengthen the ship longitudinally.

The refit was swallowing up many skilled men, when the dockyard could least afford to spare them—and particularly to work upon a ship that had already been out of action for as long as many workers could remember. So it was not surprising that The Yard requested the omission of the bulges in order to cut down the length of the refit. The Controller, however, replied: "In reply to your enquiry as to whether, with a view to reducing work, the bulge to be added to *Belfast* can be omitted, it is essential for the bulge to be fitted for stability reasons due to the addition of extra weight."

The addition of these bulges increased *Belfast*'s beam to 69 ft. and her draught to 19 ft. for'd, 20 ft. 2 in. aft, but because of this splint-like repair she did not have to lose "X" turret, like every other 6 in. triple turret ship, to compensate for added topweight in the form of the AA defence.

## Completion of twenty-six months' Refit
HMS *Belfast* recommissioned at Devonport on November 3, 1942, under the command of Captain F. R. Parham. As she slid past Drake's Island and headed for Plymouth Sound to work up her new ship's company, there were not many who would have recognized her for the splendid fighting unit she had now become. She was one of the most powerful cruisers in the world: with her speed (now reduced to $30\frac{1}{2}$ knots), considerable armour, her 6 in. rapid broadside and her new AA defence, she could outfight an 8 in. gunned ship and certainly any enemy cruiser that would have cared to take up the challenge.

A German agent ashore might have been forgiven for assuming, at a cursory glance, that *Belfast* was returning much as she was before the mining, but with her hull strengthened. On closer scrutiny he might have become aware of considerable change in the appearance of her aerials and then, awakened, he would have realized that this great ship that swept silently out of the Sound was a formidable cruiser indeed.

## The New *Belfast*: 1942/43
The RDF of 1939/40 (now known as "radar") which had been first carried by *Rodney* and *Sheffield*, had been developed apace. While the Germans had concentrated their radar effort on gunnery fire control, the British had, although realizing the importance of radar for gunnery purposes, been forced by the exigencies of aerial bombardment and U-boat warfare to throw most of their effort into long range, high definition search radar. *Belfast*, by her long refit, also enjoyed the advantage of being fitted out with the most modern radar of the day—the centimetre sets which had just been developed by British scientists—in conjunction with her new armament.

| Armament: | November 1942 |
|---|---|
| **Main:** | |
| | as at 1939 |
| *Ammunition:* | as at 1939 |
| *Radar:* | 1 × Type 284 on for'd DCT—main armament surface. |
| | 1 × Type 273 General warning, surface; in lantern aft of for'd DCT |
| | 4 × Type 283 blind barrage directors for 6 in. armament |
| | 1 × Type 252 IFF (Identification Friend or Foe) to combine with 273 |
| | 1 × Type 251 IFF |
| **High Angle:** | **November 1942** |
| *Guns and* | |
| *Mountings:* | as at 1939 |
| *Ammunition:* | as at 1939 |
| *Fire Control:* | The three HA Directors were modified to Mark IVs to take Type 285 radar for radar controlled fire |
| *Radar:* | 3 × Type 285 |
| | 1 × Type 281 *Air Warning*, Transmitter aerial on foremast; receiver aerial on mainmast |
| | 1 × Type 242 *Air Warning IFF* aerials on top of 281 receiver |
| **Close range:** | **November 1942** |
| *2-pdr. Pom-poms:* | The two Mark II mountings were replaced by two Mark VIII RPC (Remote Power Control) |
| *Ammunition:* | 1800 rounds per barrel |
| | 14 rounds per belt; 10 belts per tray |
| *Fire Control:* | The Mark II Directors were replaced by two Mark IV pom-pom directors and repositioned near the mountings |
| | 2 × Type 282 radar being fitted to the directors. The guns and directors were RPC. The weight of a director was 36 cwt |
| *Operation:* | Power or hand: maximum elevating and training speed, 16 degrees/second loading was carried out by using the energy of the recoiling barrel |
| *Sights:* | Cosine |
| *20 mm. Oerlikons* | |
| *Twins:* | Ten 20 mm. Oerlikon guns in five Mark V twin mountings equipped with tachymetric sights were fitted in exposed positions about the ship. The mountings were shielded, power controlled and later tied to radar sights; 1 on roof of "B" turret, 1 on each wing of the lower bridge, for'd; 2 right aft on the quarterdeck and protected by concave and roofed shelters |
| *Control:* | RPC through HA barrage directors |
| *Singles:* | Eight single Oerlikons, Mark IV on Mark IIIA fixed pedestal mountings were fitted, four each side on the catapult deck |
| *Ammunition:* | 2400 rounds per gun in Ready Use lockers and stowage in pom-pom magazine |
| | Though hand operated and sighted by eye-shooting using a 300 kwt. sighting ring, these single Oerlikons were comforting weapons. With an effective range of 1000-1200 yd., the gun was very versatile being manufactured in America as well as Britain and all parts being interchangeable. |
| *Details:* | Calibre: 20 mm. |
| | MV: 2725 ft./sec. |
| | Rate of fire: 465/480 r.p.m. |
| | Length: 8 ft. |
| | Weight of gun: 173 lb. |
| | Weight of pedestal: 140 lb. |
| | Elevation: 75° |
| | Training: 360° |
| *·5 in. Machine-guns:* | Removed—replaced by twin Oerlikons |

**Torpedo Department**
Six—21 in. Mark IV torpedoes were replaced by six—21 in. Mark VIII**
Depth-charge Outfit was enlarged:
15 Mark VIIs—ship
12 Mark VIII—aircraft

**Other alterations and additions carried out during the long refit**
Degaussing coils fitted.
Torpedo "B" sights power controlled from the Captain's Sight (Enemy Bearing Indicator).
Four oil fuel hoses added for fuelling destroyers at sea.
All Aluminium scuttles and ventilation trunking damaged by gun blast, were replaced with brass and steel.
The 4 in. hoists and conveyors (Scenic Railway) were modified to take the ammunition direct to the guns. Large Ready Use lockers were fitted outboard of the hangars to prevent flooding of the flight deck.
Cypher coding machines R.A.F. Type X supplied for aircrew.
The aircraft trolley base and turntable was strengthened to take aircraft up to 12,000 lb. (Sea Otters, if carried).
The Meteorological office was modernized.
Type 132 Asdic was modernized.

The following rangefinders were fitted in the DCTs to replace the original instruments:
Rangefinder unit (22 ft. Duplex and PIL FM7 rangefinder on an MR II anti-vibration mounting) with air-disturbing, desiccating and window-cleaning units.
The after DCT was fitted with 15 ft. FX2 rangefinder on an MR13 anti-vibration mounting.
The two lower Bridge rangefinders were removed.
A loud-hailer system was fitted to incorporate all close range weapons.
A Type 760 Echo Sounder was fitted.
Two extra paravanes were carried, totalling six Mark VII and Mark VII* which replaced the original outfit.

**The Aircraft**
Fearnought fire covers were fitted to the hangars.
Two Walrus amphibians were carried until June 6, 1943 when they were landed and the catapult removed.

**The Ship's Chapel**
Space was found to provide a small chapel for use by all denominations. The care of souls of the ship's company was the concern of the Chaplain who helped also with cyphering and coding.

**Communications**
Type 86 TBS was fitted; though providing voice communication, its transmission frequency interfered with the 284 radar at the Battle of North Cape.

## The Fighting Ship

HMS *Belfast* was now a new concept of cruiser, able to paralyse an 8 in.-gunned opponent. A vast amount of money and skill had been poured into the reconstruction but she was fully to justify the trust invested in her.

During the next year and a half she was to pass through the crucible of fire; without respite, she was to be almost continually operational and at the centre of some of the most momentous operations in the history of sea warfare. During 1943 and 1944, she was to reach the summit of her distinguished life.

She was not to lose touch with home, however, for, in January 1943, a happy incident occurred which reflected the affection the nation felt for its sailors.

A group of Admiralty employees in The Charnwood Engineering Company, Abbey Lane, Leicester, subscribed to sending comforts to HMS *Belfast* (the Company in peace-time made machinery for making silk stockings). This act was reflecting the generosity of towns and cities throughout the land but, in addition, these kind people presented a cup, to be known as The Charnwood Cup, for sports competitions amongst the eleven Divisions in the ship.

## Scapa Flow Again

She sailed for Scapa Flow where she became the flagship of the 10th Cruiser Squadron, Home Fleet. Vice-Admiral Robert Burnett, C.B., whose flag she flew, was an experienced destroyer man, having been RA(D) Home Fleet. He was already seasoned by the rigours of fighting through to Murmansk the convoys laden with tanks and weapons for the Russian Front.

As recently as September 1942 he had been in command of the escorting forces which had successfully battled through against the hardest and most persistent attacks which the enemy had yet mounted on an east-bound Russian convoy. Burnett was created a C.B. for this action and was awarded the D.S.O. for his courage in the Hogmanay Battle of December 31, 1942. During 1942, 6,714 tanks, over 15,600 aircraft, 85,000 vehicles, 70 million rounds of small arms ammunition, plus huge quantities of other material had been delivered by the devoted men of the Merchant and Royal Navy crews to Russia. They asked no reward but they expected gratitude; they received neither from the Russians.

The only expression of gratitude displayed to *Belfast*

(a)

(b)

(c)

(d)

(e)

(f)

(g)

*Some of the Ship's Officers.*
*(a) Cory    (b) Davison    (c) Davies    (d) Palmer*
*(e) Green    (f) Watson    (g) Byng.*
(Courtesy Lt.-Cdr. T. Sargent)

*Top left*
*The Diving Store.*    (Courtesy Lt.-Cdr. T. Sargent)

*The Rugger Team.*    (Courtesy Captain Parham)

The Bodo Raid, October 5, 1943. The Home Fleet and US Ships in Norway attack. Photo taken from Belfast. HMS Duke of York *screened by cruisers and destroyers in battle formation (USS* Tuscaloosa *in right background). Aircraft are returning from the raid and are about to land on their carrier, USS* Ranger. (IWM)

Captain Parham and Rear-Admiral Burnett lead the cheering for the USS Aircraft-carrier Ranger *who is passing* Belfast *at anchor in Scapa Flow, October 6, 1943. Note the spare PV Otter, the Flottanet and the ammunition derrick stowed on "X" gun deck.* (IWM)

USS Tuscaloosa *who took part in the Bodo attack. Her two single float planes are clearly visible.* (IWM)

HMS Belfast *as she appeared shortly before the Battle of North Cape. Note that the sheet anchor hawse pipe has been blanked over.* (IWM)

by the Soviets was when a reindeer suddenly arrived in a lighter alongside the ship on the evening of December 23, 1943. The animal was enclosed in one of the empty Walrus hangars and was therefore present at the Battle of North Cape. The shock of the broadside and the noise of battle terrified the reindeer which unhappily had to be shot by a merciful sailor.

## Arctic Convoys and the Northern Patrol

HMS *Belfast* was now entering the most active period of her life. The bland record which follows of the part she played in the operations of the next eighteen months cannot convey the feeling of the thousands of men who shared the miseries of sea warfare in these icy waters during the Arctic winter.

Never dry, always cold, short of sleep; ships overworked and desperately needing time for maintenance; every second of each hour of every day, the secret fear of a freezing death—these were the conditions which became part of life for the men who served on the Russian run. This, then, is the diary of a ship who served, HMS *Belfast*:

## Phase II Operational Wartime: December 1942—August 1945

*1942*

December 10   Left Plymouth for Scapa
December 25   Scapa, *10th Cruiser Squadron (Home Fleet)*

*1943*

February 17   Arrived Seidisfjord, Iceland

## Russian Convoys

*1943*

February 19   Off Seidisfjord in company with *Cumberland, Sheffield, Bluebell, Camellia* and destroyers
February 21   Left Seidisfjord with *Cumberland* and *Norfolk* to cover Russian Convoy JW53
March 1   Murmansk
March 2   Left Kola Inlet with *Cumberland* and *Norfolk* to cover Russian Convoy RA53

## Northern Blockade Patrol: 1943

March 29   Left Hvalfjord
Ordered to reinforce Patrol "White" with *Intrepid*—Search for Blockade Runner
March 30   Patrol "White" with *Glasgow, Intrepid* and *Echo*
April 2   Sailed to relieve *Cumberland* on Patrol "White"
April 7   On west coast of Iceland to Patrol "White"
April 13   Arrived at Hvalfjord having been relieved on patrol by *Cumberland (10th Cruiser Squadron) (Home Fleet)*
May 27   Arrived Scapa from covering minelaying operations, SN111B
June 18   Arrived Rosyth to give leave and for quick docking. Ship to sail for Scapa so as to arrive July 1
July 1   Arrived Scapa
July 7   Sailed from Scapa to the north-eastward in company with *London, Kent,* and one destroyer

*OPERATION "CAMERA"*, a diversionary sweep off Norway to exploit, during the Sicilian Landings, Hitler's continued fear of an Allied counter invasion of that country. Operation was successful because the cruisers were mistaken for a transport convoy

July 9   Arrived Scapa in company with *London* and *Kent*
July 27   Left Scapa
July 29   Arrived Scapa

*Note:*

Patrol "White" was, in the opinion of Captain Parham, one of the most arduous and unpleasant duties which the ship had to undertake.

The story is told of a sea-mist (so prevalent in the ice off Iceland) suddenly lifting to disclose HMS *Cumberland* stuck in the ice and pointing straight at a U-boat in a similar predicament. Both warships were never again seen to move so fast—in opposite directions.

## Russian Convoys: 1943

August 15   After HM the King's visit to the Home Fleet, CS10 in *Belfast,* screened by *Onslow* and *Orwell*, left Scapa to create a diversion off the South Norwegian coast—*OPERATION FN*, a covering sweep for the JW/RA Russian Convoys
August 17   Returned to Skaale Fjord with *Onslow* and *Orwell*
August 22   Left Scapa
August 28   Sailed from Hvalfjord with *Norfolk* and *Impulsive* to cover destroyers in *OPERATION "LORRY"*: stores and mail to Russia
September 3   Returned to Hvalfjord with *Norfolk* and *Impulsive: OPERATION "LORRY"* Left Hvalfjord with CS10 for reconnaissance and search in the Spitzbergen area: the enemy had landed a meteorological party on this desolate island, an action the Allies were to imitate. CS10 was ordered to investigate an intelligence report of a German raid on the island
September 10   Arrived Hvalfjord
September 25   In vicinity of Reykjanes searching to south-east *OPERATION SF;* suspected enemy break-out of blockade runner
September 27   Arrived Scapa

## Home Fleet Offensive Sweep: October 5/6, 1943

*10th Cruiser Squadron (Home Fleet)* Sailed from Scapa in company with *Duke of York, Anson,* U.S. Aircraft Carrier *Ranger* and U.S. Heavy Cruiser *Tuscaloosa* to attack shipping targets in the Bodo area with the air striking group from *Ranger*
*OPERATION "LEADER"*: diversionary, as well as offensive, to ease pressure on the Russian convoys, was successful
October 6   Scapa: self-refit, boiler-clean and leave period
October 29   Left Scapa

## Battle of North Cape:
## December 26, 1943

Four days later, the 10th Cruiser Squadron (Vice-Admiral Burnett) in *Belfast* left the Kola Inlet on December 23, 1943. In company were *Norfolk* and *Sheffield* and the task of Burnett's cruiser force, Force One, was to cover "the return of the empties", Convoy RA55A, for "its safe and timely arrival" back to the United Kingdom, via the Barents Sea. The Escort Commander was Captain Campbell in *Milne*.

Invisible, but punching eastward from Akureyri in Iceland through the heavy seas, was Force Two. This group of heavy ships was led by *Duke of York*, flagship of the Commander-in-Chief, Home Fleet, Admiral Bruce Fraser, who had relieved Sir John Tovey seven months earlier, on May 8. The task of Force Two was to destroy the German Battle cruiser, *Scharnhorst*, should she emerge as expected from her lair in Lange Fjord: Convoy JW55B was the bait.

Plodding up, also from the westward, was Convoy JW55B, routed close south of Bear Island and escorted by Captain McCoy (*Onslow*) Senior Officer (SO) of the escort.

The battle that ensued can best be described by the events themselves which have been recorded in both German and British Battle Logs:

**BATTLE LOG—British**

**22 December 1943**

**23 December 1943**
**1800** Force Two at Akureyri. Admiral Fraser meets his Captains.

**2300** Force Two sails from Akureyri.

HMS *Saumarez*

**24 December 1943**
**1200** Position of Convoy JW55B 70° 40' North, 3° 10' East.

**1400** C in C orders JW55B and Escort to reverse course for three hours. Force Two increases speed to 19kn.

**25 December 1943 – Christmas Day**
Late evening:
C in C, Home Fleet and CS10 informed by Admiralty that *Scharnhorst* was possibly at sea.

HMS *Jamaica*

**German**
*Scharnhorst* (Kapitän zur See Hintze), flagship of Rear-Admiral Bey.
Battle cruiser, 26,000 tons, 9 × 11 in., 12 × 5·9 in.
5 *Narvik* Destroyers: Fleet Destroyers, 4 × 5·9 in., 8 × 21 in. torpedoes, 38 knots.
Z–29 (Kapitän zur See Johanneson) 4th Destroyer Flottilla Leader
Z–30, Z–33, Z–34 and Z–38

**British**
*Force Two* (Admiral Bruce Fraser)
*Duke of York* (Captain The Hon. Guy Russell RN)
Battleship, 35,000 tons, 10 × 14 in., 16 × 5·25 in.
*Jamaica* Cruiser, 9 × 6 in., 8 × 4 in., 6 × 21 in. torpedoes
*Destroyer Screen*
1st. Sub-Division
*Savage* (Commander Meyrick) Divisional Leader. 4 × 4·7 in., 8 × 21 in. torpedoes, 32 knots
*Saumarez*
*Scorpion*
2nd. Sub-Division
*Stord* (Norwegian)
*Force One* (CS 10, Vice-Admiral Burnett in *Belfast*)
*Belfast* (Captain F. R. Parham) 12 × 6 in., 12 × 4 in., 6 × 21 in. torpedoes
*Norfolk* 8 × 8 in., 8 × 4 in., 8 × 21 in. torpedoes
*Sheffield* 12 × 6 in., 8 × 4 in., 6 × 21 in. torpedoes
*Destroyer Screen* (36th Division)
71st. Sub-Division
*Matchless* 6 × 4·7 in. (twins) 33 knots
*Musketeer* (Commander Fisher) Divisional Leader 6 × 4·7 in. (twins) 33 knots
72nd. Sub-Division
*Opportune* 4 × 4·7 in. All 8 × 21 in. torpedoes, 32 knots
*Convoy Escort JW55B*
*Onslow* (Captain McCoy) D 17 with 9 assorted destroyers, 1 minesweeper, 2 corvettes
*Convoy Escort RA55A*
*Milne* (Captain Campbell) with 5 assorted destroyers, 1 minesweeper, 3 corvettes (1 Norwegian)

**BATTLE LOG—German**

**22 December 1943**
**1045** Meteorological aircraft reports Convoy JW55B and Escort, course 045° at 10kn. HQ believes force to be troopships for Allied landing in Norway. *Scharnhorst* Battle Group to three hours' notice for steam.

**23 December 1943**
**1123** Luftwaffe reports contact with JW55B, identified as cargo ships and tankers en route for Murmansk sailing in seven columns. Escort reported as three or four cruisers plus nine destroyers and corvettes, co. 090°, 10kn.

**1214** Aircraft reports one cruiser, five destroyers, steering to the east, ahead of convoy. Commodore U-boats (Norway) orders U-*Gruppe Eisenbart* (eight boats) to patrol west of Bear Island.

**24 December 1943**
**1400** Air Officer Lofotens, reports to Navy (North) position of Convoy JW55B at 1220, heading 050° at 8kn.

**25 December 1943 – Christmas Day**
**0900** U-boat (Kapitänleutnant Hansen) reports Convoy JW55B passed over, steering 060°.

**1000** Reconnaissance aircraft reports JW55B.

**1215** *Scharnhorst* Battle Group comes to one hour's notice.

**1420** U-boat Hansen reports: "Convoy AB6723 (German squared chart position) course 060°, speed eight. Weather: South 7, rain, visibility two miles."

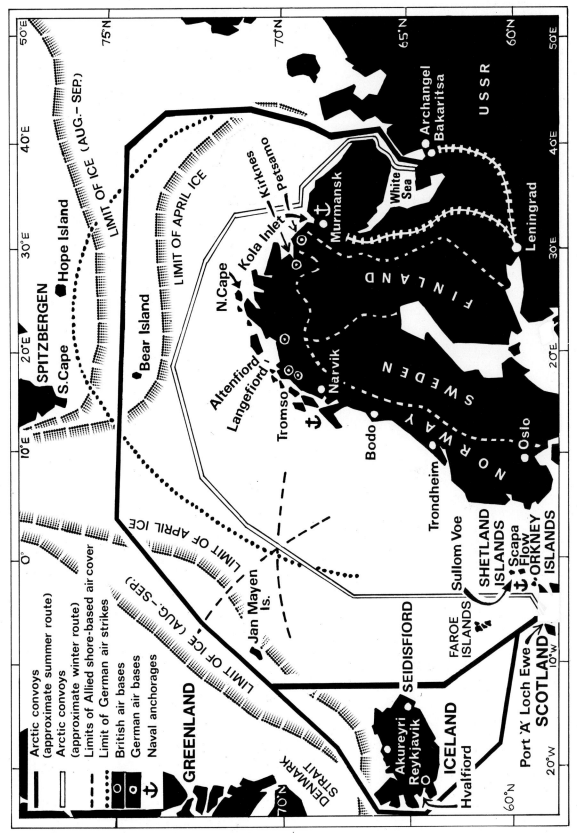

The Russian Run

SPITZBERGEN

S.Cape

Hope Island

LIMIT OF ICE (AUG.–SEP.)

75°N

LIMIT OF APRIL ICE

Bear Island

N.Cape

Kola Inlet

Kirknes

Petsamo

Murmansk

White Sea

Bakaritsa

Archangel

70°N

USSR

65°N

Leningrad

FINLAND

Tromso

Langefiord

Altenfiord

Narvik

SWEDEN

NORWAY

Bodo

Oslo

60°N

Trondheim

Sullom Voe

SHETLAND ISLANDS

Scapa Flow

ORKNEY ISLANDS

FAROE ISLANDS

SEIDISFIORD

Jan Mayen Is.

LIMIT OF APRIL ICE

LIMIT OF ICE (AUG.–SEP.)

GREENLAND

DENMARK STRAIT

70°N

Akureyri

Reykjavik

ICELAND

Hvalfiord

Port 'A' Loch Ewe

SCOTLAND

20°W

60°N

Arctic convoys (approximate summer route)

Arctic convoys (approximate winter route)

Limits of Allied shore-based air cover

Limit of German air strikes

British air bases

German air bases

Naval anchorages

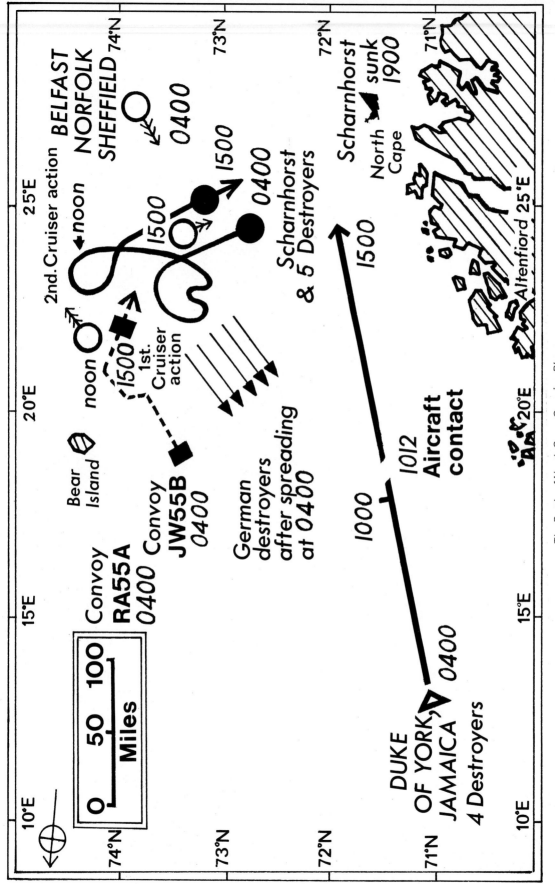

*The Battle of North Cape: Opening Phase*

HMS *Norfolk*

HMS *Duke of York*

Z-38

## 26 December 1943

**p.m.** (time of origin not known)

RA55A Convoy undetected by enemy aircraft or U-boat. C in C to Rear-Admiral (D) Home Fleet: "If you think it desirable request you (a) divert RA to northward to clear area, (b) detach four Fleet Destroyers from RA55A to join JW55B Escort."

**0339** To C in C, H/F. from Admiralty (time of origin 0319): "Admiralty appreciates *Scharnhorst* at sea."

**0430** C in C to JW55B: "Alter to due north." C in C requests position reports from D17 (JW Escort) and CS10 (Vice-Admiral Burnett in *Belfast*).

**0552** Force One steering 235°.

**0628** C in C Home Fleet signals to JW and Escort: "Alter course to 045°," and to Force One: "Close convoy for mutual support."

**0712** Force One alters to 270°.

**0815** D17 reported position, course and speed of JW Convoy. Force One adjusts to 305°, at 24kn.

### CRUISERS' DEFENCE OF CONVOY

**0840** *Belfast* in radar contact with *Scharnhorst*, range 35,000yd, bearing 295° in estimated position 73° 35' North, 23° 21' East. CS10 estimates convoy is 287°, 48 miles from him. D17 estimates *Scharnhorst* bears 125°, thirty-six miles from convoy.

**0900** *Belfast* second radar echo bearing 299° at 24,500yd. Estimates speed as 8–10kn. Assumes echo is one of the convoy and disregards. (It was probably *Z38*.)

**0915** Force One forms on a line of bearing 180°. Main echo bears 250°, at 13,000yd., speed approximately eighteen knots. Force One alters to line of bearing 160°.

**0921** From *Sheffield*: "Enemy in sight, bearing 222°, range 13,000yd."

## SCHARNHORST BATTLE GROUP SAILS

**1515** Navy (North) code signal to *Scharnhorst* Battle Group: "Eastern Front 1700. (The Group is to sail at 1700 to act against the convoy)."

**1715** Admiral Bey briefs captain of *Scharnhorst* and destroyer captains.

**1900** *Scharnhorst* begins leaving the fjord.

**1952** Commodore U-boats (Norway) orders *Gruppe Eisenbart* to attack.

**1955** *Scharnhorst* Battle Group passes Lange Fjord inner net barrage.

**2015** U-boat (Oberleutnant-zur-See Dunkelberg) fires at Convoy Escort vessel but misses. U-boat undetected by Escort, as convoy passes over.

**2037** *Scharnhorst* Battle Group passes Lange Fjord outer net barrage into main Alten Fjord.

**2100** Air Officer, Lofotens, reports Luftwaffe has lost contact with convoy.

**2200** *Scharnhorst* reaches open sea, destroyers forming screen.

**2304** *Scharnhorst* at navigational reference, "Point Lucie". Alters course to 010° at 25kn. on interception heading.

**2340** Exhortation signal from Admiral Dönitz received by *Scharnhorst*.

**2355** *Scharnhorst* to Navy/North: "In operation area, wind probably SW 6–8. Firing power of destroyers seriously impaired. Speed reduced."

## 26 December 1943

**0300** German Navy/North to *Scharnhorst*: "If destroyers cannot keep at sea, possibility of *Scharnhorst* completing task alone using mercantile warfare tactics should be considered. Decision rests with Admiral Commanding."

**0315** (approx) Destroyer Leader *(Z29)* to *Scharnhorst*: "Following sea and wind. No difficulties so far, but situation remains problematical. Expect weather to improve."

**0423** *Scharnhorst* Battle Group altered course to 030°.

**0500** *Scharnhorst* altered course to 004° to close within thirty miles of the convoy. Visibility worsening.

**0700** *Scharnhorst* to *Z29*: "4th DF to search across estimated approach course of convoy 250° speed twelve."

**0755** *Scharnhorst* to *Z29*: "Alter to 230°."

**0820** *Scharnhorst* alters course to north of west without informing *Z29*. *(This was one of the vital mistakes made by the German Admiral.)*

**0900** *Z29* sights *Z38* (also sighted by *Z30*). *Z29* makes erroneous enemy report to *Scharnhorst* believing that *Z38* (out of position to northward) is a British escort vessel.

**0930** (about) *Scharnhorst* alters to 150°, increasing speed to thirty knots; Bey signals engagement to 4th DF who is thought to be also in action.

**0935** (approx) *Scharnhorst* is hit between port III 5·9 gun and torpedo tubes. Shell fails to explode. Shell is measured and found to be 8in. She is hit again in the foretop radar which kills and wounds several AA gun-crews and destroys *Scharnhorst's* forward radar. *(This damage was the second vital disaster for the Germans.)*

**0924** *Belfast* opens fire with starshell.

**0929** CS10 to Force One: "Engage with main armament."

**0930** D17 turns JW Convoy to the north on receipt of C in C Home Fleet's orders.

**0940** *Norfolk* claims one hit with second or third salvo.

**0937** C in C Home Fleet to D17: "Detail four destroyers to join Force One with all despatch."

**0951** *Musketeer, Matchless, Opportune* and *Virago* (36th Division) are detached from JW Escort to join Force One.

**1000** Force Two picks up three shadowing aircraft on radar, relative bearing starboard quarter. Force One alters 300°.

**1014** Force One alters 305°.

**1020** Force One's radar contact with *Scharnhorst* lost. Last bearing 078°, distance 36,000yd. steering 045° at 28kn.

**1024** 4 destroyers of 36th Division join Force One.

**1030** C in C Home Fleet orders D17 to turn the JW Convoy course to 045°.

**1045** Force One's position 73° 49' North, 21° 58' East.

**1050** Convoy bears 324° from Force One, range 28,000yd. Cruisers commence zig-zagging ten miles ahead of it. 36th Division is screening ahead of CS10.

**1058** C in C Home Fleet to CS10: "Appreciate that Force Two will have little chance of finding the enemy unless some unit regains touch with him and shadows."
CS10 replies: "Weather conditions give enemy advantage of four to six knots. Consider it undesirable to split my force by detaching one or more ships to search. Am confident that enemy will return to convoy from north or north-east." *(This was the first vital moment in the battle, from the British stand-point.)*

**1100** (approx) Arctic dawn, with little light and lasting two hours. Visibility deteriorating still further. Low stratus driven by south-westerly gale kept light down to barely twilight.

**1122** C in C Home Fleet to D17: "Use your discretion regarding course of convoy."

**1137** *Norfolk* radar contact 27,000yd. but immediately loses it.

**1155** D17 brought the JW Convoy round to 125° to keep Force One between convoy and estimated approach course of enemy.

**Noon** (approx) C in C concerned about the destroyers' fuel remaining—should they reverse course or continue to Kola? Decisions depend on enemy intentions.

**1205** Convoy is nine miles on Force One's port quarter; *Belfast* makes radar contact with enemy, 30,500yd., bearing 075°.

**1219** Force One alters to 325°, the destroyers of 36th Division concentrating on starboard bow. Enemy course and speed estimated 240°, 20kn.

**1220** From *Belfast*'s plot, *Scharnhorst* seems to alter course slightly to westward.

**1221** *Sheffield* signals: "Enemy in sight." CS10 orders Force One to open fire, range then 11,000yd. 36th Division simultaneously ordered to attack with torpedoes.

**1222** *Musketeer* engages with gunfire, range 7,000yd., continuing to fire until 1226. 36th Division abandons torpedo attack because of foul weather. The range during this time between *Musketeer* and *Scharnhorst* never decreased below 4,100yd. because *Scharnhorst* was stern-on and retiring at high speed.

*Scharnhorst*

**0945** *Scharnhorst* to *Z29*: "Report your situation."

**0955** *Z29* to *Scharnhorst*: "Proceeding according to plan Square AC4413, course 230°, speed twelve."

**0955** *Scharnhorst* alters to 045° (movement is detected by *Belfast*'s radar).

Weather now Wind 7–8 from south-west. Force One's maximum speed in such conditions twenty-four kn.

**1000** U-boat (Kapitanleutnänt Lübsen): "Convoy 0945, Square AB365."

**1027** *Scharnhorst* to *Z29*: "Proceed on course 070° speed twenty-five."

*Admiral Bey addresses the ship's company of* Scharnhorst *before the Battle of North Cape. Bey was an experienced destroyer officer.* (Bibliothek für Zeitgeschichte)

**1100** (about) *Scharnhorst* receives signal from Navy/North: "Air recce reports five units to north-west of North Cape." This signal was not deemed to be of first priority because Navy/North assumes that this report referred to the German destroyers of 4th DF which were detached by *Scharnhorst* and returning.

**1135** *Scharnhorst* to *Z29*: "Alter course to 030°." *Scharnhorst* reported her position as Square AC4214 at 1120, course north, speed 27kn.

**1158** *Scharnhorst* to 4th DF: "Operate against Square AB365." Bey uses Lubsen's last enemy report.

**1217** *Z29* alters course to 280°; Johannesson signals the rest of his flotilla to close him.

**1221** *Scharnhorst* alters away to an easterly course.

*A U-boat in Norwegian waters. A boat of this type transmitted the first sighting report of Convoy JW55B.*
(Bibliothek für Zeitgeschichte)

**1233** *Norfolk* is hit: (i) through barbette of 'X' turret, the magazine having to be flooded. (ii) amidships; all radar, except Type 284, is destroyed. One officer, six ratings killed; five ratings seriously wounded. *Sheffield* is straddled, splinters ('football size' according to CS10's report) hurtling inboard.

Weather: driving snow and rain.

## THE SHADOWERS

**1241** CS10 realises that the enemy is on an interception course with Force Two.
CS10 checks fire of Force One and increases speed to 28kn. *Belfast* shadows with radar at seven and a half miles: outside visibility distance.

**1250** Enemy bearing and distance from Force One: 138°, 13,400yd. 36th Division, to westward of cruisers who are in line ahead, opens range to 20,000yd. which is maintained.

**1300** Force One alters to 345°.

**1400** C in C Home Fleet realises that should enemy maintain this course and speed, Force Two will engage at 1715 (approx).

**1405** Force One alters to southward to shadow. co. 180°. (*Belfast*'s rôle has altered to that of shadower.)

**1559** CS10 orders 36th Division to take station to westward of *Scharnhorst,* in case enemy attempts to turn back to attack the convoy.

**1603** *Norfolk* reduces speed while extinguishing a fire raging in a wing compartment.

**1610** *Sheffield* drops back, reporting that her port inner shaft is out of action. She reduces to 10kn. for 30 minutes. (*Belfast* is now in a dangerous position because she is the only ship in touch with *Scharnhorst.* If the capital ship should double back and sink *Belfast, Scharnhorst* could never have been caught.) *This was the second vital moment in the battle.*

**1617** *Duke of York,* radar contact with enemy, 020°, 45,500yd. She makes amplifying report including her own position.

**1621** *Sheffield* works up to 23kn. to rejoin the squadron.

**1632** *Duke of York*'s Fire Control Radar picks up target at 29,700yd. Enemy seems to be zig-zagging, mean course 160°.

**1637** C in C Home Fleet to 36th Division: "Take up the most advantageous position for torpedo attack, but do not fire until ordered to do so." (Destroyers are already in sub-divisions, on either bow of *Duke of York.*)
Force One radar contact with Force Two, 176°, 40,000yd. C in C Home Fleet to CS10: "Open fire with starshell." Range of *Scharnhorst* from *Belfast* 19,300yd.

**1642** Enemy appears to make alteration to port.

## THE CHASE

**1644** Force Two alters to 080° to open 'A'-arcs. Decision is made to check bearing recorder (range is not in doubt) by firing starshell in order to check for 'line' before opening fire with *Duke of York*'s 14in. guns.

**1647** *Belfast* opens fire with starshell.

**1648** *Duke of York* opens fire with starshell.
*Scharnhorst* turrets trained fore and aft, unaware that enemy ships were to the southward of her.

**1650** *Duke of York* engages with main armament. Range is 12,000 yd. but she hits enemy with first and third salvoes.

*A German destroyer, Z30.* (Bibliothek für Zeitgeschichte)

**1241** *Scharnhorst* a/c 110°, sp 28 kn. She fires at *Belfast* as she turns, shooting from "C" turret as she withdraws at speed.
*Scharnhorst* checks fire, probably because her radar was destroyed at 0935. Perhaps, also, she believed she had eluded *Belfast* and wished to remain invisible.

**1300** (approx) *Scharnhorst* abandons attack on convoy. Alters to 155°, 28kn., for escape and return to base.

**1343** *Scharnhorst* to *Z29:* "4th DF break off."

**1440** (approx) *Scharnhorst* alters course round to southward.

**1420** *Scharnhorst* to *Z29:* "4th DF return to base."

*Scharnhorst* in Norway, 1943. A photograph taken from "B" turret roof looking aft and viewing the gigantic range-finder of her Fore DCT. Note the ice on the aerials.
(Bibliothek für Zeitgeschichte)

## THE CHASE

**1708** *Scharnhorst* steers easterly course and engages *Duke of York* and *Jamaica* with main armament: she periodically turns to southward, fires a broadside, then resumes an easterly course to present an "end on" and, therefore, a difficult target.

**1652** *Jamaica* opens fire, her position being six cables astern of *Duke of York*, range 13,000yd. She continues until 1742 when the range has opened to 18,000yd.

**1655** *Scharnhorst* turns, first to the north, then back toward east, as *Belfast* prepares to fire torpedoes.

**1700** *Norfolk* rejoins *Belfast*, and opens fire with her 8in. guns. (The unannounced explosion of *Norfolk*'s broadside surprises those on *Belfast*'s bridge.)
36th Division, north-westward of *Scharnhorst* alters to follow to the east: destroyers slowly gain bearing to northward of *Scharnhorst* as they prepare to launch a torpedo attack.

**1708** *Duke of York* and *Jamaica* are to southward of *Scharnhorst*. *Savage* and *Saumarez* are astern of her and on her port quarter; *Scorpion* and *Stord*, on her starboard quarter and slowly gaining bearing preparing for torpedo attack. *Belfast* and *Norfolk* continue to engage while *Scharnhorst* remains within range.

**1713** C in C Home Fleet orders 36th Division to attack with torpedoes, but they are gaining bearing on the enemy very slowly.

**1742** All cruisers out of range of enemy.

*Machinery space,* Scharnhorst.
(Bibliothek für Zeitgeschichte)

## THE KILL

**1820** 36th Division now suddenly gain bearing as enemy loses speed. *Duke of York* abandons plan to head for Norwegian coast to cut off *Scharnhorst*. *Duke of York* steers straight for the enemy.

**1840** 1st Sub-Division *(Savage* and *Saumarez)* is astern of enemy; 2nd Sub-division *(Scorpion* and *Stord)* closes to about 10,000yd.

**1849** 1st Sub-division engages at 7,000yd., illuminating enemy with starshell. *Stord* swings for torpedo attack but enemy turns, combing tracks. *Stord* fires eight torpedoes at 1,800 yd. but all miss. *Scorpion* fires eight torpedoes at 2,100 yd: one hit. 1st Sub-division now in excellent firing position because of enemy's turn.

**1855** *Savage* with *Saumarez* rapidly train tubes to starboard when on starboard bow of enemy. *Savage* fires eight torpedoes at 3,500yd.: three hits. *Saumarez* is heavily under fire and is hit, shells passing through her director and under her rangefinder director without exploding. She is badly damaged by splinters which reduces her speed to 10kn., on one engine. One officer, ten ratings are killed, eleven ratings wounded; she is able to fire only four torpedoes, range 1,800yd. one hit.

**1901** As 1st and 2nd Sub-divisions withdraw *Duke of York* and *Jamaica* re-engage at 10,400yd. *Norfolk* also opens fire, but checks temporarily: she is uncertain of target because destroyers are still in the area. *Duke of York* is now hitting continually at point blank range.

**1911** U-boats' transmission heard by 4th DF who race to the area of North Cape until 2013 signal received: "Break off operation immediately. Avoid contact with enemy. Make at once for Scharen Islands."

**1915** *Belfast* engages, range 17,000yd. *Duke of York, Jamaica, Norfolk* are firing continually.

**1919** C in C Home Fleet to *Jamaica:* "Sink her with torpedoes."

**1920** C in C Home Fleet to *Belfast:* "Sink her with torpedoes."

**1925** *Jamaica* fires three torpedoes to port, range 3,500yd.

**1927** *Belfast* fires three torpedoes to starboard, range 3,500yd.

## THE KILL

**1800** (approx) A 14in shell from *Duke of York* hits *Scharnhorst* above the waterline and bursts in No. 1 boiler room. *Scharnhorst*'s speed is reduced to 20kn. Second hit destroys Starboard I 5·9in. gun; kills all magazine personnel.

**1815** (approx) Admiralty intercepts signal from *Scharnhorst:* "Enemy is firing at more than 18,000 metres using radar."

**1840** Confusion in *Scharnhorst*'s gunnery fire control when engaging destroyers. *Scharnhorst* regains speed to 22kn. but she fails to notice the 2nd Sub-division closing rapidly.

*Left gun of "A" turret opens fire in Arctic waters.* Scharnhorst *1943.* (Bibliothek für Zeitgeschichte)

**1906** *Scharnhorst* shifts secondary armament fire to *Duke of York* at 8,000yd; she sporadically engages *Duke of York* and *Jamaica* with the remains of her armament. Fires take hold on board *Scharnhorst*. Ammunition explodes. Her speed reduces.

**1911** Commodore U-boats to *Gruppe Eisenbart.* "Make for Square AC4940 immediately at full speed."

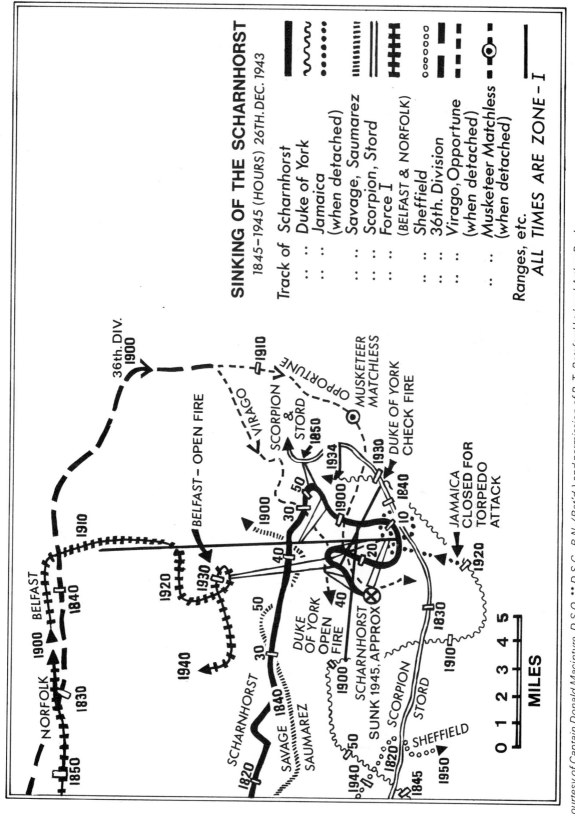

# SINKING OF THE SCHARNHORST
## 1845–1945 (HOURS) 26TH. DEC. 1943

| | | | |
|---|---|---|---|
| Track of | Scharnhorst | | |
| " | " | Duke of York | |
| " | " | Jamaica (when detached) | |
| " | " | Savage, Saumarez | |
| " | " | Scorpion, Stord | |
| " | " | Force I (BELFAST & NORFOLK) | |
| " | " | Sheffield | |
| " | " | 36th. Division | |
| " | " | Virago, Opportune (when detached) | |
| " | " | Musketeer Matchless (when detached) | |
| Ranges, etc. | | | |

**ALL TIMES ARE ZONE – I**

*Courtesy of Captain Donald Macintyre, D.S.O.,** D.S.C., R.N. (Ret'd.) and permission of B. T. Batsford Ltd and Arthur Banks.*

51

**1928** *Duke of York* ceases fire to allow torpedo attacks to continue.

**1931** 72nd Sub-division, *Opportune* and *Virago* attack. *Opportune* fires torpedoes at 2,100yd. and another salvo of four at 2,500yd.: one hit with each salvo.

**1933** 71st Sub-division, *Musketeer* and *Matchless* attack. *Musketeer* fires four torpedoes to starboard, range 1,000yd.: two or three hits between funnel and mainmast. *Matchless* training gear has been strained by a heavy sea and she cannot fire.

**1934** *Virago* fires seven torpedoes, range 2,800yd.: two hits.
72nd Sub-division retires, *Virago* firing guns.
*Duke of York* retires to northward to avoid the general confusion. *Scharnhorst* and her radar echo have disappeared. There is only a red glow in the centre of a pall of smoke.

**1935** *Belfast* runs in to fire more torpedoes but she breaks off because of the mêlée around the target.

**1937** Enemy fire ceases as *Jamaica* fires three torpedoes to starboard, range 3,750yd.: though enemy is beam on, she is concealed by a pall of smoke.

**1938** Last sighting of *Scharnhorst* by *Jamaica*, *Matchless* and *Virago*.

**1948** *Belfast* runs in for another torpedo but sees only survivors, wreckage and smoke.

**1945** Heavy underwater explosion.

**2040** Destroyers pick up 36 ratings out of a company of nearly 2,000 men. No officers survived.

**1920** *Scharnhorst* turns to northward.

*Scharnhorst's blind-folded survivors feel their way ashore across a destroyer's brow.*
(Bibliothek für Zeitgeschichte)

**1935** *Scharnhorst* lists dangerously to starboard and stops. She is out of control, with fire raging in hangar and 'A' and 'B' turret magazines. Ammunition is transferred aft to 'C' to carry on firing. Finally, her guns cannot depress sufficiently because of the heavy list.

**1945** *Scharnhorst* sinks in position 72° 16′ North, 28° 41′ East. She goes down by the bows with her propellers revolving slowly, after rolling over to starboard to the capsized position.

---

The page from the log of HMS *Belfast* for 26 December 1943 reads as follows:

**FROM THE LOG: HMS *BELFAST*: December 26, 1943**

*From Kola    To Kola*
Latitude: 73° 35′ N          Longitude: 25° 47′ E (DR)
0400   *Wind direction: SW Force 8*
       *Weather and visibility: blue sky, cloudy 6 miles*
       *Sea and swell: 56*
       *Corrected Barometric Pressure in Millibars: 992·5*
       *Sea Temperature: 42 (°F)*
0343   Reduce speed to 18 knots
0400   R/S 16 knots because of bad weather
0552   A/C 235° Cease zig-zag
0555   Recommence zig-zag
0740   I/S to 18 knots
0800   *Wind direction: SW Force 7*
       *Weather and visibility: overcast 5 miles*
       *Sea and swell: 45*
       *Corrected Barometric Pressure in Millibars: 990·0*
       *Sea Temperature: 42 (°F)*
0855   Action stations
0912   A/C 270° Cease zig-zag
1000   A/C 300° 1005 I/S to 20 knots
1015   I/S to 22 knots  1016 A/C 305°
1022   I/S to 24 knots
1040   *Norfolk* and *Sheffield* open fire. Echo lost
1200   *Wind direction: SW Force 6*
       *Weather and visibility: cloudy 5 miles*
       *Sea and Swell: 44*
       *Corrected Barometric Pressure in Millibars: 990*
       *Sea Temperature: 43 (°F)*
1220   Resume single line ahead. Course 325°
1230   Joined by *Musketeer, Matchless, Opportune, Virago*. Decrease speed to 18 knots
1300   A/C 345°
1405   Initial bearing of *Scharnhorst* 075°, 30,000 yd. A/C South Begin to shadow her to the south
1600   *Wind direction: S SW Force 5*
       *Weather and visibility: Cloudy 5 miles*
       *Sea and swell: 35*
       *Corrected Barometric Pressure in Millibars: 996*
       *Sea Temperature: no reading*
1630   Increase speed to 27 knots
1750   R/T contact with *Duke of York*
1800   I/S to 28 knots
1815   Engagement with *Scharnhorst* begins

2000   *Wind direction: S Force 4*
       *Weather and visibility: Cloudy 6 miles*
       *Sea and swell: 35*
       *Corrected Barometric Pressure in Millibars: 997*
       *Sea Temperature: no reading*
2140   Decrease speed to fire torpedoes
2145   Fire Starboard torpedoes
2150   Decrease to 16 knots to search area
2155   Searchlights used to search area where she sank
2205   Survivors confirm that *Scharnhorst* is sunk
2210   Suspicious echo
2212   Disregard
2310   I/S to 20 knots. Course 350°
2312   Recommence zig-zag
2400
       *Wind direction: SW Force 3*
       *Weather and visibility: blue sky 5 miles*
       *Sea and swell: 33*
       *Corrected Barometric Pressure in Millibars: 998*
       *Sea Temperature: no reading*

## The Analysis of the Battle

Vice-Admiral Burnett in *Belfast* had handled his cruiser force brilliantly. Always one jump ahead of his opponent, his genius gleamed when he called off his hounds at the right moment (1221 on December 26). By remaining out of visibility range and shadowing with *Belfast's* radar he set the trap for Admiral Fraser to spring. Admiral Fraser and Vice-Admiral Burnett were both honoured with the K.B.E. immediately after the battle.

Though the British outnumbered the German force, it was the superiority of British radar that was the most significant factor in this, the first major sea battle to be decided by the invisible eye of the radar beam. In the murk and darkness of the Arctic winter, the *Scharnhorst*, before the advent of radar, would almost

Jamaica *(Captain J. Hughes-Hallett, D.S.O.)* (IWM)

Saumarez *(Lt.-Cdr. E. W. Walmsley, D.S.C.) 1st Sub-Division.* (IWM)

Stord *(Lt.-Cdr. S. Storeheill) (Royal Norwegian Navy) 2nd Sub-Division.* (IWM)

Matchless *(Lt. W. S. Shaw), 71st Sub-Division.* (IWM)

Opportune *(Commander J. Lee-Barber, D.S.O.) 72nd Sub-Division.* (IWM)

Milne *(Captain M. I. R Campbell, D.S.O., Senior Officer, RA55A Escort).* (IWM)

Savage *(Commander M. D. C. Meyrick) Divisional Leader, 1st Sub-Division.* (IWM)

Scorpion *(Lt.-Cdr. W. S. Clouston) 1st Sub-Division.* (IWM)

Sheffield *(Captain C. T. Addis) (Southampton Class).* (IWM)

Musketeer *(Commander R. L. Fisher, D.S O., O.B.E.) Divisional Leader, 71st Sub-Division.* (IWM)

Onslow *(Captain J. A. McCoy, D.S.O., D17, Senior Officer, JW55B Escort).* (IWM)

Virago *(Lt.-Cdr. A. J. R. White) RA55A Escort.* (IWM)

The great Fleet Air Arm attack on Tirpitz. *April 3, 1944: Barracudas returning to land on* Furious; Belfast *on starboard quarter.* (IWM)

Kent *and* Sussex *in Seidisfjord (photograph taken from* Norfolk). *The convoy destroyer escort can be seen in the left background.* (IWM)

*November 24, 1943, Seidisfjord, Iceland:* Kent *and* Belfast *at anchor (photograph taken from "B" turret of* Norfolk—*note single Oerlikon).* (IWM)

*May 15, 1944. The King visits his Fleet at Scapa before the assault on Europe. His Majesty can be seen saluting in the bows of the MFV.* (IWM)

certainly never have been brought to action. It was *Belfast* and the skill of her company who helped to exploit this radar superiority and to set the stage to avenge *Glorious* and her two escorts, *Acasta* and *Ardent,* sunk by *Scharnhorst* in these Arctic waters three and a half years earlier. The battle was also the last challenge of Hitler's navy to wrest British command of the sea from the Royal Navy.

## The Strategic Results of the Battle of North Cape

The countless number of merchant seaman who had perished on the Russian Run had also been avenged.

*Scharnhorst* was no more: with *Tirpitz* still immobilized from the "X" craft (midget submarine) attack in September 1943, there was no longer a German fleet-in-being. The enemy sea-borne threat to the convoys had vanished with the swirls of *Scharnhorst*'s final plunge.

With the U-boats being mastered and with the growth of Allied air power, the weapons of war could once more flow along the sea lanes, carried by the Allied convoys which were now defended by escort carriers, their aircraft and more and better trained escorts.

Above all, Admiral Sir Bruce Fraser could use offensively the power of his battle fleet, now that the convoys could operate without fear of annihilation by German heavy units. He could release units of his fleet for service against the Japanese in the Far East. There was, for the first time, a scent of victory in the air during the spring of 1944.

After the battle, the captain of HMS *Belfast,* Captain Frederick Parham, D.S.O., received a letter from Admiral-of-the-Fleet, Lord Tovey, who had been Lord Fraser's predecessor as Commander-in-Chief, Home Fleet. Lord Tovey wrote in his letter:

"I was following your intercepts on the chart, and I knew that you and your fine ship flying Bob Burnett's flag would never let go of the brute unless the weather made it absolutely impossible for you to keep up. The combination of the gallant attack you and the other cruisers made on the *Scharnhorst,* coupled with your magnificent shadowing, is as fine an example of cruiser work as has ever been seen."

## The Winter of 1943/44

After sinking *Scharnhorst,* the victors returned on the next day to refuel in the Kola Inlet where *Belfast* loaded up with nineteen tons of Russian silver bullion. In company with *Norfolk* and *Sheffield,* and flying proudly the flag of CS10, she returned at high speed back to the United Kingdom where she arrived on New Year's Day, 1944, to ammunition, fuel and store at Scapa.

On January 10, 1944, *Belfast* was once again back at Rosyth, while her company enjoyed the fruits of their labours in Edinburgh.

In February 1944, the Home Fleet carried on its rôle of supporting the Russian convoys, to the strident calls from Stalin for a "Second Front". There were few in *Belfast* who could know that within three months, their ship would be playing a vital part in the greatest sea-borne invasion in history.

In March 1944, an event occurred which was to cause acute anxiety and dismay amongst the secret committees that were toiling ceaselessly to perfect last minute plans for the liberation of Europe by the free peoples of the world.

During February 1944, reports from Norwegian agents began to stream into Admiralty: *Tirpitz* had shaken herself free of the repair yard where she had lain since Lieutenants Place and Cameron's midget submarine attack in September 1943. The unsinkable leviathan, who had not yet fired her main armament in anger, had moved up to Altenfjord where she lay, surrounded by protective netting, awaiting her sea trials. In this sheer-sided fjord, there was only one way in which Admiral Sir Bruce Fraser could assault her: he now possessed that means.

## The Great Fleet Air Arm Strike: April 3, 1944

On March 30, *Belfast* left Scapa with the Home Fleet forces that were to carry out Operation Tungsten which was to be in two phases:

*Object 1:* The safe and timely arrival of Convoy JW58 from Russia.

*Object 2:* Destruction of *Tirpitz* by air strike.

| Force I (C in C H/F, Admiral Sir Bruce Fraser) *Duke of York* | Force II (Rear-Admiral Escort Carriers, Rear-Admiral A. W. la T. Bisset) *Royalist* |
|---|---|
| *Anson* flagship of Vice-Admiral 2nd Battle Squadron, Vice- Admiral Sir Henry Moore | *Furious* *Emperor* *Pursuer* *Fencer* (A/S carrier) |
| *Belfast* | *Sheffield* |
| *Victorious* | *Jamaica* |
| 6 destroyers | 10 destroyers and 2 oilers |

Convoy JW58 had reached the safe area by April 2, 1944. When *Duke of York,* 4 destroyers and the 2 oilers had rendezvoused, they reorganized as follows:

| Force 7 | Force 8 | | |
|---|---|---|---|
| *Anson* flagship of Vice-Admiral Second BS— in charge "Tungsten" | *Royalist* flagship of RA Escort Carriers | | |
| *Victorious* (21 Barracudas) | *Emperor* *Searcher* | 80 Hellcat, Wildcat, |
| *Furious* (21 Barracudas) | *Pursuer* *Fencer* | Corsair fighters |
| *Belfast* | | | |
| *Jamaica* | | | |
| 6 destroyers | | | |

*The Strike*

Protected by the strong gun protection of Force 7, Force 8 steamed to within 120 miles of Altenfjord before flying off. The 42 Barracudas, some armed with 1,600 lb. AP bombs, others with 500 SAP to explode alongside but beneath the water, skimmed the sea-crests to evade the enemy radar, until only 50 miles from the target. Then they climbed to clear the Norwegian terrain, the fighter escort soaring to 8,000ft.

When over the target, *Tirpitz* was already alerted though only half concealed by the mantle of smoke from the cylinders ashore. She was also desperately trying to proceed under way before the attack developed. For once, however, the enemy was about to taste the dose which he had so often prescribed with his Stukas.

Down from the blue sky streamed a swarm of fighters, their cannon raking *Tirpitz*'s upper deck and destroying communications. Then, as the personnel crouched from the flying splinters (her captain being

*Leaving Scapa Flow for Normandy* (IWM)

*D-Day: the small ships sweep onwards.*
(Courtesy Captain Parham)

Belfast *off the Normandy beaches, June 1944.* (IWM)

*The bombardment continues: her 4in in action. Her 44in bridge searchlight is clearly visible* (IWM)

wounded and confusion reigning) the Barracudas plummetted downwards, streaking down the sheer sides of the fjord.

All aircraft, except for one Barracuda which had been shot down, landed on their waiting carriers who were steaming off-shore under the protective power of the guns of Force 7.

Though *Tirpitz* was struck by fourteen bombs, she did not sink. So badly wounded was she however, that she remained unoperational until rolled over by the 12,000 lb. bombs delivered later by the crack blockbuster squadron of the Royal Air Force.

Operation *Tungsten* was a complete success but, to make doubly sure, the operation was repeated three weeks later on April 25. The strike was nullified by atrocious weather but the operation was not entirely abortive for, once again off Bodo, a convoy of four supply ships was sent to the bottom.

After visiting Clyde on April 17, *Belfast* refitted at Rosyth and gave leave until May 8—less than a month before the great events that lay before her.

Leaving Rosyth and now in all respects ready again for war, she had one pleasant assignment to keep: to be in the Home Fleet base of Scapa Flow when His Majesty King George VI visited his ships. 'It was a happy occasion because the King had been trained as a sailor and had served at Jutland. No doubt, also, the Sovereign wished to thank his seamen and, in his heart, wish them "God-speed" before the momentous events that lay ahead. *Belfast* enjoyed the honour of carrying the King and flying his Royal Standard.

## Normandy: June 6, 1944

There is, regrettably, no space in this work to recount in detail the part played by sea-power in the landings on June 6 upon the north coast of France. Suffice to state that beneath the umbrella of air power, the ships were able to choose the points of assault; and, the armies having secured a foothold, the navies could then transport the back-up forces of men, weapons and material. First, the initial landings *had* to succeed and the assault troops be able to exploit their landings. Constant bombardment support was therefore essential for the invading army.

A large component in the initial attacks during the grey dawn of June 6 was the pulverising gunfire which rendered immobile the German defenders manning their concrete pill boxes and gun emplacements along the sand dunes of Normandy. The best remedy for inculcating a desire to leave these undesirable residences was undoubtedly a naval shell fired from a considerable distance. Plunging fire bombardment is reputedly one of the worst horrors a static soldier can can be asked to endure.

A broadside from *Nelson* or *Rodney* would announce its impending arrival by a disconcerting flutter and cacophony through the air. The shells with a mass equalling the weight of a London omnibus, would plunge from their high parabolas to land methodically in salvoes, at spaced intervals, from guns weighing 105 tons each.

But from *Belfast,* Headquarters ship of the Bombardment Group of the Eastern Task Force, a hurricane of 6 in. shell, 96 rounds per minute, could smother and pulverize the target area.

During the forenoon of Friday, June 2, whilst last minute preparations for Overlord were being settled, a delicate situation concerning *Belfast* was coming to the boil in high places.

Winston Churchill, Prime Minister, had summoned the First Lord of the Admiralty, A. V. Alexander, and the First Sea Lord, Admiral of the Fleet, Sir Andrew Cunningham, to meet him in the map room. To their astonishment, Winston informed them that he was going to sea in *Belfast* to watch Overlord, the invasion landings. He had already arranged it, he said, with Admiral Ramsay, and Rear-Admiral Dalrymple-Hamilton who was the Commander of Force E. He glowered defensively at Mr. Alexander and Sir Andrew Cunningham, saying that he would be extremely affronted if anyone was to oppose him.

Sir Andrew Cunningham, remembering an identical performance over Pantellaria a year previously, stood up to Churchill and told him that it would be criminal for him to go. Sir Andrew did not know that General Eisenhower, the Supreme Commander, had already refused Winston who then retorted that "Ike" had no control over the administration of the Royal Navy; Winston said that there was nothing against Winston Spencer Churchill joining a ship's company.

The King, happily, intervened and settled the matter by stating that if his Prime Minister was going, the King would also go to sea as head of the three Services. So *Belfast* was not to endure the embarrassment of such a Very Important Person during the early days of the invasion.

### SPECIAL ORDER OF THE DAY TO THE OFFICERS AND MEN OF THE ALLIED NAVAL EXPEDITIONARY FORCE

It is to be our privilege to take part in the greatest amphibious operation in history—a necessary preliminary to the opening of the Western Front in Europe which in conjunction with the great Russian advance, will crush the fighting power of Germany.

This is the opportunity which we have long awaited and which must be seized and pursued with relentless determination: the hopes and prayers of the free world and of the enslaved peoples of Europe will be with us and we cannot fail them.

Our task in conjunction with the Merchant Navies of the United Nations, and supported by the Allied Air Forces, is to carry the Allied Expeditionary Force to the Continent to establish it there in a secure bridgehead and to build it up and maintain it at a rate which will outmatch that of the enemy.

Let no one underestimate the magnitude of this task.

The Germans are desperate and will resist fiercely until we out-manoeuvre and out-fight them, which we can and we will do. To every one of you will be given the opportunity to show by his determination and resource that dauntless spirit of resolution which individually strengthens and inspires and which collectively is irresistible.

I count on every man to do his utmost to ensure the success of this great enterprise which is the climax of the European war.

Good luck to you all and God speed

**B. H. Ramsay**
*Admiral*
*Allied Naval Commander-in-Chief*
*Expeditionary Force.*

## Operation Overlord: Liberation of Europe

After the King's visit to his Fleet, *Belfast* left Scapa for the Clyde where, from May 31 to June 3, she and the massive bombardment force for Operation Overlord gathered to rehearse their orders.

At dawn on Saturday, June 2, there slipped from the Clyde the bombardment groups of the Eastern Task Force: *Warspite, Ramilles,* the monitor *Roberts, Belfast,* four other cruisers and fifteen destroyers. They were to be in their bombardment positions by 0530 on June 5. The naval contribution to Overlord was code-named Neptune: its object, to land the armies at the right time—and then to keep them supplied.

The weather then turned sour. The gale raged during the long Saturday/Sunday night so that General Eisenhower, the Supreme Commander, was forced to postpone D-day by twenty-four hours. The complex armadas, all converging upon the focal point in mid-channel (The Spout), were forced to reverse courses or to anchor. The bombardment force in the Irish sea turned back, the ships reversing course until able to resume their heading again when the weather began to moderate.

## D-DAY: June 6, 1944
At 0530 on June 6, 1944, the flagship of The Commander, Force E (Rear-Admiral F. H. G. Dalrymple-Hamilton), HMS *Belfast* (Captain F. R. Parham, D.S.O.), having passed through the swept channel, opened fire at a range of about six miles upon a German battery of four 10 cm. gun-howitzers at Ver-sur-Mer: her bombardment covered Gold Beach and three miles to the westward of Courselles. *Belfast* carried out deliberate bombardment fire for two hours. At 0730 the assault forces, launched from seven miles off-shore, threshed past her and surged up the beaches. The Seventh Battalion of the Green Howards finally over-ran the 10 cm. battery where the German gunners were still cowering in their bunkers, their guns destroyed above them.

By the evening of the same day, a foothold had been secured by the Allies along the fifty-mile length of the Normandy fore-shore.

On the same day, Doenitz, the German Supreme Naval Commander, had unleashed his U-boats from the Biscay ports; the submarines entered the western Channel on June 7 and proceeded to attack the invasion shipping. Harried by ten A/S support groups and by relentless attacks of the R.A.F. Coastal Command, the U-boats made little impact upon the grand design. The Allies had landed.

On June 12 *Belfast,* in company with *Diadem,* a later *Dido*-class, bombarded the Juno beaches off Courselles and, running out of ammunition, returned to Portsmouth for ammunitioning, an evolution she repeated once more during the next month. On June 18 she sailed from Portsmouth to return to her bombardment duties in the Eastern sector. For the next ten days, she bombarded, with the battleship *Rodney* and *Argonaut,* the *Dido*-class cruiser recently refitted at Philadelphia after being torpedoed in 1943.

*Belfast* returned again to bombard in the Juno area. The bombarding force, *Belfast, Emerald,* the old 6 in. cruiser; *Roberts,* the 15 in. monitor; and *Danae,* the 6 in. light cruiser, were very vulnerable at this time due to the gallant attempts of enemy attacks by *Marders* (human torpedoes) and *Linsens* (explosive motor torpedo boats).

In addition, enemy aircraft saturated the area at night with oyster mines, so that *Belfast* could remain underway only by going slow ahead or astern on one propeller. An enterprising enemy gun continually ranged on *Belfast,* thereby forcing the ship to keep constantly on the move.

During darkness, the bombardment forces sheltered behind a smoke screen but, on one moonlight night, *Belfast* found herself at anchor well to the westward of the blanket of smoke. Captain Parham felt an intuitive uneasiness and suggested to Rear-Admiral Dalrymple-

Hamilton that the ship should weigh and return to the eastward and the benefits of concealment.

The Admiral approved. As *Belfast* disappeared into the smoke, enemy R/T transmissions between the Le Havre E-boats were intercepted. The enemy was converging on the cruiser's recent anchorage position and the R/T operators were quoting *Belfast*'s name.

Two days later, *Belfast* moved to the eastward, because General Montgomery had started his offensive and was now ready to break out of Caen. To the monstrous broadsides of *Rodney* and *Roberts, Belfast* added her salvoes, the last time in Hitler's war that she was to fire her guns in action. She had been bombarding for five weeks and she was one of the last ships to leave.

The end was at last in sight.

## *Belfast*'s War Diary: June/July 1944
| | |
|---|---|
| June 6-9 | Bombardment—assault support |
| June 12 | Area JUNO, bombarding with *Diadem,* p.m. Withdrew to sail for Portsmouth |
| June 16 | Ammunitioning at Portsmouth |
| June 18 | Sails from Portsmouth for JUNO area. Bombarding |
| June 19 | The Great Gale |
| June 22 | Overlord threatened—Mulberry harbour justifies itself |
| June 23 | Bombarding |
| June 30 | Bombarding with *Rodney* and *Argonaut* |
| July 6 | Bombarding in JUNO area with *Emerald, Roberts* (monitor) and *Danae* Danger from human torpedoes and explosive motor boats, and oyster mines |
| July 8 | Montgomery begins offensive and breaks out from Caen. *Belfast, Roberts, Rodney* bombarding in support |
| July 10 | At sea |
| July 12 | Arrives Scapa Flow |

*Belfast*'s 6 in. guns had recoiled in anger for the last time during Hitler's War. She, like her company, needed a refit, not only to refurbish but to prepare herself for the last great heave: the defeat of the most hated enemy of all—Japan.

## Tropical Refit: July 1944—April 18, 1945
On arrival in the Tyne, Captain Parham, after nearly two stenuous years in command, handed over on July 29 to Captain R. M. Dick, C.B.E., D.S.C., who was to command her during the next two years.

In addition to improving her accommodation for the tropics, the object of the refit carried out by the Middle Dock and High Shields Engineering Company was to arm her with the latest weapons and fire control for defence against the Japanese "suicide-planes", the *Kamikazes*.

When *Belfast* emerged for trials in April 1945, a few weeks after Hitler had shot himself in the Berlin bunker, she was, as before, a ship well able to take care of herself.

**ALTERATIONS and ADDITIONS: May 1945**
**4 in. HA Armament**
S3 and P3 mountings removed. Remaining Mountings S1, S2, P1, P2, modified to Remote Power Control (RPC). Auto-Selector-Alignment was fitted to the HACS Mark IV Tables.
**Pom-Poms**
2 eight-barrelled Mark VIII guns on Mark VI mountings, RP10 (Remote Power Controlled). One each side of mainmast on Pom-pom deck controlled by: 2 Pom-pom Directors, Mark IV with Gyro Rate Units

Belfast *joins the Pacific Fleet, August 1945. Note the Bofors on "B" turret (photographed from* Berwick*)* (IWM)

*Royal Marine Whaler's crew, 1945.*
            (Courtesy of B. H. Palk, R.M. Retired)

*Deck Hockey on the Quarterdeck during the Dog Watches.*
            (Courtesy of B. H. Palk, R.M. Retired)

*Transfer by Jackstay.*
            (Courtesy of B. H. Palk, R.M. Retired)

*The Ship's Band, 1945–1948.*
            (Courtesy of B. H. Palk, R.M. Retired)

*Visit to the City of Belfast October 20, 1948. The Harbour Commissioners come on board.*
(Courtesy Belfast Newsletter Ltd.)

*October 21, 1948, Sir Basil Brooke, Prime Minister of Northern Ireland, talks with Captain Le Mesurer.*
(Courtesy Belfast Newsletter Ltd.)

*The Seamen's Platoon marches past the Lord Mayor (photograph taken from the top of the Guildhall).*
(Courtesy Belfast Newsletter Ltd.)

Mark I + Type 282 radar, mounted on sponsons high up on the forward edge of the after funnel.

4 four-barrelled Mark VIII guns on Mark VII mountings, RP50, sited each side:

1 forward edge of Pom-pom deck, just abaft for'd funnel.

1 abreast after HADT on after superstructure controlled by: 4 Pom-pom Directors Mark IV with Gyro Rate Units Mark I and Type 282 radar, sited each side: 1 on sponsons, just aft of the for'd Pom-pom mounting on Pom-pom deck, 1 on after superstructure in sponsons forward of the after HADT.

### 20 mm. Oerlikons

Twelve twin mountings fitted and re-sited as follows:

6 Twin Mark V 20 mm., powered-mountings with tachymetric sights
6 newly designed hand-worked mountings with tachymetric sights

These six twin mountings were sited as follows:

1 lower bridge wings.
1 lower bridge, after corners, to replace 44 in. searchlights which were landed with the after pair.
1 B gun deck, 1 abreast forward funnel, 1 abreast after funnel, 1 on quarterdeck (2 mountings abreast of each other).

In addition, two single Mark VII mountings were sited one each side of the after super structure, in protected sponsons.

Magazine stowage was enlarged.

### Radar

In May 1945 she carried:

Type 242— IFF
,, 243— IFF
,, 253 IFF
,, 277 AA Height-finding and surface warning
,, 281 Air warning
,, 282 ⎫
,, 283 ⎭ Pom-pom Directors and blind barrage
,, 274 6 in. Armament
,, 285 HA
,, 293Q Close range height-finding and surface warning.

*44 in. Searchlights:* all landed
*Aircraft:* Hangar converted into recreation and accommodation spaces
*Catapult:* removed
*DCT Rangefinder:* for bombardment use only
*Damage Control Headquarters:* A secondary HQ was built on the port side, below the armoured deck, on the after side of 158 bulkhead, abreast "B" boiler room
*Echo Sounder:* was re-sited in the bridge plotting room
*Depth Charges:* 6 (15 spares)
*Accommodation:* The "internals" of the ship were greatly modified to make more tolerable the heat of the tropics

An interesting alteration was: "To improve laundry facilities by installing a shirt press and single sleeve form."

For the first time also can be seen the emergence of a rudimentary Action Information Organisation (AIO), the development of the complex information originally handled by the Action Plot.

*Oil Fuel Replenishment and Transfer at Sea*

The vast sea distances at sea in the Pacific had produced the Fleet Train of the huge American Task Force. It was vital therefore that *Belfast* should be modernized to the latest developments and standards of oiling at sea and she was brought up to date during this refit.

Replenishment speed was about nine knots.

*Paravanes:*

6 Mark VII Bodies with: 6–31 knot planes
2–22 knot planes
4–16 knot planes

The Starboard paravane towed from the for'd chain.
The Port paravane towed from the after chain.

## To the Far East, June 17, 1945: Sydney Refit

The refit ended on April 17, 1945 and, after kitting up with tropical rig, trials and exercises were carried out from Rosyth and Scapa. Leaving home waters on June 17, Captain Dick took his new ship to the Far East.

A short work up followed in Malta at the beginning of July when, on the twelfth, she learnt that she was to be Flagship of the 2nd Cruiser Squadron, British Pacific Fleet.

| | |
|---|---|
| June 21, 1945 | Arrived Gibraltar |
| | Malta—working up in Mediterranean |
| | To be Flagship, 2nd Cruiser Squadron, British Pacific Fleet |
| July 27 | Arrived Port Said from Alexandria |
| July 31 | Left Suez for Aden with *Hunt* destroyers, *Bleasdale, Cowdray* and *Eggesford* |
| July 31 | Arrived Aden |
| August 1 | Left Aden |
| August 6 | Arrived Colombo |
| August 7 | Left Colombo for Australia (4th Cruiser Squadron) (British Pacific Fleet) Sydney |

After recovering from the warmth of a typical Australian welcome, *Belfast* spent a few days in dockyard having her close range armament again improved. For the first time she was to carry 40 mm. Bofors, that weapon coveted by so many ships.

After her short Sydney refit in August, her armament was as follows:

$2 \times$ 8-barrelled Pom-poms ⎫
$4 \times$ 4-barrelled Pom-poms ⎭ as before

$4 \times$ single barrel Mark XVI Pom-poms with Mark XIV sights one each side, for'd end of lower bridge; one each side abreast mainmast.

2 single Bofors (Boffins), Mark V with Mark XIV sights

3 single Bofors Mark III: one on "B" gun roof; two on lower bridge wings for'd, each side.

*Note:* The original twin Oerlikon mountings were used for these single Bofors.

2 twin Oerlikons, Mark XIV sights.

4 single Oerlikons, Mark XIV sights.

## The Japanese Surrender— Aftermath: September 1945

The Atomic Bomb had exploded above Hiroshima and Nagasaki before *Belfast* reached Sydney. For the Pacific Fleet, however, these weeks immediately after the surrender were hectic and confused.

On September 9, 1945, Rear-Admiral R. M. Servaes C.B.E., commanding the 2nd Cruiser Squadron, BPF, hoisted his flag in *Belfast*. After a short call at Kiirun in Formosa (Taiwan), the ship steamed to the Yangtse Bar to anchor with other ships of Task Group III on September 18. On September 24, the Squadron was in the Whangpoo River.

## Missions of Mercy

In Shanghai were massing our emaciated survivors of the Japanese prison camps. To these British souls, both men and women, the sight of White Ensigns fluttering proudly from the great ships lying off-shore would remain an unforgettable memory. The work of mercy continued, day and night, the ships ferrying between Shanghai and Hong Kong the sick and dying who were gently lifted ashore to be tended in the hospitals manned by British medical men and nurses. On New Year's Eve, 1945, *Belfast* arrived at Shanghai for the last trip. The New Year would bring a fresh purpose to her life, because now, for a few years, her mission would be to pacify the ferment that raged in the East Indies and Far East, now that the shooting war was over.

## Uneasy Peace: 1946–48

The early months of 1946 were a difficult period for the Pacific Fleet. The East Indies were in a turmoil and the Japanese had still to be rounded up. De-mobilization had begun and men were, after seven years of war, desperately hungry to learn the ways of peace. A system, the fairest possible, of Age-and-Service Release was instituted but the inevitable upheaval disturbed the efficient functioning of the Fleets. For *Belfast*, however, the pain was bearable with the thought of the pleasant cruises that lay ahead, after her next visit to Sydney.

There in February 1946, her torpedo armament and depth-charges were landed, the bed plates being left for future contingencies. On March 6 *Belfast* arrived in Wellington, New Zealand, for the start of her Pacific Island and Japanese cruise.

**1946**

| | |
|---|---|
| March 6 | Arrived Wellington, New Zealand |
| March 7 | Departed for Napier, South Island, N.Z. |
| March 11 | Left Napier for Suva |
| March 15 | Arrived Suva, Fiji |
| March 20 | Left Suva for Tokyo Bay |
| April 12 | Arrived Kure, Japan wearing Flag of CS2 |
| April 17 | Left Kure for Kobe |
| April 18 | Arrived Kobe in company, HMAS *Warramunga* |
| April 23 | Left Kobe for Yokohama with *Warramunga* |
| April 24 | Arrived Yokohama. Rear-Admiral Servaes hauls down his flag |
| May 2 | Left Yokohama for Hong Kong, sailing east of Formosa |

## Singapore Refit: May 16—July 15, 1946

A radar teacher outfit HRB was fitted in order to train radar personnel on board, instead of sending them to schools ashore.

Air conditioning was improved to increase ventilation—the wheel had turned full circle from the days of 1942 when steam heating was installed. The health of the ship's company was a continuous source of concern when living under tropical conditions: adequate washing facilities were essential, for dreaded "dhobie's itch" and prickly heat soon took their toll. Salt water showers were provided on the upper deck.

Extra scuttles were fitted to the living spaces and those which had been blanked off in wartime, over 8 ft. above the WL, were unsealed.

Ammunitioning at sea was catered for by fitting two extra derricks, one on "B" gun, one on the quarter-deck.

A Type TCS 12 R/T transmitter was added to back up the TBS.

The Admiral's quarters and those of his staff were altered and improved, as were communications, to bring the ship up to the requirements of a Fleet Flagship on a tropical station.

Captain Dick was relieved by Captain H. B. Ellison D.S.O. on July 9, six days before the end of the refit.

## Flagship, 5th Cruiser Squadron: 1946

On July 29, 1946, a fortnight after completion of the Singapore refit, Vice-Admiral Sir Denis Boyd, K.C.B., C.B.E., D.S.C., hoisted his flag in *Belfast*. He was Captain of *Illustrious* at Taranto and, afterwards, when she endured the greatest mauling a carrier ever survived; later, he was Rear-Admiral (Air) in *Formidable* at Matapan, and Commander of the Eastern Fleet Carrier Force in *Indomitable*. *Belfast* had every reason to feel proud of her new rôle as flagship of Vice-Admiral Boyd's Cruiser Squadron.

The ship sailed from Singapore for Hong Kong and on August 15, 1946, a year after the Japanese capitulation, *Belfast* paid visits of good-will to ports of that vanquished nation. She visited China a month later, finally returning to Hong Kong on October 15. Her diary tells the story:

**1946**

| | |
|---|---|
| July 29 | 5th Cruiser Squadron: Vice-Admiral Sir Denis Boyd, C-in-C BPF |
| August 15 | Left Hong Kong for visits to Japanese ports |
| August 20 | Yokohama |

| | |
|---|---|
| August 28 | Otura |
| September 4 | Kure |
| September 11 | Kobe |
| September 18 | Arrived Woosung in series of visits to Chinese ports |
| September 20 | Nanking |
| September 25 | Shanghai |
| October 2 | Tsingtao |
| October 5 | Chinwangtao |
| October 10 | Peitaiho |
| October 15 | Arrived Hong Kong |

**1947**

| | |
|---|---|
| December 1 | Singapore, sailed same day |
| December 6 | Hong Kong—Repairs |

She spent Christmas 1946 in Hong Kong and the Spring of 1947 again visiting Japan and China. In these unsettled times, the presence of this magnificent ship had a stabilising influence upon events:

| | |
|---|---|
| March 3 | Left Kure, Japan. ETA Shanghai March 5 |
| March 5 | Shanghai |
| March 17 | Tsingtao |
| March 24 | Hong Kong |
| April 11 | sailed Hong Kong |
| May 19 | arrived Singapore for docking and refit |

## Malaya: 1947

*Belfast* spent the summer of 1947 in the vicinity of Malaya, that dependency about to be infiltrated by Chinese Communist terrorists. A refit ended at the beginning of June when the ship visited Penang on June 16; then Malacca on June 17, returning finally to Singapore on June 19.

During July she was at Hong Kong, and then, sadly, on August 20, 1947, Vice-Admiral Sir Denis Boyd hauled down his flag: *Belfast* was on her way home to Portsmouth with eighty service passengers, to pay off into reserve.

## The Reserve Fleet and Long Refit: October 15, 1947—October 15, 1948

HMS *Belfast*, it seemed, had reached a trough in the record of her faithful service: *"Reserve"*—that evocative term of despair for the future of a fighting ship. On November 20, Captain Ellison left her, Commander J. R. Westmacott being appointed In Command to relieve him whilst the ship underwent a long refit in reserve—her turbines were opened up and long-overdue maintenance was carried out. By the end of the refit, four more Bofors, Mark VIIs, had been added, two each side abreast both funnels.

The country was passing through an inevitably depressing and unhappy phase: men were too pre-occupied with establishing themselves in civvy street to bother about the state of the nation or the Navy: ". . . leave that to the politicians."

*Belfast*, happily, was alerted to serve again, for there were rumblings of discord once again in the Far East. On January 20, 1948, Commander Westmacott was relieved by Commander O. S. Stevinson who looked after the ship until September 22 when she re-commissioned with Captain E. K. Le Mesurer in command.

## Visit to City of Belfast: October 20, 1948

She left Portsmouth, kitted up for the tropics, on October 15, 1948, but before leaving home waters she had a long-standing appointment to keep: the presentation of the magnificent silver bell, the gift of the loyal people of Belfast which had been guarded safely throughout the long days of the blitz.

On October 20, 1948 the ship arrived in the City of

*Trafalgar Day, City of Belfast. The Royal Marine Band leads the march past.* (Courtesy Belfast Newsletter Ltd.)

*The Seamen's Platoon marches past the Lord Mayor.* (Courtesy Belfast Newsletter Ltd.)

*The ship is presented her crest by the High Sheriff, October 22, 1948. Motto:* Pro Tanto Quid Retribuamus.
(Courtesy Belfast Newsletter Ltd.)

*The Boys' Platoon.*     (Courtesy Belfast Newsletter Ltd.)

*Presentation of the Silver Bell; the Prime Minister is at left.*
(Courtesy Belfast Newsletter Ltd.)

*God speed.*     (Courtesy Belfast Newsletter Ltd.)

# 1943 GUNNERY PRINCIPLES

Radar    Human Observation    Secondary

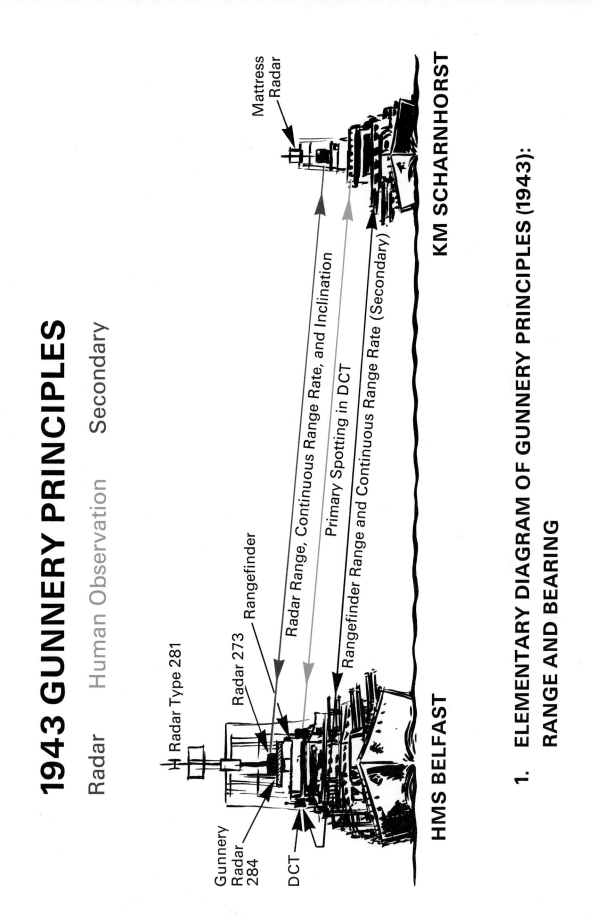

Mattress Radar

Radar Type 281

Radar 273

Rangefinder

Gunnery Radar 284

DCT

Radar Range, Continuous Range Rate, and Inclination

Primary Spotting in DCT

Rangefinder Range and Continuous Range Rate (Secondary)

HMS BELFAST

KM SCHARNHORST

1.  ELEMENTARY DIAGRAM OF GUNNERY PRINCIPLES (1943): RANGE AND BEARING

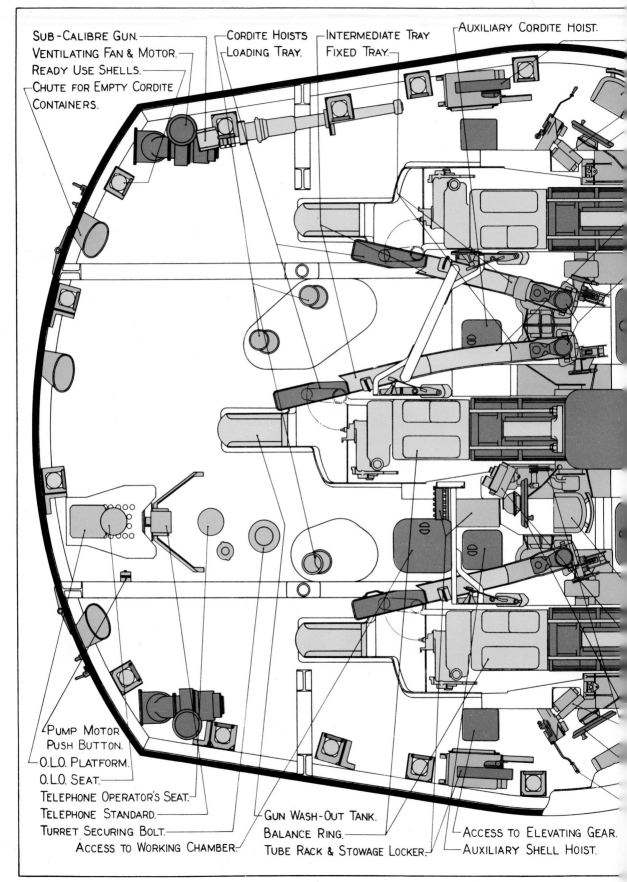

SUB-CALIBRE GUN.
VENTILATING FAN & MOTOR.
READY USE SHELLS.
CHUTE FOR EMPTY CORDITE
CONTAINERS.

CORDITE HOISTS
LOADING TRAY.

INTERMEDIATE TRAY
FIXED TRAY.

AUXILIARY CORDITE HOIST.

PUMP MOTOR
PUSH BUTTON.
O.L.O. PLATFORM.
O.L.O. SEAT.
TELEPHONE OPERATOR'S SEAT.
TELEPHONE STANDARD.
TURRET SECURING BOLT.
ACCESS TO WORKING CHAMBER.

GUN WASH-OUT TANK.
BALANCE RING.
TUBE RACK & STOWAGE LOCKER.

ACCESS TO ELEVATING GEAR.
AUXILIARY SHELL HOIST.

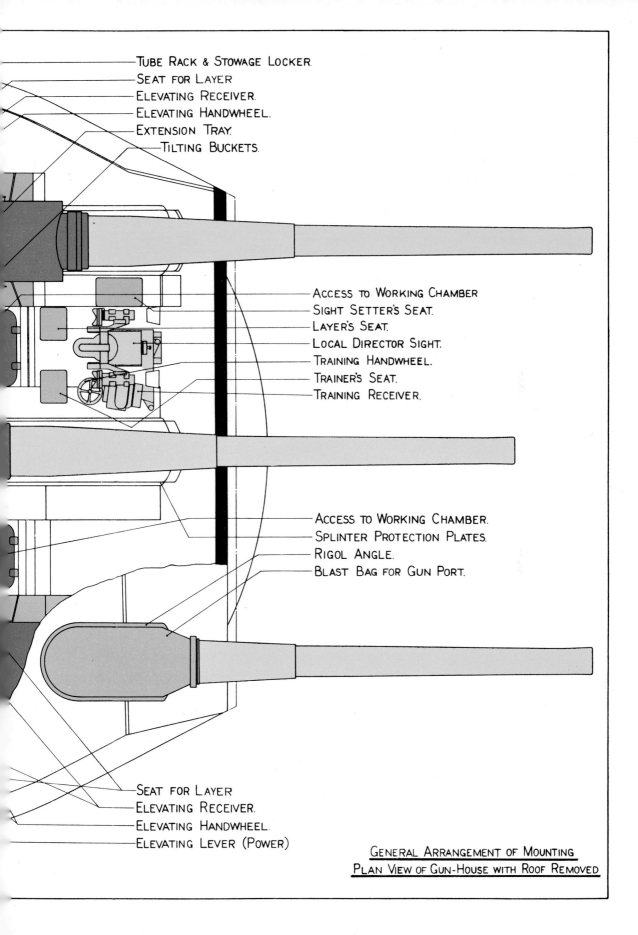

TUBE RACK & STOWAGE LOCKER.
SEAT FOR LAYER
ELEVATING RECEIVER.
ELEVATING HANDWHEEL.
EXTENSION TRAY.
TILTING BUCKETS.

ACCESS TO WORKING CHAMBER
SIGHT SETTER'S SEAT.
LAYER'S SEAT.
LOCAL DIRECTOR SIGHT.
TRAINING HANDWHEEL.
TRAINER'S SEAT.
TRAINING RECEIVER.

ACCESS TO WORKING CHAMBER.
SPLINTER PROTECTION PLATES.
RIGOL ANGLE.
BLAST BAG FOR GUN PORT.

SEAT FOR LAYER
ELEVATING RECEIVER.
ELEVATING HANDWHEEL.
ELEVATING LEVER (POWER)

GENERAL ARRANGEMENT OF MOUNTING
PLAN VIEW OF GUN-HOUSE WITH ROOF REMOVED

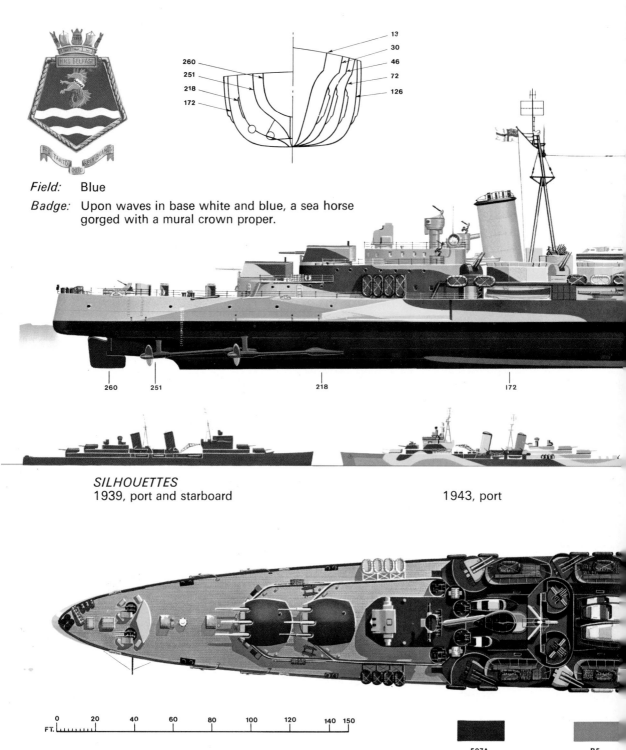

*Field:* Blue

*Badge:* Upon waves in base white and blue, a sea horse gorged with a mural crown proper.

*SILHOUETTES*
1939, port and starboard                    1943, port

```
0    20    40    60    80    100    120    140  150
FT.
```

507A
HOME FLEET DARK GREY                              B5

HMS *BELFAST* is depicted in the Admiralty Disruptive Camouflage Type 25 she wore as she went into action at the Battle of North Cape on 26 December 1943.
At that date, the Admiral's barge would have been covered and both Walrus amphibians had been landed on 6 June 1943, the flight being disbanded in September.
A second battle ensign would have been flying at the foremast.

*James Goulding © Profile Publications Ltd.*

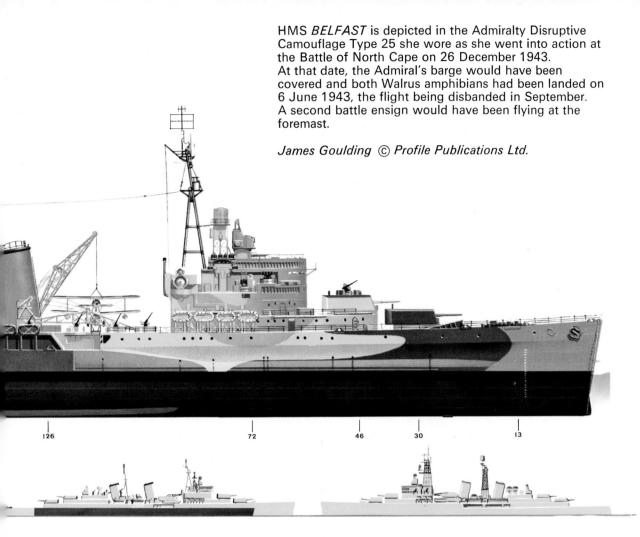

|   |   |   |   |   |
|---|---|---|---|---|
| 126 | 72 | 46 | 30 | 13 |

1945, British Pacific Fleet, port and starboard          1956, port and starboard

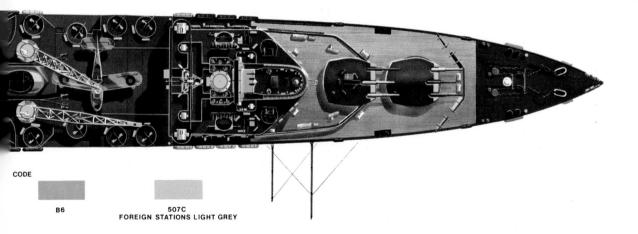

CODE

B6          507C
FOREIGN STATIONS LIGHT GREY

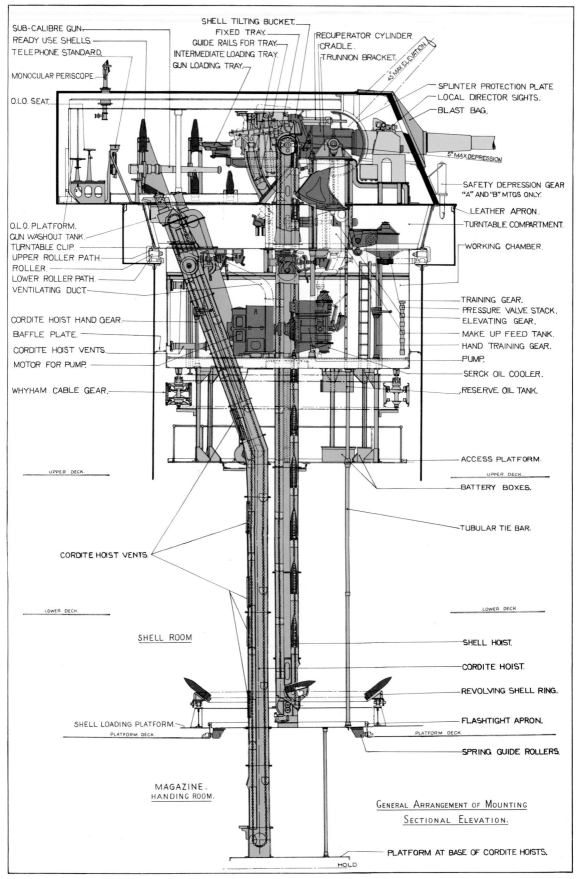

SUB-CALIBRE GUN.
READY USE SHELLS.
TELEPHONE STANDARD.
MONOCULAR PERISCOPE.
O.L.O. SEAT.

SHELL TILTING BUCKET.
FIXED TRAY.
GUIDE RAILS FOR TRAY.
INTERMEDIATE LOADING TRAY.
GUN LOADING TRAY.
RECUPERATOR CYLINDER.
CRADLE.
TRUNNION BRACKET.
45° MAX. ELEVATION.
SPLINTER PROTECTION PLATE
LOCAL DIRECTOR SIGHTS.
BLAST BAG.
5° MAX DEPRESSION.
SAFETY DEPRESSION GEAR "A" AND "B" MTGS ONLY.
LEATHER APRON.
TURNTABLE COMPARTMENT.
WORKING CHAMBER.

O.L.O. PLATFORM.
GUN WASHOUT TANK.
TURNTABLE CLIP.
UPPER ROLLER PATH.
ROLLER.
LOWER ROLLER PATH.
VENTILATING DUCT.
CORDITE HOIST HAND GEAR.
BAFFLE PLATE.
CORDITE HOIST VENTS.
MOTOR FOR PUMP.
WHYHAM CABLE GEAR.

TRAINING GEAR.
PRESSURE VALVE STACK.
ELEVATING GEAR.
MAKE UP FEED TANK.
HAND TRAINING GEAR.
PUMP.
SERCK OIL COOLER.
RESERVE OIL TANK.

UPPER DECK.
UPPER DECK.
ACCESS PLATFORM.
BATTERY BOXES.
TUBULAR TIE BAR.

CORDITE HOIST VENTS.

LOWER DECK.
LOWER DECK.

SHELL ROOM.
SHELL HOIST.
CORDITE HOIST.
REVOLVING SHELL RING.
FLASHTIGHT APRON.

SHELL LOADING PLATFORM.
PLATFORM DECK.
PLATFORM DECK.
SPRING GUIDE ROLLERS.

MAGAZINE.
HANDING ROOM.

GENERAL ARRANGEMENT OF MOUNTING
SECTIONAL ELEVATION.

PLATFORM AT BASE OF CORDITE HOISTS.

HOLD.

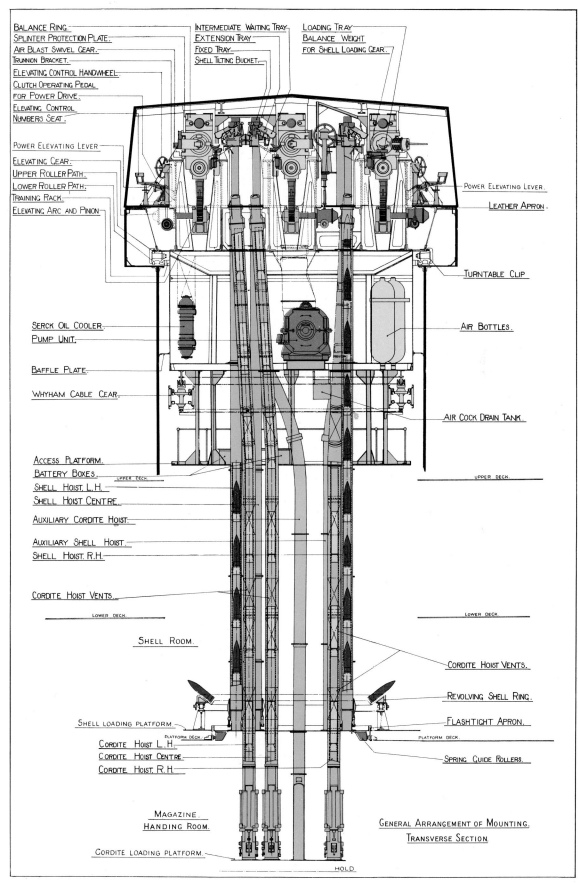

BALANCE RING.
SPLINTER PROTECTION PLATE.
AIR BLAST SWIVEL GEAR.
TRUNNION BRACKET.
ELEVATING CONTROL HANDWHEEL.
CLUTCH OPERATING PEDAL FOR POWER DRIVE.
ELEVATING CONTROL NUMBERS SEAT.

INTERMEDIATE WAITING TRAY
EXTENSION TRAY
FIXED TRAY
SHELL TILTING BUCKET.

LOADING TRAY
BALANCE WEIGHT FOR SHELL LOADING GEAR.

POWER ELEVATING LEVER.
ELEVATING GEAR.
UPPER ROLLER PATH.
LOWER ROLLER PATH.
TRAINING RACK.
ELEVATING ARC AND PINION.

POWER ELEVATING LEVER.
LEATHER APRON.

TURNTABLE CLIP

SERCK OIL COOLER.
PUMP UNIT.

AIR BOTTLES.

BAFFLE PLATE.
WHYHAM CABLE GEAR.

AIR COCK DRAIN TANK.

ACCESS PLATFORM.
BATTERY BOXES.
SHELL HOIST, L.H.
SHELL HOIST CENTRE.
AUXILIARY CORDITE HOIST.
AUXILIARY SHELL HOIST.
SHELL HOIST. R.H.

UPPER DECK.

UPPER DECK.

CORDITE HOIST VENTS.

LOWER DECK.

LOWER DECK.

SHELL ROOM.

CORDITE HOIST VENTS.

REVOLVING SHELL RING.

SHELL LOADING PLATFORM.

FLASHTIGHT APRON.

PLATFORM DECK.

PLATFORM DECK.

CORDITE HOIST L.H.
CORDITE HOIST CENTRE.
CORDITE HOIST R.H.

SPRING GUIDE ROLLERS.

MAGAZINE.
HANDING ROOM.

GENERAL ARRANGEMENT OF MOUNTING.
TRANSVERSE SECTION.

CORDITE LOADING PLATFORM.

HOLD.

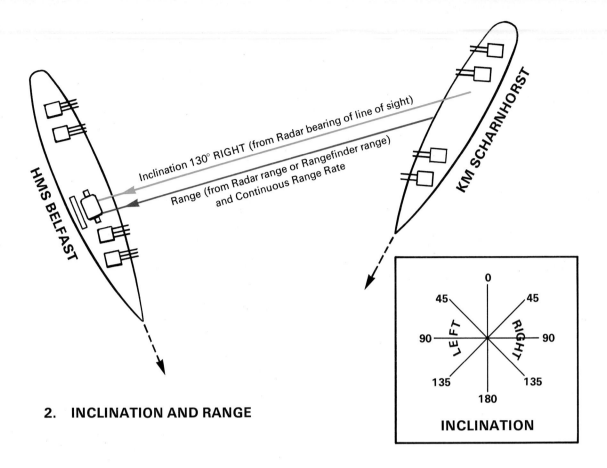

Inclination 130° RIGHT (from Radar bearing of line of sight)

Range (from Radar range or Rangefinder range) and Continuous Range Rate

HMS BELFAST

KM SCHARNHORST

**2. INCLINATION AND RANGE**

INCLINATION

The Range, Continuous Range Rate and Bearing of the enemy are received by the DCT and passed to the Transmitting Station (TS) where calculations are made in the Admiralty Fire Control Table to produce the Total Corrections.

The resultant Gun Elevation and Gun Training is then passed electrically to the guns.

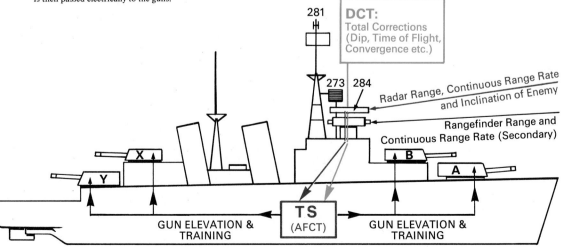

281

**DCT:**
Total Corrections
(Dip, Time of Flight,
Convergence etc.)

273 284

Radar Range, Continuous Range Rate and Inclination of Enemy

Rangefinder Range and
Continuous Range Rate (Secondary)

X

B

Y

A

**TS**
**(AFCT)**

GUN ELEVATION & TRAINING

GUN ELEVATION & TRAINING

Belfast to be welcomed by the Harbour Commissioners who came on board. That evening the Lord and Lady Mayoress, Sir William and Lady Neill, entertained the ship's Officers at a reception in The Guildhall.

The next day, Trafalgar Day, the ship's Company, led by the Royal Marine Band, marched past the Lord Mayor, the City Elders and Sir Basil Brooke, Prime Minister of Northern Ireland, who were assembled outside the Guildhall. On October 22, the ship returned the hospitality of the City by inviting the Civic Authorities on board where, on the quarterdeck, the Lord Mayor handed over the silver bell and a carving of the ship's crest to the safe-keeping of Captain Le Mesurer.

There followed an afternoon and evening of entertainment for the ship, a degree of hospitality that only Ulstermen could provide and, on the next morning, October 23, 1948, her silken ensign fluttering, the ship slipped for the last time silently out of Belfast Lough.

A pleasing postscript to this happy visit can be added: on January 4, 1949 the Lord Mayor of Belfast, Sir William Neill and the First Lord of the Admiralty, Lord Hall, signed an agreement setting out the conditions of custody for the ship's bell.

While the ship was in commission, the bell was to hang on board; out of commission, in the Royal Navy Barracks of her port; if there was no ship in the Royal Navy bearing the name of HMS Belfast, the bell was to be returned to the custody of the City of Belfast.

## The Peace-keepers: The Royal Navy, International Representative of Goodwill

Wherever the White Ensign flies in these days of non-war, those who see it know instinctively that the ship who flies it does so in the name of peace. Belfast was upholding this tradition as soon as she left the United Kingdom: on passage through the Mediterranean a seaman from the American steamship Eastport, of the Eastship Steam Corporation, was suffering from acute abdominal pains. He was transferred at sea to Belfast where Surgeon-Commander Hamilton removed his appendix in the ship's operating theatre: the man recovered, made excellent progress and the Steamship Company expressed its gratitude.

## The Far East: Spring 1949

Belfast arrived at Hong Kong during the last days of December to relieve Sussex who, as flagship of the 5th Cruiser Squadron, was flying the flag of Vice-Admiral A. C. C. Madden, C.B., C.B.E., C.B.E., Second-in-Command of the Far East Station (FES), the Commander-in-Chief being Admiral Sir Patrick Brind, K.C.B., C.B.E..

Tension in the Far East was by then electric. The Communists under Mao-tse-tung were in the throes of hurling out the forces of Generalissimo Chiang Kai-shek. The task of the 5th Cruiser Squadron was to provide the force-in-being in the area of the Yangtse, to restrain the Chinese and to protect our nationals. International incidents in the New Year of 1949 were therefore highly to be deprecated. Politicians and apathetic democracies will never learn until it is too late, that a strong navy in peace-time is an essential investment and, however expensive, the most economical means whereby to ensure peace.

On January 12 an R.A.F. Vampire force-landed on the west shore of Bias Bay on Tai Pang Wan beach: a secret aircraft on Chinese territory.

Belfast steamed into the Bay and, under the protection of her guns, sent a party inshore to salvage the Vampire. Her seamen hauled the aircraft on to a pontoon which was towed out by the ship's boats to the cruiser lying stopped in the bay. Belfast's crane whisked the aircraft on board and the ship returned to Hong Kong: competent seamanship, considering that Belfast's ship's company were barely shaken down and still under training.

St. George's Day, April 23, 1949: Belfast had by now relieved Sussex in the Nanking/Shanghai area which was still a powder-barrel with the fuse burning. For, on St. George's Day, April 23, which was being honoured by Belfast, an international incident occurred which, though a stirring deed in the best tradition of the Royal Navy, was an indication of things to come.

The story of the little sloop, Amethyst, and of Lieutenant-Commander Kerans and his men, is of such gallantry in the face of adversity that the saga should be repeated briefly because Belfast was involved, albeit inactively, as flagship of the Station.

## The Amethyst Incident: April 20, 1949

Against a background of the Chinese civil war, when Mao's Communists hurled Generalissimo Chiang Kai-shek and his Nationalists out of the country, the Royal Navy was endeavouring to protect our own people and trading interests up the Yangste as far as Nanking. The Chinese Communists were on the left bank of the three mile wide river below Nanking, the Nationalists being encamped on the opposite side.

On April 20, 1949, three days before St. George's Day, HMS Amethyst (Black Swan sloop) with White Ensign flying, was steaming slowly up the Yangtse to Nanking to relieve the guardship, Consort. On reaching a position off Kiang Yin Island, she was suddenly attacked by the guns of a Communist battery from the north bank. The ship stopped, then again proceeded slowly up river. At 0930, she was again viciously attacked from shore batteries on the Communist bank.

Her Captain, Lieutenant-Commander B. M. Skinner, was killed outright; her First Lieutenant, Lieutenant G. L. Weston D.S.C., was gravely wounded. Losing consciousness intermittently, he nevertheless took command and during the next twenty-four hours refused to leave the ship.

Amethyst stopped, out of control with her steering destroyed. She immediately went aground on the western shore of Rose Island where, with only "X" gun firing (her two for'd 4 in. mountings "A" and "B" had been knocked out) she remained a sitting target for the concentrated Communist gunners. A signal by W/T was transmitted to our Consul in Nanking that Amethyst had suffered twenty-two dead and thirty wounded.

At 1145 Consort, a modern Fleet destroyer armed with four 4·5 in., cleared Nanking at 15 knots, with seven White Ensigns and three Union Flags flying, two being draped over the ship's side. She was soon fired on but her 4·5s demolished the opposition as she increased speed to 27 knots. She sighted Amethyst at 1345 when she swept round Rose Island. Shooting at the batteries that had now opened fire, her speed took her two miles south of the Island. As she turned, she

*H.M.S.* Amethyst, *1949.* (Tom Molland Ltd.)

*Lieutenant-Commander J. S. Kerans, D.S.O., R.N., on board H.M.S.* Amethyst, *on arrival at Hong Kong after her dash down the Yangtse river.*
*Courtesy of Captain Donald Macintyre, D.S.O.,** D.S.C.*
(Keystone Press)

*Admiral Sir Patrick Brind, K.C.B., C.B.E.*

slowly retraced her track towards the stricken sloop to silence four more batteries as she proceeded.

At 1400 the destroyer had reached a position within one-and-a-half miles of *Amethyst*, when *Consort* was herself hit on the bridge and forward. The Coxswain was killed in the wheel-house; "A" and "B" guns were knocked out. With the gyro, W/T office and the TS destroyed, and by using emergency steering from the tiller flat, there was little more *Consort* could do: having fired 240 rounds of 4·5 in. ammunition, she turned and steamed downstream to reach the mouth of the estuary at Woosung. There she transferred her wounded to *London* who was waiting in support with *Black Swan*.

## Cutting-out Attempt

During the darkness that night, *Amethyst*, at 0100 on April 21, evacuated her wounded by Carley floats. Those who were fit swam for it, the survivors being helped ashore by the Nationalists. The ship then steamed slowly three miles up river, to anchor at a point equi-distant between two batteries.

At first light, an R.A.F. Sunderland, handled with considerable coolness and skill, landed close to *Amethyst*. An R.A.F. doctor and vital supplies were transferred and the sloop's Gunnery officer was taken off to liaise with the rescue force. Unable to return to the Sunderland, which was now under heavy fire, the doctor remained in *Amethyst* to care for the casualties until the incident was over. The Sunderland took off under a hail of fire.

As daylight broke on the morning of April 21, the massive silhouette of *London* (Captain P. G. L. Cazalet, D.S.O., D.S.C.), flying the flag of Vice-Admiral Madden, with *Black Swan* following astern, moved silently up-river from Woosung, White Ensigns prominently displayed. When the rescuing force had reached a position nine miles below *Amethyst*, intense fire from the heavy Communist batteries struck the 8 in. gunned cruiser. Though "A" and "B" turrets were not penetrated, 23 shells (one in "B" shell handing room) exploded inboard. The 4 in. Director was knocked out and 50% of the HA armament. As men fell at their action Close Range stations, others, entirely untrained in the drill, leaped forward to take the places of their dying messmates.

The shell-fire ripped through the 4 in. gunshields and terrible casualties were suffered—70 killed in all, with 35 seriously wounded. The total casualties between both ships (*London* and *Black Swan*) was nearly one hundred. *London*, having silenced the batteries with her 8 in. in local control (155 rounds were fired in addition to the 4 in., with shell VT fused) swung round and, with *Black Swan*, returned to anchor in Woosung.

There was no more that the relieving force could do.

## Break Out

Among the three Staff at Nanking was Lieutenant-Commander J. S. Kerans R.N. and he was sent down to take command of *Amethyst*. She was now anchored in a creek where her damage had been patched up below the waterline with concrete.

The incident had now developed into a world crisis: a ship of the Royal Navy was trapped up the Yangtse, unable to move without the sanction of the local Communist Commander, Colonel Kang. As the days of waiting grew into weeks, considerable pressure was brought to bear on Kerans by Kang who was endeavouring to extract from him a signed statement to the effect that *Amethyst* had provoked the Communist Chinese troops.

Admiral Sir Patrick Brind was in *Belfast*, at a buoy in Hong Kong, and he was continually in touch by W/T with *Amethyst* who by now was using an elementary one-time code devised from a simple manual common to both the flagship and the sloop. While time passed, *Amethyst*'s stocks of oil fuel rapidly dwindled as the typhoon season approached. The Commander-in-Chief was convinced that the opportune moment had arrived for a break-out but, secrecy being vital to the operation, no means of ordering *Amethyst* to proceed could be devised. Fortuitously, a typhoon being imminent, Kerans signalled to his Admiral:

"Request advice on my action if menaced by a typhoon."

Admiral Brind replied:

"The golden rule is to make an offing and to take plenty of sea room."

Unfortunately, Kerans, exhausted by the non-stop work of preparing his ship for her dash down-river, failed to interpret his Admiral's signal, so it was to be a day or two before he was finally to break out.

*Amethyst* now had insufficient fuel by which to escape, in spite of repeated demands on Kang by Kerans who had ordered that 50-gallon drums of oil fuel, which were stacked on the bund in Nanking, were to be delivered on board by junk. Kang continued to play cat-and-mouse with the ship by prevaricating with the delivery of the fuel.

During the early part of the night of July 30, the 50-gallon drums of oil fuel suddenly arrived alongside *Amethyst*, carried in a junk: Kang's administrative machine had slipped up and the official cancellation had not reached the supplier in time.

So, during the darkness of the night, six weeks after the original outrage, Kerans slipped anchor and silently turned the darkened *Amethyst* across the strong current. While she swung, a brightly illuminated Chinese steamer thrashed up river between the erupting gun batteries and the escaping sloop. By this miracle of good fortune, the gunners were temporarily blinded and *Amethyst* was away, slipping swiftly down stream as she worked up to 23 knots. She had been hit by only one shell which caused little damage.

The river at this time of year was in full spate, the water level being high up the banks and thereby concealing the normal navigational hazards. Kerans conned his little sloop down the middle of the lit channel (buoyed by the British), his destination Woosung.

On board *Belfast*, Admiral Brind and his Staff were spending an anxious night. To allay any suspicions of a break-out that evening, the Admiral had deliberately laid on a formal dinner party for the local society in his quarters in *Belfast*. In full mess dress, the dinner had proceeded traditionally but at 2230 precisely the guests had been tactfully ushered ashore.

As the last visitor left, the table was swept of its

glass and silver; signal pads and maps were hurriedly spread on the polished table in preparation for the night's work which had already begun some 600 miles away up a dark and hostile waterway. For the rest of that night, the Admiral and his Staff, still in tropical Mess dress, sweated it out in the Admiral's cabin.

*Amethyst* was reporting her position by W/T every fifteen minutes. At one tense period there had been no communication for a 45-minute interval. Even Admiral Brind was betraying anxiety, when suddenly up came another transmission from Kerans. (It appeared that the two telegraphists were, in fact, in touch with each other, but *Belfast*'s operator had not reported the fact to the Staff!)

*Amethyst* swept downstream all that night, carving her way through a junk in the process, until finally at first light she glimpsed before her the darkened silhouette of *Concord*, the duty ship of the Yangtse Patrol, who had come up-river to meet her. The rendezvous took place at dawn (0600) on July 31, 160 miles from Nanking.

Five-hundred miles away on board *Belfast* in Hong Kong, the Admiral and his Staff breathed again: the *Amethyst* incident was now closed.

*Belfast* remained in the area of the Yangtse for several weeks while waiting for events to calm down. The Communists were still about to cross the river from the north bank of the Yangtse and the ship stood by to evacuate civilians but, in the event, few came out.

She had once again become Flagship of FO2 and the Second Cruiser Squadron. There was still much to do in preserving peace as her diary shows when she again visited Malaya which was still in the throes of its Emergency:

## 1949
August 8    Hong Kong ETD for Malayan area
            ETA Singapore Roads August 16
                Penang August 20
                Singapore Dockyard August 26
                Hong Kong September 3
            ETD Singapore August 29
            ETA Hong Kong September 2
            ETD Hong Kong September 9
            ETA Kure September 9
            ETD Kure September 19
            ETA Hong Kong September 23
            North China Patrol (FOC5CS and FO2 i/c FES)
            Hong Kong

## Working for Peace: 1949
During the night of October 31/November 1, *Belfast* went to the assistance of a Nationalist Landing Ship (Tank), the *Cheung Hsai* who had grounded on the Pratas Reef, in the middle of the northern section of the South China Sea. *Belfast* saved 226 passengers, assuring thereby considerable goodwill as can be seen from the copy of the letter from the Commanding General. The ship continued to operate from Hong Kong, occasionally visiting Saigon which was already a trouble spot. Christmas 1949 was celebrated in Hong Kong but *Belfast* was now due for refit and on January 18, 1950, she left the friendliness of Hong Kong and sailed to Singapore Dockyard.

November 12, 1949
Chinese Marine Headquarter
Nantow Formosa China

Dear Capt Le Mesurer
    All the distressed people whom rescued by your ship from R C 5 Chung-Sin have safely arrived their destinations on Nov. 5. Please accept my heartly gratitude to you and all the members of your ship. Their honorable heroic deeds are deeply grateful and will bear in the minds of the favoured eternally.
    Now I am devoting myself in the course for building the Chinese Marine Corps. That is a new trail anyhow. I do hope you will give me some advices and any training lectures about the Royal Marines.
    Here with all my best wishes to you and your ship's company. I am
                            Sincerely yours
            (Signed)  CHUO HUAN
                            *Commanding General*
                            *Chinese Marine*
                            *Second Division*

## Singapore Refit:
## 23 January—14 March 1950
The ship was docked, her bottom scrubbed and anti-fouled, her boilers cleaned and examined. Her starboard outer propeller was found to have one chipped blade, probably a result of the rescue operation off the Pratas Reef. For the first time in her career, there was concern over the effect that her added topweight was having on her stability. The opportunity to carry out a stability test was probably seized upon and from then onwards all additions were carefully scrutinized.

In addition the following alterations took place:
  (i)   Six Tachymetric Directors replaced the Pom-pom Directors Mark IV for the RP50 Mark VII and the RP10 Mark VIA Mountings.
  (ii)  The Range-finder was removed from the for'd 6 in. DCT.
  (iii) Showers were fitted throughout, instead of baths.
  (iv)  The fitting of a Type 268 radar was begun, but not completed until 1951.
  (v)   The numbers of refrigerators were brought up to scale.
  (vi)  The sick-bay was given air conditioning.
  (vii) The Kelvin Sounding machine and boom were removed.
  (viii) Two for'd 20 in. signalling projectors were removed.

Trials were satisfactorily completed on March 25, 1950 and on April 8, Captain le Mesurer was relieved by Captain Sir Aubrey St. Clair-Ford, Bt. D.S.O.* who received a letter of good wishes from the Lord Mayor of Belfast: "The Citizens of Belfast will always follow with pride and interest the exploits of HMS *Belfast* and they look forward with pleasure to the day when they will welcome once again the officers and men of the ship which bears the name of no mean city."

The ship worked up and by May 12 was back in Hong Kong where FO2 and FO CS5, Rear-Admiral W. G. Andrewes, C.B., C.B.E., D.S.O., hoisted his flag in *Belfast*. In company were *Kenya* and *Jamaica*.

## The Far East Station, Summer Cruise 1950
On May 12, 1950, the Far East Fleet began its summer cruise during a period of intense international tension. The cruise was to last barely six weeks before an event was to occur which was to affect the history of mankind. On June 25, when *Belfast* was visiting Hakodate, the North Koreans, aided and abetted by the Russians and the Communist Chinese, crossed the 38th Parallel and marched into South Korea. This was bare-faced and unprovoked aggression.

Belfast *at speed off Korea. Note her new Bofors armament*

Belfast *at anchor, 1951. The five Bofors around the bridge structure have been fitted.*
(Courtesy Lt.-Cdr. G. R. Potier, R.N. (Ret'd.))

*Off Korea, 1951.* Belfast *at speed. Note the bridge personnel, the Union Jack emblem on "A" turret and the Bofors armament.*
(Courtesy Lt.-Cdr. G. R. Potier, R.N. (Ret'd.))

*Korea, 1951. Bombardment at anchor in wintry conditions. The ship is at action stations with close range weapons closed up.* (Courtesy Lt.-Cdr. G. R. Potier, R.N. (Ret'd.))

For the first time in the history of the world, the nations of the Free World, under the flag of the United Nations, rallied to the defence of the aggressed.

## The Korean War:
## June 25, 1950—September 26, 1952
The words of *Belfast*'s Gunnery Officer, Lieutenant-Commander H. G. G. Ogilvie R.N. (now Commander) best recalls those tragic hours:

"I was duty Lieutenant-Commander and I well remember that night. After the usual Sunday evening cinema I saw the Admiral walking up and down the quarterdeck with the Flag Captain. They were undoubtedly discussing the grave situation which had arisen when the North Koreans had invaded South Korea that morning, and its implications for us in the Fleet.

In my hearing, the Admiral stopped and turned to the Captain and waiting staff officers: "You had better raise steam as soon as possible and prepare to sail as soon as you can. See that the ship is darkened."

There followed much activity by the staff ordering the ships to sail from their ports in Japan and to rendezvous with the flag. We also had a busy night in the *Belfast* and sailed at 0100 with the ship darkened.

We rendezvoused with other ships of the Fleet in the morning and proceeded to Okinawa to join up with the United States 7th Fleet. We had the *Kenya* and *Jamaica* and the carrier *Triumph* and destroyers of the 8th Destroyer Squadron and a number of frigates. We formed an impressive sight as the *Belfast* led the British Fleet into Okinawa. By this time the British Government had ordered that our naval forces should at once join up with the Americans and operate in Korean waters in accordance with the United Nations decision to come to the aid of South Korea. The whole Fleet sailed shortly afterwards with the U.S. 7th Fleet units towards Korean waters.

Meanwhile we fuzed all the shells with warheads and prepared for war as we steamed North. We carried out the preparations for action so familiar to some of us on board, but a new experience for the young members of our peacetime crew. We were manned with a peace complement and this allowed us to man 9 of the 12 six-inch guns, one turret being unmanned. We worked all the 4 inch twin mountings and half the close range weapons, but had only skeleton ammunition supply parties. We had a fine, well worked-up ship's company who had been in commission for 18 months with few changes.

It was, I think, on July 6th, 1950 that we went into action for the first time and thereafter we bombarded the advancing North Korean troops for many days and nights, answering calls for fire from the hard pressed army. We carried out indirect bombardments when mostly under way, and the fall of shot was spotted sometimes by Forward Observers on shore, and sometimes by aircraft. The aircraft were either British or American and we quickly became accustomed to working with either. Sometimes we carried out a direct shoot but usually it was indirect, at a range of 20,000 yards. Several times we bombarded at our extreme range of 24,000 yards.

On one occasion, I recall that in response to an urgent call for support we fired 24 nine gun broadsides in 'rapid broadsides' procedure into a village packed with enemy troops at a range of 18,000 yards. The results, we were told, were devastating and our American spotting aircraft observer was enthusiastic over the air. "Boy, you sure hit the jackpot . . .," he said.

On many occasions by day and by night the *Belfast* and the other cruisers of the British and U.S Fleet answered calls for support from the hard-pressed troops. The *Belfast* gained a name for rapid, accurate shooting, and hard hitting. The Americans found it hard to believe that our 6 inch triple turrets were hand worked. We were fortunate in having three fine turrets' crews that had had no changes for a long time, and were trained up to a peak and were keen rivals with each other. As was customary, two turrets were manned by the seamen and one by the Royal Marines. This made for the keenest competitive spirit.

The most unusual shoot from the Gunnery point of view was our bombardment of moving trains proceeding along the coastal railway. This was an unorthodox Gunnery exercise when carried out by the 4 inch batteries controlled by the High Angle Fire Control System in Low Angle procedure. The Lieutenant of Marines in the HA director became an expert in knocking off a moving train with his four inch battery. Sometimes we would illuminate a train with starshell and let fly at it with the six inch as it appeared out of a tunnel. One great advantage from the Gunnery Officer's point of view was that no analysis was ever required.

And so the service of the *Belfast* continued: it was, in a nutshell, to provide the Army with the fire support of her 6 inch guns with their range of 12 miles, week after week, month after month. During this time the ship wore out her six inch guns and had to go down to Singapore to have twelve new ones installed. She fired several thousand rounds, far more than she had expended in the whole of the Second World War. The ship, and her Gunnery Officer, were fortunate in having a very accurate Gyro sight in the Forward Director Tower and a very good Fire Control Table manned by a most experienced Transmitting Station crew. We were able to put the first round of a shoot usually within 200 yards of a target and very soon were pouring in rapid broadsides in fire for effect. We were very lucky in having a superlative navigating officer in Commander Peter Cardale who would fix our initial position again and again, with unerring accuracy.

During these operations the ship was always under war routine and closed up at Anti Aircraft Defence or Cruising Stations, with always one or two 6 inch turrets manned. Often we would open fire with a defence watch closed up and with the bombardment controlled by perhaps the Torpedo Officer or whoever was the P.C.O. on watch. The ship would spend about a month or more at sea and would then return to Sasebo, our operational base, for a short period of about 4 days.

In October 1950, the *Belfast* was ordered to return home to Chatham to recommission for further service on the station. We steamed home at 24 knots. We stayed in Chatham for 17 days and sailed again having recommissioned with a full war complement of over 900. It included some reservists who had been called up and many retained men who would have been dis-

The Korean War, May 1951—'that straight-shooting ship'. (IWM)

Korea, 1951. Note "B" turret's Bofors sight.
(Courtesy Lt.-Cdr. G. R. Potier, R.N. (Ret'd.))

Korea, September 1951. A helicopter hovering near Belfast in the Yellow Sea. (IWM)

charged, time expired. We worked up for a month at Malta and then steamed on to the Far East. I recall that on arrival in Korea we immediately started to bombard the same target that we had left before we went home. The ship was now able to man all twelve 6 in. guns, the whole of the 4 in. armament and control positions and the whole close range armament of Pom-poms, Bofors and Oerlikons. We also had full supply parties down below. Under these conditions the ship was very crowded.

I left the ship in August 1951 but she continued her service off Korea right up to the end of the war. She was never attacked by aircraft, or hit by shore batteries, and had no casualties.

I next saw the *Belfast* in 1961 at Trincomalee, when serving as N.A. Ceylon. Once more she was the spick and span Flagship of the Far East Fleet, gleaming in her enamel and brightwork, and with her quarterdeck a picture of peacetime smartness. She was now under the command of Captain, now Rear-Admiral, Morgan Giles and flew the flag of Rear-Admiral John Frewen, now Admiral Sir John Frewen. As soon as one went on board it was possible to sense the same high morale and pride of the crew in their ship. The *Belfast* was always a happy ship with a proud ship's company. Even when over-crowded and hard-worked, with very little shore leave as in the Korean war, she was still the happiest of ships, the crew realizing that she was doing a real job and doing it well.

She was the best ship I served in in my 36 years."

The history of *Belfast's* part in the Korean War is more fully described from the records.

## *Belfast's* Diary of the Korean War: June 25, 1950—September 26, 1952

*1950*

| | |
|---|---|
| June 25 | Arrives Hakodate |
| July 1 | Arrives Okinawa |
| July 3 | Arrives Pyongyang |
| July 13 | Arrives Sasebo |
| July 28 | Arrives Hong Kong |
| August 6 | Sailed for U.K. |
| October 6 | Chatham |
| October 18 | Paid off and recommissioned |
| October 27 | Sailed U.K. for Far East |

*1951*

| | |
|---|---|
| January 31 | Sasebo |

The Far East Fleet was immediately placed at the disposal of the U.N. Peace-Keeping Force.

*Belfast* left Hakodate and steamed at full speed to Yokosuka to refuel and to allow Rear-Admiral Andrewes to confer with the Americans and with the Commander-in-Chief, Far East Station, Admiral Sir Patrick Brind, K.C.B., C.B.E.. Sailing the same day, *Belfast* steamed to Okinawa to join the U.S. Navy Task Force 77 on July 1; in company were *Triumph*, *Cossack* and *Consort*.

## War: the Yellow Sea, July 1—August 6, 1950

A period of intense activity followed in this, a hideous, bloody and ruthless war: unnecessary and fought by the Free World with one hand behind its back.

In company with USS *Rochester*, *Philippine Sea* and eight destroyers, the RN Ships operated as a carrier task force in the Yellow Sea where air strikes were launched upon targets in the Pyongyang and Haeju areas on July 3 and 4. More profitable use could be made of the cruiser and destroyers than remaining tied to the carrier force and so they were detached on July 5; they proceeded to Sasebo, the main Royal Naval base for Korean operations during the next two years.

## "A Straight-Shooting Ship"

On July 9, *Belfast* and two destroyers sailed for the first of many west coast patrols to prevent the enemy seaborne infiltration and supply-running. This was a short patrol, however, for she returned to Sasebo on July 13, only to sail again on the 17th for the east coast, down which the North Korean Army was advancing. Harassing bombardments and observed shoots by *Belfast* took place between July 17 and 21.

Mokko harbour installations were shelled on the 18th; in a brief bombardment of the nearby shore *Belfast* managed to demolish a substantial slice of both cliff and road. From July 19 she operated in company with USS *Juneau* (12×5 in. cruiser), both ships supporting the fighting around the town of Yongdok.

On July 19 she fired 350 accurate rounds from her main armament, a feat which drew praise from the US Navy Admiral for the precision of her bombardment and for her "fast-firing crew". From then onwards she was known on the station as, *that "straight-shooting ship"*, a term used by the American Admiral.

Under cover of *Belfast's* gunfire, a radio station was destroyed, the army of the Korean Republic recapturing Yongdok on July 21; she then returned to Sasebo.

The west coast was revisited between July 29 and August 2. On August 1, *Belfast* fired 56 rounds of 6 in. against a battery in the Seoul River approaches which had engaged HMAS *Bataan*, an Australian Tribal destroyer. *Belfast* returned to this part of the coast on August 5 when, with *Kenya* and two destroyers, she bombarded barracks, oil storage tanks, an electrical equipment factory, a power station and railway installations at Inchon, firing 252 rounds of 6 in. On the next day, she returned to Sasebo where she de-ammunitioned, de-stored and disembarked the Admiral's staff. She sailed the same day for the United Kingdom where she was to recommission.

## Recommissioning, October 19, 1950

*Belfast* arrived at Sheerness on October 6 and proceeded to Chatham to pay off on October 18. She recommissioned on October 19 and sailed from England on the 27th—fast work for a ship of over 800 souls. She worked up at Malta from November 2 to 17 and eventually returned to Sasebo on January 31, 1951.

During *Belfast's* absence, the situation ashore in Korea had twice changed dramatically: the United Nations had broken out of the Pusan perimeter into which they had been forced by the initial invasion and, by November, they were approaching the borders with

The west coast of Korea, 1951—memories of arctic convoys in 1943–44.
(Courtesy Lt.-Cdr. G. R. Potier, R.N. (Ret'd.))

"Away motor-boat", in icy conditions. Korea, 1951.
(Courtesy Lt.-Cdr. G. R. Potier, R.N. (Ret'd.))

Turning through the ice off the west coast of Korea, 1951. Note the single Pom-pom in the port waist. An auxiliary is secured alongside.
(Courtesy Lt.-Cdr. G. R. Potier, R.N. (Ret'd.))

Action Stations, Korea 1951. The single Bofors, the single Pom-pom and a Pom-pom Director are clearly visible. All hands are wearing tin hats and anti-flash clothing.
(Courtesy Lt.-Cdr. G. R. Potier, R.N. (Ret'd.))

Rear-Admiral Scott-Moncreiff welcomes on board the President of South Korea.
(Courtesy Lt.-Cdr. G. R. Potier, R.N. (Ret'd.))

Korea, 1951. Direct hit by Communist shell.
(Courtesy Lt.-Cdr. G. R. Potier, R.N. (Ret'd.))

Peaceful contrast: ship open to visitors, Kobe 1952. Note the close-range weapons.
(Courtesy Lt.-Cdr. G. R. Potier, R.N. (Ret'd.))

China and the Soviet Union. Then the Chinese Army intervened and the United Nations had been swept south again, overwhelmed by numbers and fanaticism.

When *Belfast* returned to her wartime billet, the Chinese were being driven back to the 38th Parallel but they were still south of Seoul. As the opposing armies fought up and down the Korean peninsula, so United Nations ships moved with them, bombarding, assaulting, blockading, minesweeping and evacuating. This period of the campaign was a unique example of sea-power.

## 1951
The Chinese were recoiling after their winter advance. To help them on their way, a feint landing in their rear at Inchon was organized, an operation in which *Belfast* took part when on February 6 she sailed from Sasebo. The landing was cancelled when United Nations troops were found to be about to enter the port.

## West Coast Patrols
*Belfast*'s first west coast patrol began on February 2 and continued until February 14, 1951. For the first days, she was busy bombarding Inchon and the surrounding islands; and conducting "Harassment and Interdiction" shoots at night. Thereafter she patrolled, returning to bombard as necessary.

The east coast was visited on February 19, 1951, 127 rounds of 6 in. and 27 rounds of 4 in. being fired at the harbour of Wonsan which was under siege. Air spotting was provided by an American carrier: it was hoped to deny the harbour to the enemy and to cut the main lines of communication running through the city. The neighbouring islands had first to be cleared and, on February 19, *Belfast* bombarded artillery batteries on Sin Do, before it was occupied by South Korean Marines.

These operations were carried out in very rough weather. Summer typhoons and winter gales, ice and snow were features of Korean waters. *Belfast* had tasted these conditions before but such conditions exacerbated supply problems, the warships often re-fuelling and re-ammunitioning whilst steaming at sea.

*Belfast* returned to the west coast four days later and remained on station until March 4. Towards the end of this patrol she took part in a major diversionary operation which simulated an amphibious assault in the Taedong Estuary. This operation involved carrier strikes, minesweeping operations and an assault ship formation, as well as the cruiser and destroyer bombardment force. *Belfast* fired by day and night, expending 410 rounds of 6 in., 217 of 4 in. and 24 of starshell. The feint was successful, the enemy moving a complete division into the area.

## *Belfast*'s Breathing Spaces: March 1951 and Annual Refit, June 1951
A week on patrol from March 13 to 20 was followed by a six-day visit to Yokosuka as part of the programme of farewell calls by Vice-Admiral Sir William Andrewes. Still flying FO2FE's flag, *Belfast* returned to Sasebo before continuing to Hong Kong on April 11, 1951 to exchange Vice-Admiral Andrewes for Rear-Admiral A. K. Scott-Moncrieff, D.S.O.*.

In late April she carried out one more west coast patrol: she spent a day with Task Force 77 and on May 3, while the new FO2 met the United Nations Naval Commander. On June 1 she docked at Singapore for her annual refit. Her turbines were inspected, sabotage during the last refit being suspected for the over speeding, on December 9, 1950, of the starboard outer turbine. The starboard inner was also vibrating but this was believed to be the result of the mining, eleven years earlier. It was decided, after inspection, to limit the stern power of the ship and to open up the turbines at the next United Kingdom refit.

The work-up was completed on August 16 and *Belfast* returned direct to the patrol area, where she arrived on August 31. The next three months proved to be the busiest of her Korean career: six west patrols, harassment and interdiction and counter-battery shoots—and three visits to the east coast—becoming a routine affair.

## Salvage Expedition
The first patrol, in late September 1951, was a five-day operation during which she supported a raid by .41 Commando RM. Reports had also indicated that a Russian-built Mig-15 jet fighter had crashed in shoal water off the west coast of Korea. *Belfast* stood by to ward off air attack, while *Glory*'s aircraft located the wreck and then guided an LSV through the narrow channels to recover it. By July 22, 1951, the Mig-15 was on its way to Inchon for expert examination.

The next operation on October 10 and 11 was a sea/air attack on the town of Kojo, in which *Belfast* joined HMAS *Sydney*, USS *New Jersey* and six destroyers in bombarding, bombing and blockading. This was a very successful operation, *Belfast* firing another 529 rounds of 6 in.

The dose was repeated at Hungnam on November 20 and 21, 1951. On this occasion, *Belfast* was the senior ship of Task Group 95.8, a truly United Nations force which comprised, in addition to the RN cruiser and the Australian carrier, one RN, one Canadian, one US Navy, one Netherlands, and two Australian destroyers. The cruiser and destroyers shelled targets with air spotting from *Sydney* and fired flak suppression barrages immediately prior to air strikes. Altogether 200 tons of bombs, rockets and shells were landed on Hungnam during those two days.

*Belfast* now enjoyed a break of a full month from operations. The "rest" commenced with a visit to Yokosuka, where Captain A. C. A. C. Duckworth, D.S.O., D.S.C., relieved Captain St. Clair-Ford on November 23, 1951 and where the Vice-President of the U.S.A., Senator Alben Barkley, visited the ship. She then proceeded to Hong Kong, where FO2 FE was to confer with the civil authorities; she did not return to the operational zone until December 23, 1951.

## The New Year: 1952
Christmas and New Year were spent off the west coast of Korea, the festivals being celebrated by deliberate bombardment of troublesome batteries on the Amgak Peninsula which were detected by naval aviators. As one Fleet Air Arm pilot has described:

"The Amgak batteries I do mention, as every aviator who served on the west coast and with whom I

1951. The Bofors on the twin Oerlikon mounting can be seen on the port lower bridge for'd; the Bofors on "B" turret is protected by a zareba. (MOD)

Replenishment at sea, July 1952, off Korea. Rear-Admiral A. K. Scott-Moncreiff, C.B., D.S.O., is transferred by jackstay from the carrier Ocean. Hawker Sea Furies of 802 Squadron are on the Flight Deck. (IWM)

Transfer by jackstay: Rear-Admiral Scott-Moncreiff about to board Belfast. The hands on the fo'c'sle are running away with the inhaul. The port PV chain is clearly visible. (IWM)

June 30, 1959. A good view of the modernised ship showing her new close-range armament of twin Bofors. The gash-chute hangs over the side at the break in the port waist. (MOD)

The Royal Marine Band of Belfast raises morale ashore in Korea, September 1952. (IWM)

At Pulau Langkawi, Centaur and Belfast. Top right, Lincoln (A/D Frigate), Loch Killesport (Bay Class), 2 Indian Type 12 Frigates (A/S), an Indian Minesweeper and, at left Cavalier. In centre background, a "T" class submarine. (IWM)

have spoken, has related with deep emotion his loathing for them; they controlled the landward approaches to Choda Island, the largest UN-held island off the North Korean coast and they were protected by numerous well-concealed flak batteries. The main batteries had a habit of remaining silent for days on end, only to open fire on some incautious destroyer or frigate as she passed within range. For the next few days thereafter, the duty cruiser would hide behind Choda in the hopes that the batteries would fire at a destroyer sent out deliberately to trail her coat and draw fire, whereupon the cruiser would enliven the Communists' day still further . . ."

The military situation had now reached stalemate, on the line of what is now the *de facto* border between North and South Korea.

## West Coast Again
The west coast patrols had as their main tasks the blockade of coastal shipping, the disruption of land communications where they could be reached, and the maintenance of guerrilla and regular garrisons on offshore islands. *Belfast* took part in 18 west coast patrols between mid-January and September 27, 1952, but all followed much the same pattern of H & I firing, counter-battery shoots, bombardments in the Han River and Haeju areas, and the occasional gunfire support mission with guerrilla forces making minor raids. On these patrols she alternated with *Kenya, Ceylon* and *Newcastle*, each of the two cruisers in the Korean theatre being accompanied on patrol by a pair of destroyers.

## Her First Korean War Casualties
Although short ranges were necessary for deliberate shoots against the well-camouflaged coastal batteries, it was not until July 29, 1952 that *Belfast* was hit by return fire. While engaging a battery on the island of Wolsa-ri, a 76 mm. shell struck forward, killing one Chinaman in his hammock (scalded to death by a fractured steam pipe) and wounding four other Chinese ratings—a cruel irony for them. This was the only occasion on which *Belfast* was hit by enemy action during her 404 days spent on patrol.

## Peace
On September 26, 1952, the Korean war ended. After 27 months of useless slaughter both sides were back where they started—but a principle had been established which even the Communists could not now flaunt: aggression would not be tolerated by the nations of the Free World.

On September 22, Rear-Admiral Scott-Moncrieff hauled down his flag in *Belfast*. On September 27, 1952, *Belfast* was relieved on patrol by *Newcastle* to whom she handed over her LCP(L) which she had carried for the duration; and on station, by *Birmingham*. *Belfast* had steamed over 80,000 miles in the combat zone and had fired over 8,000 rounds of 6 in.—an average speed of 8·31 knots and a round from the main battery every 72 minutes.

The UN police action dragged on until July 1953 but the agony was no longer *Belfast's*. She returned home to enjoy the fruits of her labours, paying off in Chatham on November 4, 1952. She was accepted at Devonport into Class III reserve on December 1, 1952, where her fate was to be determined.

## Belfast's future in the balance
*Belfast's* fate was in doubt and during the discussions to decide her future, she was commanded by Commander J. L. Blackham from November 27, 1952, when he relieved Captain Duckworth. On January 12, 1953, Commander A. W. Langridge, D.S.C., took over until relieved by Commander J. C. Richards, D.S.C., on January 26, 1953. He remained her captain until December 1, 1953 when she was finally placed in Class III Reserve. Her future seemed hardly bright, her existence depending upon decisions of great moment affecting the future of the United Kingdom.

The transfer of independence to the Colonies and to the Protectorates; the diminishing Empire; our new rôle in world affairs, with the advent of the nuclear deterrent. These and many other issues were the fundamental questions which the Board of Admiralty, with Earl Mountbatten at the head of the Royal Navy, had to resolve. A new Navy was to be built. In March 1955, the board approved the modernization of *Belfast*.

## Modernization
The Deputy Controller on December 22, 1955, stated that the design and drawing office work was too much for Devonport Dockyard because of the work already in hand. The Controller therefore decided on January 6, 1956 that the work should be undertaken during an extended refit.

The work that was started in 1956 at Devonport Dockyard was to transform HMS *Belfast* into the ship she is today. As the minute, dated May 11, 1956, from The Director, Tactical Ships, stated:

"The alterations to the gun armament bring *Belfast* up to a standard similar to that known as *Birmingham* standard. This is defined as, able to defend themselves against present-day air attack in all conditions, and other ships, to a limited extent in blind fire.

The main limitation is that of range in using MRS8 with radar Type 262R for 4 in. guns.

Torpedo armament is removed to allow top weight and, particularly, space for other alterations. The electrical system can be described as no more than adequate, but the naval staff agreed that this must be accepted.

Main machinery will last the ship about 10 years after completion of the extended refit but there may be some reduction in endurance.

Alterations to the accommodation affect the largest improvement to the ship. Provision of centralized messing and a reasonable area in Messes and Mess decks have been achieved by reduction in the complement and by building in a large portion of the upper deck, which later has been possible because of the removal of torpedo tubes."

## Extended Refit:
## January 6, 1956—May 12, 1959
The appearance of the ship was radically altered and the HA armament was brought up to date.

Modern living conditions were installed, complete with air conditioning for ABCD (Atomic, Biological and Chemical Warfare Defence) State and for tropical conditions. The principal features of the modernization were:

*Structure.* The advent of possible nuclear and/or chemical warfare demanded an air-tight citadel, inside

Belfast *leaves Plymouth after her long refit. She is now modernised: July 1959.* (IWM)

which a slight positive pressure had to be maintained. The profile of the ship changed when a newly designed enclosed bridge replaced the structure that had seen so much action and service.

*Bridge.* The superstructure was considerably altered by the requirement to enclose the bridge. A five-sided tiered arrangement was the result: functional, but not so pleasing on the eye.

A new enclosed compass platform was built. The Operations Room, combining Air Direction, Gunnery Direction and Radar Direction rooms, was fitted on one level in the Bridge above the Compass Platform.

An Admiral's Bridge was provided.

*Funnels.* It was proposed to substitute upright funnels of equal height but the proposal was dropped.

*Watertight Integrity.* To improve the ability of the ship to withstand heavy underwater damage, all main transverse bulkheads, excepting those at 117, 238, 248, 258 and 262 stations, were made intact below the upper deck. Watertight integrity was brought up to date.

*Gas-tight citadel.* A citadel inside the ship, at a slight positive pressure, was built, all services (drinking water etc.) being safeguarded.

Pre-wetting of the superstructure, for use against nuclear attack, was arranged.

Two extra cleansing compartments for gas-attacks were fitted.

Emergency blanking arrangements for ship's side scuttles were fitted.

Secondary lighting was fitted in the Sick Bay and Damage Control Headquarters, fore and aft.

*Mast and Decks.* The tripod masts were replaced by lattice structures. All timber decks were removed, except on the quarter deck. The steel decks were painted with anti-slip paint and anti-slip strips were attached to the steel deck.

## ARMAMENT

1. The 6 in. turrets were retained
2. The two DCTs were replaced by modern 6 in. Directors, fitted with RP40

*The Fire Control* was brought up to date by:
 (i) fitting an auto-cross level system Mark II
 (ii) fitting a starshell transmitter unit Mark II and starshell deflector calculator Mark V

3. The 4 in. twin RP52 mountings were replaced by four 4 in. RP51 Mark XVIV* mountings
4. The three 4 in. HADTs were removed and the 4 in. control system replaced by four MRS8 directors, sited on a platform between the funnels, adjacent to the 4 in. mountings.
5. A clean sweep was made of the existing Close Range armament and its control systems. They were replaced by fitting six Twin Bofors Mark V mountings controlled by four MRS8 Directors sited between each pair of mountings. (2 directors each bridge wing— 4 twin mountings; 2 directors after superstructure—2 twin mountings)
 Three months later, four portable saluting guns were added

6. The barrage director was removed
7. All torpedo tubes, torpedoes, torpedo control systems; all depth charges and the quarterdeck D/C chute were to be removed (completed 1.7.57.)
8. Type 174/176 Asdic was fitted

*Navigation.* Loran type SPN 7A was fitted. An ARL Mark XIII replaced the existing plotting table. A Decca QM4 navigational position-finder was fitted.

The Type 758N Echo Sounder was replaced by a Type 765. The two pattern 1015 Admiralty Gyro Compasses were replaced by two Pattern 2005.

*Meteorology.* The Met. Office was modernized.

*Machinery.* The turbines were lifted, examined and repaired. The steering motor was fitted with shock-proof units. The propeller shafts were rubberised.

Improvements were made to the forced draught, distilling and refrigerating plants.

*Aircraft.* A deck landing pad for helicopter use was fitted on the quarterdeck. "Y" gun had to be trained abeam when operating helicopters.

*Communications.* Internal communications were fitted for: replenishment at sea, navigating and machinery operation.

The W/T fit was brought up to date.

*Electrical System.* Augmented, but DC installation remained.

*Accommodation.* Accommodation was modernized and enlarged for a Ship's Complement of 956.

*Complement Bill:*
Admiral
Captain
55 Wardroom Officers
10 Gunroom Officers
190 CPOs and POs
699 Junior ratings
Total Ship's complement: 956.

Full centralized messing was provided, electric galleys replacing the oil-fired arrangements.

Centralized air-conditioning was provided throughout, including the Bridge action spaces and the communication spaces.

*Radar.* Types 262   Gunnery close range
            274   Main armament
            277 Q  Heightfinding and surface warning
            293 Q  Close range H/F and surface warning
            960 M  Air warning
            974   Warning surface

*Stability.* An inclining experiment was carried out on completion of the refit, the final act before allowing the ship to proceed on trials.

Plymouth, June 1959 after modernisation. Her new
Bofors armament and the HA Directors are shown plainly.
Her silver bell hangs on the after screen          (IWM)

Her stern, Plymouth Sound, 30 June 1959          (MOD)

A good photograph of her enclosed bridge after
modernisation

## A Modern Ship: 1959/1960

HMS *Belfast* commissioned at Devonport on May 12, 1959, under the command of Captain J. V. Wilkinson, D.S.C., G.M. The ship, having worked up her new company in the use of her up-to-date equipment, sailed from England on August 20 for the Far East where she was to fly the flag of FO2, Rear-Admiral V. C. Begg, C.B., D.S.O., D.S.C. She spent September working up in Malta, then docked in Singapore for a bottom scrub and anti-fouling on December 16, 1959.

## SEATO Exercise SEALION

Nearly ten years had elapsed since the outbreak of the Korean war and conditions in the Far East were still far from being settled: the seeds of future tragedy had already begun to germinate.

The Free World's SEATO defence organization therefore carried out a joint exercise, SEALION, in which *Belfast* took part. To prevent an expected show of strength by the Communists on June 25, the Flag Officer, Vice-Admiral Begg (promoted on May 21) took the Fleet to Inchon in Korea during May 1960.

## Korea: Tenth Anniversary, 1960

Flying his flag in *Belfast*, FO2 sailed from Singapore on April 29 to visit Hong Kong, India, Ceylon and finally Australia. Then, in company with the carrier *Albion*, the frigates *Salisbury, Scarborough, Torquay* and the RFA *Tideflow*, she called at Manila between May 3 and 4 for a final briefing on SEALION. The exercise terminated on May 11 when FO2 took his fleet to Hong Kong where it was reinforced by the Royal Australian Navy, the carrier *Melbourne* and two destroyers. A Fleet Air Arm Pilot from *Albion* has recorded the tension that existed in those days, when all that lay between peace and war was the presence of a powerful force of warships:

"A week there and off again, this time to Inchon via the passage between Taiwan and China—an interesting day that, with ships at DC State 1 and wearing anti-flash gear, sitting in the cockpit ready strapped to the catapult at Condition One (non-war is a terribly subjective experience). Inchon was a good visit—there was a riot in Seoul which trapped over 150 of us from the Fleet in Seoul for a while. Then to Japan—*Albion* and *Salisbury* to Yokohama and Yokosuka, *Belfast* to Kure and the other eight ships to odd spots. *Albion* went sick at Yokosuka but although we left three days late, *Belfast* seems to have waited for us, for we did a tracking exercise with her two days out from Yokosuka, before we arrived off Okinawa for a weapon training session. Thereafter, we went back to Singapore, lingering a while in Hong Kong (from about July 3 to 9) and getting back to Singapore on July 12, 1960.

We were told that the purpose of the cruise north of Hong Kong to Inchon and Japanese ports at that time was to deter the Communists from commemorating the 10th anniversary of the invasion of South Korea. There were 14 Commonwealth ships (including RFAs) in the Inchon anchorage from about May 21 to 27, 1960 as well as a number of American ships, and at Yokosuka there were two USN Attack carriers and all the "heavies" of the 7th Fleet up to the time we left—

the evening of June 25. We were convinced that we had stopped World War III."

## Singapore: Annual Docking and Refit 1960

*Belfast* was still flexing her muscles during that summer, working up and training her ship's company. On August 3 she was towing splash targets for *Albion* in the Malacca Straits and operating with the Indian cruiser *Mysore* (ex-*Nigeria*). She transferred the flag of Vice-Admiral Begg to *Albion* and then went to Singapore in October for her annual docking and refit.

She had spent 210 days at sea during 1960, her diary covering a wide area:

| Period | | Place or | No. of days |
|--------|----|----------|-------------|
| From | To | Locality | not underway |
| 16.12.59 | 19.12.59 | Singapore | 3 |
| 19.12.59 | 2.1.60 | Hong Kong | 10 |
| 2.1.60 | 10.1.60 | Borneo | 1 |
| 10.1.60 | 29.2.60 | India and Ceylon | 19 |
| 29.2.60 | 13.4.60 | Australia | 9 |
| 13.4.60 | 13.5.60 | Philippines | 15 |
| 13.5.60 | 13.7.60 | Japan | 26 |
| 13.7.60 | 12.8.60 | Singapore | 21 |
| 12.8.60 | 29.8.60 | Hong Kong | 8 |
| 29.8.60 | 12.10.60 | Singapore | 43 |
| | | | 155 |

The ship had refurbished but her men also needed refreshment: the ship's company paid off and flew home to the United Kingdom. *Belfast* recommissioned on January 31, 1961 under the command of Captain Morgan Giles, D.S.O., O.B.E., G.M.

## The Royal Navy Keeps the Peace

When people ask, "Why spend money on defence?" the short answer is, "so we can sleep 'o nights." While we continue to take our Fighting Services for granted, it is a sobering thought that the rôle of the Royal Navy and the navies of our NATO allies is the only shield between our shores and a Russia that now possesses ten times as many submarines as the U-boats with which Germany nearly brought us to our knees in 1940-41.

The rôle of the warships of the Royal Navy in peacetime is unpublicized and often monotonous. It is true to say that the duties carried out by the Far Eastern Fleet during 1959 and 1960 reflected accurately the influence that an efficient and powerful navy can exert towards keeping the peace.

Happily, the military presence of a fleet-in-being is not the only part played by our ships in peacetime. A more pleasant duty, that of international goodwill, is as important a contribution: *Belfast*'s next commission illustrates the other rôles which ships of the Royal Navy are called upon to play and in which they have always excelled.

## Last Foreign Commission: 1961–1962

It is good for a ship to finish her active life at the peak of her form. *Belfast*, always a happy ship since those dreary days of 1939, some twenty-one years earlier, could now look forward to a foreign commission that would long be remembered by those who served in her.

This, her last foreign commission, was to epitomise the work of a peacetime ship: the vital function which a ship of the Royal Navy plays in keeping the peace.

Apart from the tragedy of Vietnam, the political climate in the Far East was certainly no worse, the confrontation in Indonesia still lying in the not too-distant future.

By Sir JOHN DAVID LUCE, *Knight Commander of the Most Honour-able Order of the Bath, Companion of the Distinguished Service Order, Officer of the Most Excellent Order of the British Empire. Admiral in Her Majesty's Fleet and Commander-in-Chief of Her Majesty's Ships and Vessels employed and to be employed in the Far East Station.*

### H.M.S. *BELFAST* – Recommissioning Order

The Lords Commissioners of the Admiralty having directed that Her Majesty's Ship *Belfast* recommission at Singapore on 31st January, 1961, you are to proceed to recommission her accordingly and to prepare her for a Foreign Service Commission.

Until further notice Her Majesty's Ship *Belfast* will be administered by the Flag Officer Second-in-Command, Far East Station. You are to bring to the immediate notice of the Flag Officer Second-in-Command, Far East Station any reason you may have for dissatisfaction with the state of training, discipline or welfare of the ship's company or with the general state of her material or any part of her.

May God's blessing be upon the ship and company hereby entrusted to your command, and may your joint endeavours to uphold the highest traditions of the Royal Navy in the service of Her Majesty the Queen be crowned with success and happiness.

Given under my hand at Her Majesty's Naval Base, Singapore, this 25th day of January, 1961.

Admiral

Captain M. C. Giles, D.S.O., O.B.E., G.M., Royal Navy
    Her Majesty's Ship *Belfast*

*Copy to:*
    The Flag Officer Second-in-Command, Far East Station.

*Commissioning Day: January 31, 1961.* The new ship's company flew out to Singapore to join their ship, air transport revolutionizing the hardship of long separation from families. Though it was winter, the climate was hot and sticky, an abrupt change for the young men in tropical rig who were savouring the East for the first time.

The ship's company assembled on January 31 for the Commissioning Ceremony when her Captain read a signal from the Commander-in-Chief, Far East Station, Admiral Sir David Luce, G.C.B., D.S.O.,* O.B.E.

"Best wishes for your commission. HMS *Belfast* has a great reputation out here and I am sure you will add lustre to it."

The ship and her company were blessed by the Chaplain in the name of Almighty God: her last foreign commission had begun.

*Work up: February 1961. Belfast* had only three weeks in which to become efficient before taking part in the Far East Station's annual exercise, JET '61, which was to begin on February 23.

The ship shook off the dust of Singapore on February 3 and steamed to Pulau Tioman in which area she worked up. During firing and tracking exercises on a Sea Vixen of 890 Squadron from HMS *Hermes,* the plane crashed into the sea 20 miles from *Belfast;* the prophets of doom suggested that by some quirk of fortune, *Belfast*'s gunnery department had, at that stage of her work up, actually hit the target.

Anxiety was acute when only an oil slick was discovered, *Belfast*'s whaler recovering wreckage. An RAF Shackleton and an RN helicopter arrived and soon reported the survivors, the observer in his dinghy enjoying a smoke of his pipe. When later he left the ship, he noted in the Ward Room's visitors' book, "Glad to be on board."

Four days later, the intention to exercise a Replenishment-At-Sea (RAS) with the oiler, RFA *Fort Langley* was hastened by a signal from her asking for urgent medical attention: a Chinese rating had been hurt.

*Belfast*'s surgeon went across by whaler and shortly after the rating was transferred back to *Belfast*. After a few weeks of RAS exercises no transfer method other than by jackstay would have been considered.

### Exercise JET '61

With four of the 8th Destroyer Squadron (the terminology of Destroyer/Frigate had altered in 1951) and HMAS *Quickmatch* and *Voyager* (later to be tragically sunk) *Belfast* steamed through the Samoa Straits on February 24 to join Blue Force. To some in *Belfast*, the sailing over that exact position where HMAS *Perth* and USS *Houston* had been sunk by the Japanese nineteen years earlier was a sad memory.

During the exercise, FO2, Rear-Admiral M. Le Fanu, C.B., D.S.C., hoisted his flag in *Belfast;* he was shortly to reach the peak of his profession by becoming a most successful and highly respected First Sea Lord.

History, as always, repeats itself: during the exercise, *Belfast* represented a commerce raider, much as she did in 1939. Disguised, this time, as a Shell oil tanker, she was again discovered and exposed for what she was by six Venoms from the carrier, HMAS *Melbourne*. *Belfast* returned to Trincomalee harbour on March 10, now a deserted expanse of blue water surrounded by the depressing sight of decaying buildings from World War II: "Scapa Flow in technicolour," said the Captain.

### The Amphibious Commitment: April 1961

When *Belfast*'s future hung in the balance in early 1956, a suggestion was made to convert her into an assault cruiser, as a complement to the Commando carrier *Bulwark;* and a prototype trials vessel for the *Fearless*-type assault ship. The proposal was not approved but on April 19, 1961, *Belfast* took part in Exercise **Pony Express,** a multi-nation operation of the SEATO organization to rehearse large scale amphibious landings. Units from Thailand, the Philippines, Australia, New Zealand, U.S.A. and the United Kingdom took part, France and Pakistan sending observers.

*Pony Express.* A hilarious concert party was enjoyed on the quarterdeck of *Belfast,* one sketch, "The Compass Platform at Sea", being played by The Commander (The Gyro Repeater), Commander (L) (Windscreen Wipers) and the Gunnery Officer (Covering Guns).

Exercise **Pony Express** began in early April, the early part involving *Belfast* with much helicopter work on her quarterdeck, both announced and unheralded. The ship was detailed to lead the Firex Group to bombard Balam Bangan, an island off North Borneo.

*Tragedy.* During the same afternoon a Scimitar on ground support duties from *Victorious* crashed near the island. The pilot ejected and was picked up twenty minutes later by one of *Bulwark*'s helicopters. *Belfast* steamed round the island in company with the frigate *Llandaff* to search for wreckage. She anchored while

91

*Exercise JET '62: 6 in. bombardment off the Nicobar Islands.* (Courtesy Commander S. Ferguson, R.N. (Ret'd.))

*Llandaff* carried out a square search with her Asdic until she gained a contact in deep water. The Fleet Clearance Diving Team, who went down the next day to investigate, had to desist because of the concentration of sharks in the area. Eight days later, *Belfast* was shocked to learn that the pilot had died from his injuries.

On May 4 all landing parties had been re-embarked in the ships and *Belfast*, flying again FO2's flag, steamed for Hong Kong where she arrived on May 8.

### *"Libertymen fall in"*—Hong Kong, May 8, 1961

*Belfast* had not stopped for three months: men, as well as machines, required refit. Before arriving at Hong Kong she was to call at Inchon; but instead, she had to remain at sea for two days to ride out the fury of Typhoon Alice.

Hong Kong, the perfect run ashore, *". . . if you are disappointed with Hong Kong, there is nothing left."* So says the sailor—and he is right. The author of *Belfast's* Ship's Magazine best describes her visit:

"I remember standing one evening on the balcony of a friend's flat situated on the Peak, looking down in faint disbelief at the truly breath-taking panorama below. Strains of music filtered through the windows from the radiogram, the night air was still, humid and sweet with the scent of hibiscus and frangipani, and a myriad of lights blinked and glowed from the darkness below. The distant hum of traffic wafted up to us from 'central' Hong Kong, the 'West End', where the neon lights of expensive restaurants and plush night clubs glowed to welcome the clientèle of free-spending tourists. The towering monoliths of the Hong Kong and Shanghai Bank and the China Fleet Club were unmistakable.

The never ceasing shuttle of the Star Ferry across to Kowloon claimed attention, its brightly illuminated boats looking like fireflies flitting across the dark waters of the harbour; so too did *Belfast*, dignified and impressive, illuminated at anchor in the centre of the harbour, her ghostly outline contrasting starkly with the dark background of the mainland and Kowloon. And away to the right, the countless lights and throb of activity that never sleeps, where every other building is a bar and '. . . every third drink is free.'

Wanchai is a world apart; the world of Suzie Wong . . . a world of desperate poverty, squalor and overcrowding, such that the West has never known; where families live on rooftops, in lobbies, in shacks and in the streets; where the pitiful sight of a wizened old man, resigned, impassive, squatting on a landing and surrounded by his pathetic bundle of earthly possessions, becomes so familiar as to warrant little more than a passing glance from the tourist. How utterly remote and foreign this is to anyone from the West and how easy it is to dismiss it from our minds as one of the unpleasant realities of life to be ignored as quickly as possible."

*Belfast did not pass by on the other side.* The following extract is taken from her magazine:

### *". . . but the greatest of these is charity"*

#### A Home for a Chinese Refugee Family

During our visit to Hong Kong in May 1961, the Padré took some of the ship's company to visit the St. James' Settlement in the Wanchai area. There they saw the welfare work that is being done to assist some of the thousands of Chinese who live in the overcrowded tenement buildings. During the visit the party met the wife and children of Mr. Ng Sekcheung, a 46 year old caretaker, and later the men went with the family to see their bed-space home in a tenement flat which they shared with seven other families. The size of the bed-space occupied by this family of ten was about the size of an ordinary bathroom!

H.M.S. *Belfast* decided to rehouse this family and it was proposed to buy the type of bungalow being built by the World Lutheran Service scheme of resettlement in a suitable rural area. A garden and pigsty would be included in the property and the family would be taught to be self-supporting. The ship's company raised the necessary £250 and early in August the family moved to their new home in the village of Sai Kung on the Kowloon side of the Colony.

We paid our second visit to Hong Kong in November and shortly after our arrival the Captain and Mrs. Giles accompanied a number of the ship's company on a visit to the new house. Mr. and Mrs. Ng Sekcheung and their eight children gave us a very enthusiastic welcome and whilst we were with them the Captain presented a ship's plaque to the family. The mother was delighted to show her house to the visitors and the father was anxious to show them the garden and the pigs and chickens. The whole family was a little overawed by our visit and especially by the number of cameras that were used to record the occasion. The following day the family came to the ship and they had tea in the Junior Rates' Dining Hall. The boys were taken on a tour of the ship and before leaving the children received gifts of toys and clothing. The family are now happily resettled in their new home and the mother has written to express her grateful thanks to the members of the ship's company of H.M.S. *Belfast*.

> 34, Hung Fa Village,
> Sai Kung,
> New Territories.
>
> Dear Captain,
> I thank you with my heart for resettling my family at House No. 34, Hung Fa Village, Sai Kung. The stone cottage is so nice that not only help us to have a house to live in but also there is land for us to cultivate, beside we have a pigsty for raising pigs and at the moment we are raising 3 pigs. Every month Lutheran World Service give us food stuff and help my children to go to school. We live happily at Hung Fa Village now. I with the names of my family members to thank you again.
>
> Wu Hsi Chang, Chang Yao Hsin.

**A Guide Dog for a Blind Person**
A second venture during the commission had been to raise the money to pay for a guide dog for a blind person. Since August a regular fortnightly lottery had been held and large prizes had been handed over to the lucky winners by C.E.R.A. N. Brown (Welfare) who had given much of his time to this work. A proportion of the ticket money had gone to the charity fund and by the time the ship reached home we had reached the necessary target of about £250.

## Japan: Nagasaki, May 24—May 31, 1961
Leaving Hong Kong nostalgically astern, *Belfast* steamed to Nagasaki where she arrived on May 24, a visit to Korea having been cancelled. She entered the harbour on May 27 where she stayed until the end of the month. The Peace Statue on the purported Ground Zero of the atomic bomb blast was a reminder that mankind has to work for peace: it was the laissez-faire attitude of peace-time democracies in the twenties and thirties that led ultimately to the monstrosities of the two atomic bombs. A naval peace-time force, powerful enough to stop aggression and, more importantly, to know what is going on, is the best and most economical means by which to enforce upon an imperfect world the discipline of keeping the peace.

## Kure and Hiroshima: June 1–5
The coloured streamers parted as *Belfast* pulled gently away from the jetty when finally she left Nagasaki on May 31. Through the Shimonoseki Strait to Kure, centre of shipbuilding where, waiting on the jetty for their British sailors, was an attractive reception party: complete with flowers, they had travelled from Nagasaki to meet again their possible future husbands. It was at this time too that the Japanese custom of bowing in salute was temporarily adopted by the ship.

At Kure, transport took the men of *Belfast* to Hiroshima, the rebuilt city and monument to man's folly. On June 6 the ship sailed for Tokyo.

## Tokyo: June 6—July 13, 1961
At the head of an impressive line of ships, *Belfast* sailed majestically through the Inland Sea with its incredibly beautiful scenery and its myriads of islands.

The visit was memorable, if only for the prices. Preparation for the 1964 Olympic Games were in progress, though the Japanese were somewhat sceptical at the proposed date: the height of the typhoon season.

One major crisis developed during the final arrangements of the Squadron's farewell functions for the Japanese: the official cocktail affairs and the children's parties. Up-wind of the anchored frigates, *Rocket* and *Queenborough*, a merchantman suddenly arrived intent on discharging its cargo of soya beans: the parties were doomed to be engulfed in soya dust.

Prompt action postponed the unloading till the morrow, but the incident was inscribed for posterity by the ship's poet (to the tune, "*I think that I shall never see—a poem, lovely as a tree*"):
> "I think that I have never seen
> A frigate spread with soya bean."

The ship sailed on June 14; she was not to see Japan again—*Sayonara* . . .

*Emergency Medical Case.* In company with the Fleet, some ships turning off into Hong Kong during the passage, *Belfast* sailed southwards for her six-monthly docking. When two days out from Singapore, she increased to full speed to land a rating who needed urgent hospital care. The sick man was taken off by pinnace in Singapore Roads and the ship proceeded to the Johore Shoal Buoy. Important acceptance trials on a secret device were about to take place on the morrow.

*Belfast Anti-shark Net, Mark I: Swimmers, for the Use of.* Designed by the Captain and made up by the sail-maker, an anti-shark net was rigged out from the ship's side (see pictorial record by the ship's artist). It was rumoured that if the sharks were hungry they would swallow the corks and netting as an *hors d'oeuvres*, on their way to the main course in the net.

## Singapore Docking and Kuwait Emergency: July 13—August 4, 1961
The ship had de-stored and the Engine Room staff had begun to dismantle machinery, when Iraq began to rattle its machine-guns in the direction of the Sheikdom

*The anti-shark net, Type M/G Mark I.*
(Courtesy Rear-Admiral Morgan Giles)

93

*Homeward bound. Leaving Guam, April 1962.* (MOD)

*Leaving Guam, April 1962.*
(Courtesy Aubrey Bowden, Esq. and IWM)

*A bow view of the ship leaving Guam, April 1962; her paying-off pendant streams to leeward.*
(Courtesy Aubrey Bowden, Esq. and IWM)

of Kuwait which, fourteen days earlier, had been granted its independence. Ships of the FES were diverted to Kuwait; *Belfast*, from being at 48 hours' notice for steam, was ordered to 8 hours' notice. To her credit and to that of the Dockyard staff, she achieved the impossible overnight.

The crisis evaporated a few days later and the ship docked on the date originally planned, July 14. The ship's company went on station leave to the more remote parts of Malaya, invited by the people of that hospitable country.

The refit finally ended, the ship leaving Singapore on August 5, 1961, in company with *Caesar, Carysfort, Crane, St. Bride's Bay* and RFA *Wave Master*.

The Squadron was on its way to take part with the Australian Fleet in Exercise TUCKER BOX. *Belfast* and her smaller consorts, whom she kept supplied with the essentials of life, steamed through the Karimata and Wetar Straits, across the Java and Timor seas and through the Torres Straits to the Great Barrier Reef. Her concern for her accompanying brood caused *Caesar* to make this signal:

From: *D 8*   To: *Belfast*
Date: 22.8.61
  Benediction must be said
  For supplies of eggs and bread
  Smoke markers concealed in bags,
  And bales and bales and bales of rags.
  Nor does this long list define
  All that *Belfast* did,
  She even passed by heaving line
  Tons of simulated squid.

On completion of Exercise TUCKER BOX in the Coral Sea, *Belfast* steamed to Melbourne where she arrived on August 28.

## Australian Cruise:
## August 28—September 14, 1961

*Melbourne.* To a Pommie, Melbourne at first glance was reminiscent of some Midland town—not only the architecture, but the dress and language of the people were familiar—a contrast to the uniqueness of the Orient. The life, however, was very different. The Six O'clock Swill between five and six, when the pubs shut, was the greatest difference with home but the Australian hospitality would never be forgotten.

*Sydney.* To Sydney next, after only four hectic days in Melbourne, the bad weather of the passage being noticed only by those on watch because the residue were asleep.

On September 2, *Belfast,* followed by *Wave Master,* steamed through the Heads on a beautiful morning, the sky clear and blue. Sydney looked its best, the span bridge framing the harbour that was indeed a wonder for those who saw it for the first time. *Belfast* secured alongside in Woolloomooloo Bay.

Sydney's hospitality—that of those Australians who invited "Belfasts" to their homes—some ratings even staying on a sheep station 250 miles away—was its traditional best. The visit was all too short, however, and once again the ship was sailing away from friends: one successful rating, trying to jump on board the ship as the brow was being hoisted, was presented with a gigantic Koala bear by a sorrowing lady on the jetty.

## Singapore again and Exercise FOTEX

"Boomerang" was the ship's company's code name for the passage back to Singapore which was reached on September 26. An official visit was made by King Neptune and his Queen as the ship crossed the line in longitude 106° 21′ East, the traditional rituals of the Kingdom being exercised.

Ten days in Singapore with Self Maintenance and then she prepared for Exercise FOTEX, an intensive sea-going evolution, which was carried out at sea and at Pulau Tioman. Here an important exercise took place: the Fleet Banyan, a colossus of a picnic.

## Hong Kong: Princess Alexandra's visit

An intended visit to Saigon was cancelled, so the ship stayed longer in Singapore than originally planned: on November 2 she sailed for Hong Kong to be present for the visit of HRH Princess Alexandra who reviewed the Fleet from the Commodore's barge, escorted by an Inshore Minesweeper from the Hong Kong Flotilla. *Belfast* provided the Guard at the Cenotaph on Remembrance Sunday and then, on November 22, she sailed for Singapore, en route for Tanganyika for the Independence Celebrations. The Royal Marine Band of the Commander-in-Chief was embarked at Singapore and the ship then proceeded on November 28 to East Africa.

## Gan and Mombasa: December 4, 1961

*Belfast* called at the R.A.F. base at Gan where she exercised her ceremonial drill and where her divers helped to remove obstructions in the harbour. Then on to Mombasa which was reached on December 4 and where Rear-Admiral A. A. F. Talbot, FO Middle East, and his wife joined the ship for passage to Dar-es-Salaam.

Kenya was suffering from severe flooding so the expeditions to climb Kilimanjaro and the visits to Nairobi had to be cancelled. Two days were spent in this happy African country and then she sailed on December 6 for Dar-es-Salaam, with *Rhyl* and *Loch Alvie* in company.

## Royal Representative: Tanganyika
## Independence Celebrations, December 8,
## 1961

*Belfast* was welcomed by thousands of Africans and Europeans when at the early hour of six o'clock on Thursday, December 7, she entered the harbour of Dar-es-Salaam. The Governor of Tanganyika, Sir Richard Timball, came on board to inspect the Guard of Honour provided by the Royal Marines and in the evening, the Prime Minister and his cabinet were entertained on the quarterdeck.

Friday, December 8 was Independence Day when the Duke of Edinburgh, representing Her Majesty Queen Elizabeth the Second, formally granted independence to the country. *Belfast* provided the guard at the hauling down for the last time of the Union Jack and, for the first time, the hoisting of the Tanzanian flag. At this time of writing, when the same ship moors for the final phase of her life opposite the Tower of London, it is still less than ten years since this historic moment in African and world history.

Traditional parties and entertainments took place over the week-end, the Duke of Edinburgh dining with the Admiral on board *Belfast*.

Before the ship left on the next morning, Monday, December 11, the Prime Minister of Tanganyika sent a message of thanks. Thousands thronged the foreshore as *Belfast* steamed symbolically out of the harbour and away, over the horizon, never to return. She called at Mombasa to land Rear-Admiral and Mrs. Talbot and then set course for the Malacca Straits. The Ship's Pantomime enlivened the passage back to Singapore and by the time she returned to the Roads she had steamed over 10,000 miles since leaving Hong Kong; and, from the beginning of the commission since January 1961, 44,314 miles.

## Malayan Waters:
## December 1961—March 25, 1962
Christmas 1961 and New Year were spent in Singapore and then, on January 4, 1962 *Belfast* sailed for Subic Bay and Olongapo in Luzon, where the Americans gave the ship a wonderful welcome, "a foretaste of American hospitality," as one member of the ship's company observed. On passage back to Singapore, the dreaded Sea Inspection by the Admiral's Staff took place, but the ship survived unscathed.

On February 6 *Belfast* left Singapore to visit the small harbour of Penang; then Vizagapatnam, the port in the state of Orissa on the east coast of India, where INS *Circars*—a Boys' Training Establishment—entertained the ship; and finally to Tricomalee in Ceylon to rendezvous with the Fleet for Exercise JET '62.

*JET '62.* The annual large scale SEATO exercise took place in the Indian Ocean, *Belfast* joining in with the ships of five other navies: Indian, Australian, New Zealand, Malayan and, for the first time, three ships from the Canadian Navy. The Fleet was thoroughly exercised in A/S, surface and carrier operations, and anti-atomic defence.

The Fleet returned to Singapore, the Royal Navy acting as hosts to their brother navies: but *Belfast* had, at the same time, to prepare for the Admiral's Departmental and Harbour Inspection which took place on Saturday, March 24, 1962. *Belfast's* account in the Far East had closed.

## Journey Home: March 26—June 19, 1962
On Monday, March 26, 1962, *Belfast* sailed for the last time out of Singapore Roads. Sailing east-about, her passage home was to take almost three months and to remain a memorable cruise for those taking part: across the Pacific, through the Panama Canal, across the Atlantic and Home.

There were only two days in which to say "good-bye" to Hong Kong and to stock up for the last time with "rabbits", those hordes of presents for the families with whom the company were soon to be re-united. Two days is not long, twenty-four hours to each watch for men to acquire tailored garments: "amidst the confusion," so the record goes, "fluttered tailors and shoe-makers, measuring everyone who stood still for more than a couple of minutes."

The ship, to bring men to their senses, sailed out of Hong Kong and straight into appalling weather, the worst she experienced during the whole commission.

For four days the storm raged, then, as suddenly, the blue of the Pacific, a calm and gigantic ocean, stretched ahead from horizon to horizon.

## Guam and Pearl Harbour: April 1962
An all-too-short two days were spent in Guam, the US Navy base in the Marianas, where the ship was made very welcome on passage to Pearl Harbour. *Belfast* crossed the International Date Line, where King Neptune again visited the ship, on Saturday, April 14, and, after ten days' steaming, she arrived in Pearl Harbour on April 18.

Pearl Harbour, an evocative name by any account, is the American Pacific Naval Base. An account of *Belfast's* entry to the harbour is best described by a ship's officer:

"... As we entered Pearl Harbour we were surrounded on all sides by massive carriers, guided missile ships, conventional and nuclear submarines and hosts of smaller ships—a truly impressive sight. We sailed past the famous 'Battleship Row' where seven battleships were sunk or damaged by the Japanese attack in December 1941. One of the battleships, the USS *Arizona,* carried over 1,100 men to the bottom of Pearl Harbour, where they remain entombed to this day. The ship has never been taken out of commission and today a lonely flag marks the spot where *Arizona* lies. HMS *Belfast* paid the normal marks of respect to a ship in commission as we passed by. A memorial to those who lost their lives in the Japanese attack is now being built over the remains of the *Arizona.*"

The magic of Oahu Island captured the visitors from the British cruiser, but England lay ahead: on Easter Sunday, April 22, *Belfast* sailed on her 2,100 mile passage to San Francisco.

## 'Frisco: April 28, 1962
Guarded by the Golden Gate, San Francisco was a city that *Belfast* would never forget: the hospitality was overwhelming and, in return, the ship was opened to vistors who streamed on board in their thousands. *"I left my heart in San Francisco"* was heard floating across the water for weeks after *Belfast* sailed on May 5 for Seattle. The ship would not forget 'Frisco, but it is interesting to read what the Californian San Franciscan thought of HMS *Belfast.*

"Her Majesty, Queen Elizabeth II, had 600 ambassadors of goodwill in San Francisco for the week. These were the officers and men of the ship HMS *Belfast.*

On one occasion while here in San Francisco the ship was host to hundreds of blind and deaf Californians. The crew had voluntarily offered to show the blind around their ship. The men of *Belfast* were extremely gallant to these people. One of the crew, who had his hands full with an extremely large woman who was blind, was most attentive to her condition and should receive special commendation. However, he merely said, 'We are here for goodwill and it is a pleasure to show our ship.'

The men of *Belfast* swarmed over San Francisco and were welcomed into the businesses and the homes of the city as probably no ship ever before. Throughout their stay, no words of reproach have been voiced as to their conduct. Usually, when any of the larger vessels tie up at strange ports, there is resentment of one sort

*Homeward bound, April 1962. The starboard flag hoist indicates her signal letters.* (MOD)

*Course is set for Pearl Harbour, April 1962. An excellent view of her Bofors armament.* (MOD)

*Hands still fallen in on the upper deck, the ship steams for Pearl Harbour.* (Courtesy Aubrey Bowden, Esq. and IWM)

*Leaving Guam, April 1962.* (Courtesy Aubrey Bowden, Esq. and IWM)

or another that leads to at least a little misunderstanding. The crew of *Belfast* conducted themselves in such a manner that no one has anything but good to say of them.

The Commanding Officer of the *Belfast,* her officers, and her crew, are commended for their conduct which reflects nothing but the finest on the Navy and Her Majesty."

## Seattle: May 7, 1962

"On the way to Seattle, *Belfast* gave a very creditable imitation of the *Marie Celeste,* only those on duty being seen above decks . . ." So runs the record: the rest were asleep.

But on Monday, May 7, she steamed majestically into Puget Sound to visit Seattle, Washington State, where the World's Fair was being held. The Sound in the early morning, with the snow peaks of the mountains forming a backdrop in the far distance, the forests running down to the stillness of the water's edge, was a breath-taking sight.

Four sailors, four Royal Marines and two Sergeants RM from *Belfast* were selected to man the British Pavilion in the Fair. When the ship left on May 11 for Victoria, BC, this party was left behind to join later, half in Victoria, half in Panama.

Again, the ship's record should be quoted:

"With the exception of the passage through the Panama Canal, which lay ahead, Seattle represented our last visit to American soil. It must be said that the Americans have no superior anywhere in the world in the realms of hospitality and friendliness. During the commission we visited the Philippines, Guam, Pearl Harbour, San Francisco and Seattle, and always found a tremendous welcome. We can only hope that the Americans enjoyed our company as much as we certainly enjoyed theirs."

## British Columbia:
## Vancouver, Victoria, Esquimalt

Those three wonderful ports of call, all "home" to ships of the Royal Navy and, in particular, those of the America and West Indies Squadron of pre-war days, were visited next.

The CPR Pier in "downtown" Vancouver, where the ship berthed, was not far from HMCS *Discovery,* the RCNR shore establishment. A hectic six days of sport, song and dance followed when, on Thursday, May 17, *Belfast* sailed for Victoria, capital of British Columbia.

She anchored overnight in Pember Sound to arrive at daylight on Friday when the High Commissioner for Canada, Lord Amory, boarded the ship.

The ship proceeded to Esquimalt, the Canadian Navy's Pacific Base, three miles outside Victoria whose Centenary Parade on Monday, May 21, *Belfast* had come to honour.

The Centenary celebrations of service marches, parades (American style), bands and floats took three and a half hours to pass by. *Belfast*'s men were honoured by being privileged to lead the Parade: they were cheered the whole length of the route.

## Panama: June 2–3, 1962

The forests of British Columbia receded astern of her as she sailed south on that Monday morning of May 22. Down the whole length of the North American continent she steamed, in leisurely fashion, unlike another cruise some twenty-four years earlier. During the Munich Crisis of 1938, HMS *York* (later sunk at Crete), Flagship of the A & WI Squadron, had steamed at full speed from Vancouver Island to the Panama Canal in order to intercept a suspected German Pocket-Battleship in the Caribbean.

*Belfast* made the transit of the Panama Isthmus on June 3, 1962. Forty-four miles long, the canal is an incredible feat of engineering considering that it was constructed sixty-five years ago (1906). It rises to 82 ft. above mean low water level (this height is the difference between the two oceans, the Pacific being lower than the Atlantic.

The ship was taken up from Balboa through the locks to the Gatun Lake which is 115 ft. above mean water level: then she was dropped down again into the Atlantic, at Cristobal where she refuelled.

## Port of Spain, Trinidad: June 6, 1962

On the eighteenth anniversary of the Normandy landings, HMS *Belfast* steamed into Port of Spain where she lay for three days at anchor. The attractions of "the limbo" and the steel bands made up for the twenty-minute boat trips. The ship was sad at leaving after three days, when she weighed and began to turn to seaward, at last on her last passage homewards across the Atlantic. At that moment, a man fell overboard; he was wet but unharmed when picked up.

## "And dear the land that gave you birth . . ."

*Belfast* was a few days out into the Atlantic when she received a signal from a merchant vessel asking for urgent medical assistance for a seriously injured seaman. *Belfast* altered course to close the ship but, sadly, the casualty died before a rendezvous was made.

Shortly afterwards, one of *Belfast*'s own company developed acute appendicitis; the ship's Principal Medical Officer operated successfully but, in case of complications, *Belfast* increased speed to reach the nearest hospital ashore.

On Sunday, June 17, the tower of Eddystone climbed above the horizon and there, the red and green topped cliffs of Devon showing behind, stretched the home of Drake: Plymouth and its Hoe.

Refuelling on Monday, June 18 from RFA *Wave Baron,* *Belfast* was clearing the harbour when the Officer of the Watch sighted a body at the foot of the cliffs some distance away. The ship delayed her sailing by sending away a boat and calling up the life-boat and a police launch. The armada converged on the sinister shape which, when within a few yards, sat up and waved: a man and a woman were sharing a sleeping bag.

## "Hoist Paying-off Pendant . . ."

*Belfast* anchored in Spithead during the forenoon of June 19, 1962 when the Custom and Excisemen cleared the ship. Then, her paying-off pendant streaming lazily in the wind, she steamed slowly up the channel, past Fort Blockhouse and Wylie's Tower and into Portsmouth Harbour.

There, on the South Railway Jetty were the families,

*Another aerial view: leaving Guam, April 1962.*

(Courtesy Aubrey Bowden, Esq. and IWM)

friends and relations for whom, for so long, the men of HMS *Belfast* had waited.

A bugle sounded. Turning for'd and aft, the files of men on the upper deck were dismissed. Precisely at 1400, the wires went across.

HMS *Belfast* had come home.

## Home Sea Service 1962

The ship paid off and recommissioned on the same day, July 2, 1962, for Home Sea Service. Captain M. G. R. Lumby, D.S.O., D.S.C., a Submarine Officer, relieved Captain Morgan Giles. On the next day, Vice-Admiral J. G. Hamilton, C.B., C.B.E., Flag Officer Flotillas, Home Fleet, hoisted his flag in *Belfast*. She spent the next six weeks working up her new company but in Devonport on August 16, 1962, the command partnership was changed, due to pressing demands elsewhere.

Captain W. R. D. Gerard-Pearse, M.V.O., relieved Captain Lumby and Rear-Admiral F. R. Twiss, C.B., D.S.C., became Flag Officer.

On August 21, 1962, she sailed from Plymouth to continue with working up exercises in the Channel Area. On October 31 she left Portland, the Fleet Training Base, to pay a courtesy visit to Amsterdam, that great commercial port belonging to one of our most dependable NATO partners.

Four days later, she called at Portsmouth on her way to the City of Belfast, for her last visit on November 23-29, 1962.

She arrived at Greenock on 30th, exercising in the Clyde Area, and finally returned to Portsmouth on December 3 where she gave Christmas leave.

She left Portsmouth for Devonport on January 30, 1963 where she paid off into reserve on February 25. Her sea-going life was drawing to a close.

## Last Commission:
## July 16, 1963—August 23, 1963

It was fitting that she should be commissioned for the last time for service to the officers and men of the Royal Naval Reserve. The Admiral Commanding Reserves, Rear-Admiral H. C. Martell, C.B., C.B.E., hoisted his flag in HMS *Belfast* and, leaving Devonport on July 16, he sailed up Channel to exercise the reserve ship's company by whom she was manned.

She left Portsmouth on August 10 and, with 16 coastal minesweepers, steamed down to Gibraltar, steering southward to the sun for the last time.

She entered the Mediterranean to continue Exercise ROCKHAUL (for the first time W/T and V/S were combined in one Communication Department). Communication exercises, manoeuvring and fleet operations were carried out and then she finally turned back for the Atlantic and The Bay. She reached Devonport on August 24, 1963, where she hauled down an Admiral's flag for the last time. She had finally paid off into reserve: she had earned her rest, having steamed nearly half a million miles during her operational life.

## Reserve

*Belfast* could now see her end, the abyss of the scrapyard looming before her. She could still serve, however, in a passive rôle: she was in Plymouth for Navy Days in August 1965 and, in May 1966, she was moved to Portsmouth where she was re-classified as a Harbour Accommodation Ship for the use of the Reserve Ships Division at Portsmouth.

A floating barracks, she was still serving a vital purpose for the efficient maintenance and disposal of the reserve fleet. For four years, from 1966-1970, she was the living ship for HMS *Bellerophon,* the name of the Portsmouth Division of Reserve Ships.

It seemed at last that her end had come. In 1971, after 32 years of service, she was prepared for her own funeral: on May 4 she was "Reduced to Disposal" and, moored in Fareham Creek, measures began on her last rites.

## Her Last Battle

Quietly, behind the scenes since 1967, a team of devoted men had been working to preserve for the heritage of the nation the last examples of these great ships that had borne the brunt of the defence of our Islands and of civilisation throughout the world.

Eighty years previously, sail had reluctantly moved aside for steam and the all-big-gun-ship. Now it was the turn of these last descendants of the *Dreadnought* era to fade into history. Steam has been overtaken by gas-turbine and nuclear propulsion; the gun, by missile rocketry. Beneath the blanket of the sea there roam the lonely battleships of the present day, the nuclear submarines with their monstrous payloads—but, para-doxically for mankind, keeping the peace.

The Imperial War Museum had already successfully preserved a pair of 15 in. guns which were mounted outside its entrance. Then, in 1967, the Director, Doctor Noble Frankland, and his Staff considered the possibility of preserving a complete 6 in. turret before the species finally vanished. A visit to a turret on board *Gambia,* who was lying in Portsmouth, was made on April 14, 1967, and from that moment was conceived the dream of preserving for the nation an entire cruiser.

*Gambia,* unhappily, had deteriorated rapidly while lying in Fareham Creek for disposal, so attention was centred on *Belfast* in whom the visitors had been entertained to lunch.

A joint Imperial War Museum-National Maritime Museum-Ministry of Defence Committee was set up to report on the practicality of the project. The Committee's work included several nights and many days spent on board the ship, visits to likely berths, technical and historical research, and a world-wide survey of all preserved ships. In June 1968, it reported that the scheme was a practicable and economic one, but early in 1971, their hopes were dashed: the Government decided not to preserve the ship as a national museum.

This decision did not prevent a group of private individuals from trying to save her. THE HMS *BELFAST* TRUST was set up under the chairmanship of Rear-Admiral Morgan Giles, D.S.O., O.B.E., G.M., M.P., the IWM's experience and past work being placed at the disposal of the Trust.

In July 1971, the Government agreed to hand over the ship to the Trust and Vice-Admiral Sir Donald Gibson, K.C.B., D.S.C. was appointed its Director.

## Operation Seahorse

At a Press Conference in the Imperial War Museum on August 17, 1971, the Chairman of The *Belfast* Trust announced officially the plans for *Belfast*'s future: they were designated Operation SEAHORSE, from the emblem of the ship's badge.

The ship was to be towed by private contractors from Portsmouth during the first week in September, up the English Channel for the last time and into Tilbury for a final docking; and then to the dolphins at Hay's Wharf where, opposite the Tower of London, she would lie afloat for years to come.

**OPERATION SEAHORSE: September-October 1971**
The final journey of her sea-going life was planned as follows:

*Wednesday, September 1*
1330   Unmoored from berth in Fareham Creek
1500   Steamed alongside Middle Slip Jetty, HM Dockyard Portsmouth, to disembark unnecessary gear
*Thursday, September 2*
1000   Slipped and proceeded under tow of tugs, bound for Thames Estuary through the Straits of Dover
*Friday, September 3*
        Secured at Lay-by berth in Tilbury
        Fitted out as Museum Ship
*Monday, October 4*
        Entered King George V Dock, Tilbury
*Thursday, October 14*
        Undocked. Towed up river to her permanent berth in the Pool of London

*Trafalgar Day, October 21, 1971*
The First Sea Lord, Admiral Sir Michael Pollock, G.C.B., M.V.O., D.S.C., addressed the assembled company on behalf of the Royal Navy.

Mr. Peter Kirk MP, the Navy Minister, handed over the Ship's Ensign to the Lord Mayor of London, Sir Peter Studd, G.B.E., M.A., D.Sc., who accepted it on behalf of The HMS *Belfast* Trust.

The Ensign was then hoisted where it streamed once again from the ensign staff on the quarter deck.

After thirty-two years, HMS *Belfast* was continuing to serve the nation.

## The Future

". . . not an exercise in nostalgia, but an act of faith for the youth of the future."

With these words, the Chairman of The *Belfast* Trust summed up the object of preserving this ship, the first to be so honoured since Nelson's *Victory*. Twice in our history, this nation has been within weeks of starvation because of blockades to our sea routes. As future generations gaze upon this great ship lying in London River, may they recall with pride the maritime tradition represented by HMS *BELFAST*.

Belfast *alongside Middle Slip Jetty, HM Dockyard, Portsmouth, Thursday, September 2, 1971, having left Fareham Creek the day before.* (Author's collection)

Belfast *clears Wylie's Tower on her final journey up-Channel. The pilot cons the ship from the upper bridge by R/T. The skeleton steaming party is fallen in on the fo'c'sle.* (Author's collection)

*Proceeding up river.* (G. A. Osbon)

Top right
*The tugs have her under complete control before entering the lock.* (G. A. Osbon)

*Entering the King George V Dock, North Woolwich.* (G. A. Osbon)

*Passing under Tower Bridge. Hidden in the overhead structure of the bridge is a man waiting with a hacksaw.* (G. A. Osbon)

*Manoeuvring alongside: the bearer which has been fitted to the hull abreast the bridge will ride up and down on the tide, against the nearer of the two dolphins.* (G. A. Osbon)

## ACKNOWLEDGEMENTS

The author wishes to acknowledge the great debt he owes to those who have given their knowledge, their patience and their encouragement. In particular, he expresses his gratitude to the following:

The HMS *Belfast* Trust.
The Imperial War Museum.
The National Maritime Museum.
The Public Record Office.
The Naval Repository, Hayes, Middlesex.
The Controller, HM Stationery Office, for his permission to reproduce Crown Copyright photographs and diagrams.
The Ministry of Defence.
Rear-Admiral Morgan Giles, D.S.O., O.B.E., G.M., M.P.
Admiral Sir Frederick R. Parham, G.B.E., K.C.B., D.S.O.
Admiral Sir Horace R. Law, K.C.B., O.B.E., D.S.C., *Commander-in-Chief, Portsmouth.*
Lady Burnett.
The Admiral Superintendent, Portsmouth.
The Commanding Officers:
HMS *Collingwood.*
HMS *Dryad.*
HMS *Excellent.*
HMS *Mercury* and DGW(N), DNS.
HMS *Vernon.*
Captain H. E. Howard, D.S.C., R.N., *Captain of the Port, Portsmouth.*
Lieutenant M. Twells, R.N., *Ships' Disposal Officer, Portsmouth.*
Commander Stuart Ferguson, F.I. MechE., R.N. (Ret'd.).
Captain Donald Macintyre, D.S.O.,** D.S.C., R.N. (Ret'd.).
Commander H. G. G. Ogilvie, R.N. (Ret'd.).
Captain Peter Dickens, D.S.O., M.B.E., D.S.C., R.N.
Professor Dr. Jurgen Rohwer.
Lieutenant-Commander M. Ogden, R.N. (Ret'd.) for his kind permission to make use of the battle logs in his book, *The Battle of North Cape,* published by William Kimber Ltd.
Lieutenant-Commander G. R. Potier, D.S.M., R.N. (Ret'd.).
Lieutenant-Commander R. M. Herbert-Smith, R.N. (Ret'd.).
W. P. Brooke Smith, Esq.
The Navy League.
B. H. Palk, Esq., Royal Marines (Ret'd.).
B. T. Batsford Ltd., Publishers.
Arthur Banks, Esq., Mapmaker.
Aubrey Houston Bowden, Esq.
G. A. Osbon, *Department of Pictures, National Maritime Museum, Greenwich.*
John Magee Ltd., Fine Art Dealers, Belfast.
Lieutenant-Colonel H. Wylie, R.S.M.A.
Century Newspapers Ltd., Belfast.

## Bibliography

The War at Sea, Vols. I–II (H.M.S.O.)—S. W. Roskill.
Jane's Fighting Ships—Sampson Low, Marston & Co.
Warships of World War II (Ian Allan)—H. T. Lenton, J. J. Colledge.
The Battle of North Cape (William Kimber)—Michael Ogden.
A Sailor's Odyssey (Hutchinson)—Admiral of the Fleet Viscount Cunningham of Hyndhope.
The Naval War against Hitler (Batsford)—Donald Macintyre.
HMS *Belfast* (paper): (I.W.M.)—Martin Brice, Esq.
HMS *Belfast*: 1961–62—Ship's Magazine.

## Official Records

The Ship's Book and Records—HMS *Belfast.*
The Ship's Covers—MOD and National Maritime Museum.
'Pink Lists' (Disposition of HM Ships)—Admiralty Library.
Ships' Histories—Public Record Office.
Ships' Plans—Imperial War Museum.
Photography—Imperial War Museum,
National Maritime Museum, Greenwich,
Ministry of Defence,
Private collections as credited,
The Controller, HM Stationery Office
Bibliothek für Zeitgeschichte.

## HER CAPTAINS

| | |
|---|---|
| 5.8.39 –4.1.40 | Captain G. A. Scott, D.S.O., R.N. |
| 18.6.40 –19.6.40 | Lt.-Cdr. H. W. Parkinson, R.N. |
| 20.6.40 –4.7.40 | Captain C. M. Blackman, D.S.O., R.N. |
| 3.11.42 –28.7.44 | Captain F. R. Parham, D.S.O., R.N. |
| 29.7.44 –8.7.46 | Captain R. M. Dick, C.B.E., D.S.C., R.N. |
| 9.7.46 –20.11.47 | Captain H. B. Ellison, D.S.O., R.N. |
| 21.11.47–20.1.48 | Commander J. R. Westmacott, R.N. |
| 21.1.48 –21.9.48 | Commander O. S. Stevinson, R.N. |
| 22.9.48 –7.4.50 | Captain E. K. Le Mesurer, M.V.O., R.N. |
| 8.4.50 –22.11.51 | Captain Sir Aubrey St. Clair-Ford, Bt., D.S.O.*, R.N. |
| 23.11.51–26.11.52 | Captain A. C. A. C. Duckworth, D.S.O.*, D.S.C., R.N. |
| 27.11.52–11.1.53 | Commander J. L. Blackham, R.N. |
| 12.1.53 –25.1.53 | Commander A. W. Langridge, D.S.C., R.N. |
| 26.1.53 –1.12.53 | Commander J. C. Richards, D.S.C., R.N. |
| 12.5.59 –30.1.61 | Captain J. V. Wilkinson, D.S.C., G.M., R.N. |
| 31.1.61 –1.7.62 | Captain M. C. Giles, D.S.O., O.B.E., G.M., R.N. |
| 2.7.62 –15.8.62 | Captain M. G. R. Lumby, D.S.O., D.S.C., R.N. |
| 16.8.62 –7.2.63 | Captain W. R. D. Gerard-Pearse, M.V.O., R.N. |

## FLAG OFFICERS

| | |
|---|---|
| 1943 | Vice-Admiral Sir Robert Burnett, K.B.E., C.B., D.S.O. |
| 1944 | Vice-Admiral F. H. G. Dalrymple-Hamilton, C.B. |
| 1945–6 | Rear-Admiral R. M. Servaes, C.B.E. |
| 1946–7 | Vice-Admiral Sir Denis Boyd, K.C.B., C.B.E., D.S.C. |
| 1948–9 | Vice-Admiral A. C. G. Madden, C.B., C.B.E. |
| | Admiral Sir Patrick Brind, K.C.B., C.B.E. |
| 1950–1 | Rear-Admiral W. G. Andrewes, C.B., C.B.E., D.S.O. |
| 1951–2 | Rear-Admiral A. K. Scott-Moncrieff, C.B., C.B.E., D.S.O.* |
| 1959–60 | †Vice-Admiral V. C. Begg, C.B., D.S.O., D.S.C. |
| 1961–62 | †Rear-Admiral M. Le Fanu, C.B., D.S.C. |
| | Rear-Admiral J. B. Frewen, C.B. |
| 1962 | Vice-Admiral J. G. Hamilton, C.B., C.B.E. |
| 1963 | Rear-Admiral F. R. Twiss, C.B., D.S.C. |
| 1963 | Rear-Admiral H. C. Martell, C.B., C.B.E. |

†*Later to become First Sea Lords.*

---

## THE LIFE OF HMS *BELFAST* (*Edinburgh* Class Cruiser)

| | |
|---|---|
| Aug. 1, 1939 | At Belfast, Northern Ireland. |
| Aug. 3, 1939 | Left Belfast for Portsmouth. *(2nd Cruiser Squadron)* |
| Aug. 5, 1939 | Arrived Portsmouth. (To leave Portsmouth Aug. 14 for exercises, returning to the port about Aug. 23). *(2nd Cruiser Squadron)* |
| Aug. 14, 1939 | Left Portsmouth for Humber. *(2nd Cruiser Squadron)* |
| Aug. 21, 1939 | Left Humber for Portsmouth. (Eventually to relieve HMS *Glasgow* in 2nd C.S. Home Fleet). *(2nd Cruiser Squadron)* At Scapa Flow. *(2nd Cruiser Squadron—3rd Division)* At Scapa. *(18th Cruiser Squadron)* *(Under Command of R.A.D. (H.F.))* |
| Aug. 31, 1939 | Left Scapa to patrol (18th C.S.). |
| Sept. 5, 1939 | Left Scapa (18th C.S.). At Scapa (18th C.S.). |
| Sept. 8, 1939 | Left Scapa (18th C.S.). (Sailed from Scapa on Sept. 8, 1939, in company with HM Ships *Hood*, *Renown* and *Edinburgh* to form patrol between Iceland and the Faroes with object of destroying raiders and for contraband control). |
| Sept. 15, 1939 | Arrived Sullom Voe, Shetlands. |
| Sept. 18, 1939 | Left Sullom Voe to patrol. |
| Sept. 20, 1939 | Arrived Scapa. |
| Oct. 1, 1939 | Left Scapa—patrolling. At Scapa. |
| Oct. 2, 1939 | Left Scapa. Captured in 64°N 08'W (50' N.W. of Faroes) the German M.V. *Cap Norte* (13,615 tons) Hamburg Sud-Amerika Line from Pernambuco. |
| Oct. 14, 1939 | Arrived Port A. (In company with HM Ships *Nelson*, *Rodney*, *Hood*, *Furious*, *Aurora* and 10 destroyers covering the Armed Merchant Cruisers of the Northern Patrol). (With H.M. Ships named above covering the Armed Merchant Cruisers off the North East coast of Iceland). |
| Oct. 22, 1939 | Arrived Port A. |
| Oct. 23, 1939 | Left Port A. |
| Oct. 24, 1939 | Arrived Clyde. Clyde—Docking and repairs. Completed Nov. 6 approx. |
| Nov. 6, 1939 | Left Clyde for Rosyth. Rosyth. |
| Nov. 11, 1939 | Left Rosyth (2nd C.S.). (In company with H.M. Ships *Southampton*, *Glasgow*, *Aurora* and 4 Tribal Class Destroyers, left Rosyth 0430 Nov. 11). *(2nd Cruiser Squadron)* |
| Nov. 17, 1939 | Arrived Rosyth. |
| Nov. 21, 1939 | Rosyth—Damaged. (Struck by mine or torpedoes in Firth of Forth). Rosyth—Damaged—Docked. To be paid off. Damage repairs. (To be paid off in C and M Jan. 4, 1940). (Under C-in-C, Rosyth from Dec. 14, 1939). |
| June 1940 | Considered transfer to a port for permanent repair—extensive under-water machinery and electrical damage. (Will require at least 6 months in dock). |
| July 1940 | Rosyth—Damage Repairs—ready for transfer to another port for permanent repairs. (Ready for transfer to Plymouth for permanent repairs which will be completed about June 1941). |

# THE LIFE OF HMS *BELFAST* (Edinburgh Class Cruiser)

| | |
|---|---|
| June 28, 1939 | Left Rosyth for Plymouth. |
| June 30, 1939 | Arrived Plymouth. |
| | *(Western Approaches Command)* |
| | Plymouth—Repairs—Completed in about 12-15 months from July 7, 1940. Plymouth—Dockyard Control—Repairs completed. |
| | *(1st Cruiser Squadron). (Home Fleet)* |
| | Plymouth. |
| Dec. 10, 1942 | Left Plymouth for Scapa. |
| | *(10th Cruiser Squadron). (Home Fleet)* |
| | Scapa. |
| Feb. 17, 1943 | Arrived Seidisfjord. |
| Feb. 19, 1943 | Off Seidisfjord in company with H.M. Ships *Cumberland, Sheffield, Bluebell, Camellia* and destroyers. |
| Feb. 21, 1943 | Left Seidisfjord with H.M. Ships *Cumberland* and *Norfolk* to cover Convoy JW53. |
| | Murmansk. |
| March 2, 1943 | Left Kola Inlet with H.M. Ships *Cumberland* and *Norfolk* to cover Convoy RA53. |
| March 29, 1943 | Left Hvalfjord. |
| | Ordered to reinforce Patrol "White" with HMS *Intrepid*—Search for Blockade Runner. |
| March 30, 1943 | Patrol "White" with H.M. Ships *Glasgow, Intrepid* and *Echo.* |
| April 2, 1943 | Sailed to relieve HMS *Cumberland* on Patrol "White". |
| April 7, 1943 | *Denmark Straits Patrol*—On west coast of Iceland to Patrol "White". |
| April 13, 1943 | *Northern Patrol.* Arrived at Hvalfjord having been relieved on patrol by HMS *Cumberland.* |
| | *(10th Cruiser Squadron). (Home Fleet).* |
| May 27, 1943 | Arrived Scapa from covering mine-laying operations S.N.111B. |
| June 18, 1943 | Arrived Rosyth to give leave and for quick docking. (Ship to sail for Scapa so as to arrive July 1). |
| July 1, 1943 | Arrived Scapa. |
| July 7, 1943 | Sailed from Scapa to the North-Eastward in company with H.M. Ships *London, Kent,* and one destroyer. *Operation "CAMERA".* |
| July 9, 1943 | Arrived Scapa in company with H.M. Ships *London* and *Kent.* |
| July 23, 1943 | Left Scapa. |
| July 29, 1943 | Arrived Scapa. |
| Aug. 15, 1943 | C.S.10 in *Belfast,* screened by H.M. Ships *Onslow* and *Orwell,* left Scapa to create a diversion off the South Norwegian coast. *Operation F.N.* |
| Aug. 17, 1943 | Returned to Skaale Fjord with *Onslow* and *Orwell.* |
| Aug. 22, 1943 | Left Scapa. |
| Aug. 28, 1943 | Sailed from Hvalfjord with H.M. Ships *Norfolk* and *Impulsive* to cover destroyers in *Operation "LORRY".* (Stores and mail to Russia). |
| Sept. 3, 1943 | Returned to Hvalfjord with *Norfolk* and *Impulsive. Operation "LORRY".* Left Halfjord with C.S.10 for Spitzbergen area re enemy raid reported. |
| Sept. 10, 1943 | Arrived Hvalfjord. |
| Sept. 25, 1943 | In vicinity of Reykjanes searching to South-East. *Operation S.F.* |

| | |
|---|---|
| Sept. 27, 1943 | Arrived Scapa. |
| | *(10th Cruiser Squadron). (Home Fleet).* Sailed from Scapa in company with H.M. Ships *Duke of York, Anson,* U.S. Aircraft Carrier *Ranger* and U.S. Heavy Cruiser *Tuscaloosa* to attack shipping targets in the Bodo area with the air striking group from *Ranger.* *Operation "LEADER"* successful. |
| Oct. 16, 1943 | Scapa. |
| Oct. 29, 1943 | Left Scapa. |
| Oct. 30, 1943 | Arrived Seidisfjord with H.M. Ships *Norfolk* and *Kent.* Operation F.R. |
| Nov. 1, 1943 | Left Seidisfjord in company with HMS *Kent* for Akureyri, Iceland to refuel. *Operation F.S.* |
| Nov. 9, 1943 | Arrived Hvalfjord from *Op. F.S.* |
| Nov. 22, 1943 | Left Hvalfjord for Scapa. *Operation F.T.* |
| Nov. 23, 1943 | Arrived Akureyri, Iceland. |
| Nov. 28, 1943 | Left Akureyri, Iceland to cover North Russia convoys, in company with H.M. Ships *Anson, Musketeer, Obdurate, Ashanti* and *Matchless.* |
| Dec. 4, 1943 | Arrived Scapa. |
| Dec. 12, 1943 | Left Aultbea. *Operation F.V.* E.T.A. Seidisfjord 1900 Dec. 13, 1943. |
| Dec. 19, 1943 | Arrived Kola Inlet in company with H.M. Ships *Norfolk* and *Sheffield* from covering Convoy JW55A. |
| Dec. 23, 1943 | Left Kola Inlet to cover Convoy 55A in the Barents Sea. |
| Dec. 26, 1943 | C.S.10 (Vice-Admiral Burnett) in *Belfast* with *Norfolk* and *Sheffield,* while covering a North Russian convoy made contact with *Scharnhorst* about 80 miles South-East of Bear Island—*Scharnhorst* sunk 2035 Dec. 26, 1943. |
| Dec. 30, 1943 | Left Kola Inlet. |
| Jan. 1 1944 | Arrived Scapa with H.M. Ships *Norfolk* and *Sheffield.* (With 19 tons of Russian Bullion). |
| | Rosyth. |
| Jan. 24, 1944 | Left Rosyth for Scapa. |
| | Scapa. |
| March 5, 1944 | Left Greenock. |
| March 6, 1944 | Arrived Scapa. |
| | At sea. |
| April 6, 1944 | Arrived Scapa from *Operation "TUNGSTEN".* |
| | Clyde. |
| April 23, 1944 | Arrived Rosyth. |
| May 8, 1944 | Rosyth—Repairs—Completed. |
| | Scapa. |
| May 31, 1944 | Arrived Clyde. |
| | At Sea. |
| June 6, 1944 | *Operation "NEPTUNE".* In Eastern Task Force. *D-Day Landings.* |
| June 9, 1944 | Successfully attacked enemy concentrations in Normandy. |
| June 12, 1944 | With HMS *Diadem* engaged targets in area Juno. |
| | Sheerness. |
| | At sea. |
| June 18, 1944 | Left Portsmouth. |
| June 30, 1944 | With H.M. Ships *Rodney* and *Argonaut* engaged enemy shore targets in Eastern Sector. |

| | |
|---|---|
| July 1, 1944 | Bombardment Forces—HMS *Belfast* to leave Assault Area.—Due to be taken in hand for docking in Tyne about July 5/6. Arrived Belfast, Northern Ireland. |
| July 6, 1944 | In company with H.M. Ships *Emerald, Roberts* and *Danae* in bombardment force Juno Area because of menace of human torpedoes. |
| July 8, 1944 | Engaged shore targets with H.M. Ships *Rodney* and *Roberts* in support of the Caen offensive. At sea. |
| July 12, 1944 | Arrived Scapa. |
| April 17, 1945 | Tyne refit—completes ex-trials. |
| May 6, 1945 | Arrived Rosyth. Scapa. |
| June 21 1945 | Arrived Gibraltar. Malta—Working up in Mediterranean. To be Flagship, 2nd Cruiser Squadron, British Pacific Fleet. |
| July 27, 1945 | Arrived Port Said from Alexandria. |
| July 28, 1945 | Left Suez for Aden with H.M. Ships *Bleasdale, Cowdray* and *Eggesford*. |
| July 31, 1945 | Arrived Aden. |
| Aug. 1, 1945 | Left Aden. |
| Aug. 6, 1945 | Arrived Colombo. |
| Aug. 7, 1945 | Left Colombo for Australia. *(4th Cruiser Squadron). (British Pacific Fleet).* Sydney. *(2nd Cruiser Squadron). (British Pacific Fleet).* Sydney. Manus. |
| Sept. 10, 1945 | Arrived Kiirun, Formosa. At sea for Shanghai. |
| Sept. 18, 1945 | Arrived and anchored off Yangtse Bar with other ships of Task Group 111.3. |
| Sept. 19, 1945 | Arrived Shanghai. Hong Kong. |
| Sept. 31, 1945 | Arrived Shanghai. |
| March 6, 1946 | Arrived Wellington, New Zealand. |
| March 7, 1946 | Departed for Napier, South Island N.Z. |
| March 11, 1946 | Left Napier for Suva. |
| March 15, 1946 | Arrived Suva, Fiji. |
| March 20, 1946 | Left Suva for Tokyo Bay. |
| April 12, 1946 | Arrived Kure, Japan, wearing Flag of C.S.2. |
| April 17, 1946 | Left Kure for Kobe. |
| April 18, 1946 | Arrived Kobe in company with H.M.A.S. *Warramunga*. |
| April 23, 1946 | Left Kobe for Yokohama with *Warramunga*. |
| April 24, 1946 | Arrived Yokohama. |
| May 2, 1946 | Left Yokohama for Hong Kong, sailing east of Formosa. |
| May 16, 1946 | Arrived Singapore—Refit. |
| July 15, 1946 | Refit completed. *(5th Cruiser Squadron).* |
| Aug. 15, 1946 | Left Hong Kong for visits to Japanese ports. E.T.A. Yokohama Aug. 20, Otura Aug. 28, Kure Sept. 4, Kobe Sept. 11. |
| Sept. 18, 1946 | Arrived Wosung in series of visits to Chinese ports. E.T.A. Wosung Sept. 18, Nanking Sept. 20, Shanghai Sept. 25, Tsingtao Oct. 2, Chinwangtao Oct. 5, Peitaiho Oct. 10, Hong Kong Oct. 14. |
| Oct. 15, 1946 | Arrived Hong Kong. Singapore E.T.D. Dec. 1, 1946. Hong Kong E.T.A. Dec. 6, 1946—Repairs. |

| | |
|---|---|
| March 3, 1947 | Left Kure, Japan E.T.A. Shanghai March 5, 1947, Tsingtao March 17, Hong Kong March 24. *(5th Cruiser Squadron). (British Pacific Fleet).* |
| April 11, 1947 | E.T.D. approx. Hong Kong for Singapore for refit. Singapore. Penang. E.T.A. Malacca June 17, 1947. Singapore June 19, 1947. Hong Kong. |
| Oct. 15, 1948 | Leaves Portsmouth. |
| Oct. 20, 1948 | Arrived Belfast where she remained until Oct. 23 when she proceeded to the Far East to relieve H.M.S. *Sussex* at Hong Kong during December 1948. (While at Belfast, Ship's Bell (silver) presented to the ship by Belfast Corporation). |

DEDICATION AGREEMENT—H.M.S. *BELFAST*

(1) The gift of a Silver Ship's Bell which forms the subject of this Agreement is presented by the citizens of Belfast.

(2) When H.M.S. *BELFAST* is in Commission the gift is to be kept on board in such place as the Commanding Officer may select, and when she is not in Commission is to be deposited with, and kept in the custody of, the Commodore of the Royal Naval Barracks at the Port to which she may be attached.

(3) It is intended that the gift shall be an ornament in H.M.S. *BELFAST* so long as she remains in the Royal Navy, and shall descend to her successors of the same name. If at any time there shall be no ship in the Royal Navy bearing the name of H.M.S. *BELFAST* the gift shall be returned to the custody of the Lord Mayor of Belfast.

DATED this 4th day of January 1949.

*Present when the Corporate*
*Seal of the City of Belfast*
*was affixed hereto.*
*Lord Mayor*
*Town Clerk*

Approved
*Hall*
FIRST LORD OF THE ADMIRALTY

| | |
|---|---|
| Jan. 12, 1949 | Hong Kong—Ship salvaged an R.A.F. jet Vampire which force-landed on Tai Pang Wan beach on the West shore of Bias Bay. A salvage party from *Belfast* hauled her on to a pontoon which was then towed to the ship where the aircraft was hoisted for the passage home. *(Far East Fleet).* Hong Kong. |
| Aug. 8, 1949 | Hong Kong E.T.D. for Malayan Area. E.T.A. Singapore Roads Aug. 16, 1949. Penang Aug. 20. Singapore Dockyard Aug. 26. Hong Kong Sept. 3. E.T.D. Singapore Aug. 29, 1949. E.T.A. Hong Kong Sept. 2. E.T.D. Hong Kong Sept. 9. E.T.A. Kure Sept. 9. E.T.D. Kure Sept. 19. E.T.A. Hong Kong Sept. 23. North China Patrol (F.O.C. 5.C.S. and F.O.2. i/c F.E.S.) Hong Kong. |

# THE LIFE OF HMS *BELFAST* (*Edinburgh* Class Cruiser)

| | |
|---|---|
| Oct. 31 —<br>Nov. 1, 1949 | Assisted Chinese L.S.T. *Cheung Hsai* aground on Pratas Reef and embarked passengers for mainland.<br>Hong Kong.<br>E.T.D. Hong Kong Dec. 9, 1949.<br>E.T.A. Saigon Dec. 12.<br>E.T.A. Hong Kong Dec. 20.<br>E.T.D. Saigon Dec. 17.<br>E.T.A. Hong Kong Dec. 20.<br>E.T.D. Hong Kong Jan. 18, 1950.<br>E.T.A. Singapore Jan. 23 for refit.<br>Singapore—Refit.<br>E.T.D. Hong Kong May 12, 1950.<br>E.T.A. Kure, Japan May 16.<br>*Far East Station Summer Cruise.* |
| May 12, 1950 | Leaves Hong Kong. |
| May 16, 1950 | Arrives Kure. |
| May 20, 1950 | Arrives Yokosuka. |
| June 8, 1950 | Arrives Ominato. |
| June 25, 1950 | Arrives Hakodate. |
| July 1, 1950 | Arrives Okinawa. |
| July 3, 1950 | Arrives Pyongyang. |
| July 13, 1950 | Arrives Sasebo. |
| July 28, 1950 | Arrives Hong Kong. |
| | *War in Korea began June 25, 1950— September 26, 1952*<br>Japanese waters. |
| May 12, 1959 | Recommissioned at Devonport for service on the Far East Station Singapore—<br>Self-refit and docking— |
| Dec. 17, 1959 | Completed. |
| April 28, 1960 | With Far East Fleet in S.E.A.T.O., Exercise SEALION beginning. |
| May 1960 | Visited Inchon, Korea. |

| | |
|---|---|
| July 13, 1960 | Arrived back in Singapore having visited Korea, Japan and Hong Kong. |
| Dec. 5 1960 | Singapore—Completed Refit. |
| Aug. 28, 1961 | Paid visits to various Australian ports (Melbourne Aug. 28, 1961) after exercise in Coral Sea, and returned to Singapore last week in Sept. |
| Sept. 1961 | Arrived Hong Kong.<br>Left Hong Kong for Tanganyika—Independence celebrations, on arriving at Dar-es-Salaam. |
| Dec. 6 1961 | |
| April 22—<br>May 22, 1962 | Sailed from Pearl Harbour, Hawaii—visited San Francisco, Seattle, Vancouver and Victoria, British Columbia. |
| June 19, 1962 | Arrived Portsmouth.<br>Recommissioned for H.S.S. and as Flagship F.O.Flotilla, Home Fleet. |
| Nov. 2–8, 1962 | Visited Amsterdam. |
| Aug. 10, 1963 | Wearing flag of A.C.R., sailed from Portsmouth for the Mediterranean (Exercise ROCK HAUL—R.N.R.)<br>To be retained in Reserve at Plymouth. |
| Aug. 1965 | At Plymouth for Navy Days.<br>To be removed from Reserve and to be reclassified as a Harbour Accommodation Ship for the use of Reserve Ships Division at Portsmouth Reserve Ships—Plymouth Division—H.M.S. *Orion*.<br>Reserve ships—Portsmouth Division—H.M.S. *Bellerophon*.<br>Portsmouth—Living Ship for Reserve Ships. |

**Final Report of circumstances attending the explosion in H.M.S. *Belfast* in the Firth of Forth on Tuesday, November 21, 1939.**

H.M.S. *BELFAST* November 29, 1939

Sir,

I have the honour to forward the accompanying final report in connection with the explosion which occurred in H.M. Ship under my command on November 21, 1939.

2 H.M.S. *BELFAST* sailed from Rosyth at 0917 on Tuesday November 21, in company with the Vice-Admiral Commanding the Second Cruiser Squadron in the *Southampton,* and two destroyers, to carry out an exercise programme in the Firth of Forth.

3 At 1030 the *Southampton* was about to carry out a sub-calibre practice, and at this time the *BELFAST* was 4 cables astern of her; course 025 degrees, speed 17 knots.

4 At 1037 course was altered together to 295 degrees, at 1042 to 115 degrees, and at 1049 to 060 degrees.

5 The rudder had just been put amidships at the conclusion of the last alteration of course—the ship's head at the time being about 065 degrees—when, at 1052, a violent explosion occurred, apparently under the foremast. At this time the *Southampton* bore 030 degrees, approximately $4\frac{1}{2}$ cables.

6 The order "Stop Both" was given, and subsequently "Half-ahead Both" — "Hard-a-Starboard". The ship answered the rudder until she lost steerage way and was put on a course for Inchkeith, but the main engines were out of action from the moment of the explosion.

7 The tracks of both ships are shown from 1035 in Enclosure I on a scale of 1'' to 1,000 yds.

8 The explosion occurred in position 56° 06' 49'', N, 2° 54' 36'', W, in approximately 18 fathoms of water. Little or no tidal stream was running at the time: this position was about 4 cables to the Eastward of the original line of advance of 025 degrees.

9 The weather was calm.

10 The maximum number of lookouts were closed up at the time, and no track of torpedo or discharge bursts was observed; opinions vary as to the number of explosions. Officers situated forward felt one explosion. Some of those aft considered there was more than one explosion, and two columns of water. A large column of water and smoke came up abreast the mainmast starboard side.

11 All doors, valves etc., not already shut, were promptly closed, and preparations were made to be taken in tow. The fresh water system was switched off; and such floats and rafts as were available were prepared for lowering over the side if required.

12 A number of destroyers and escort vessels closed immediately after the explosion, and I ordered them to keep on the move screening round the *BELFAST*.

13 In the meantime every endeavour was being made to ascertain the nature of the damage to the ship, and at 1116 a signal was made to the Commander-in-Chief, Rosyth, to the effect that it was improbable that steam could be raised (vide Enclosure II).

14 By 1133 the Tug *Krooman* had closed to within a cable of the *BELFAST,* and she was ordered to slip the targets which she had been towing, and to take the *BELFAST* in tow. Shortly after 1140 she commenced to tow, and the ship began to move slowly in the direction of Inchkeith. H.M.S. *BELFAST*'s steering gear continued to work normally throughout the operation.

15 At 1148 a further signal was made to Rosyth with the information that the *Krooman* was towing, but that more assistance was urgently required, and at 1259 a more comprehensive signal giving the known state of the ship, and adding that it was essential to drydock immediately, was sent to the Commander-in-Chief, Rosyth.

16 At 1302 the Tug *Brahman* arrived from Rosyth and commenced to tow from forrard with the *Krooman,* and between 1314 and 1333 the Tugs *Grangebourne, Oxcar* and *Bulger* arrived and were secured on port and starboard quarters and on the starboard side amidships respectively.

17 From the moment of the *Brahman*'s arrival H.M.S. *BELFAST* continued to make good progress and Inchkeith was passed at 1411 and the Gate at 1520. At 1700 the *BELFAST* was secured in the lock in Rosyth dockyard, and the work of landing the casualties commenced (vide Appendix IV).

18 The handling of all tugs was good throughout, the operation of taking the *BELFAST* into the lock, conducted by the Tug *Brahman*, being particularly well carried out.

19 H.M.S. *BELFAST* was subsequently moved and secured in dry dock at 2230.

20 In view of the large alterations of course immediately prior to the explosion, and the fact that nothing was seen although a number of His Majesty's Ships were in the vicinity, I consider it most unlikely that the damage was caused by submarine attack. In my opinion, the *BELFAST* struck a mine; possibly more than one, though I do not think this was so.

21 The conduct of all officers and men was beyond praise; there was a complete absence of panic and all work was carried out in a quiet and normal manner. I have, in Appendix X, submitted to you the name of one rating who in my opinion is particularly deserving of your favourable consideration. Furthermore, I desire to draw your especial notice to Commander James Gregson Roper, Royal Navy, my executive officer. I cannot speak too highly of his work as Commander of the ship: his abilities and untiring devotion to duty have, in my judgement, had their reward in that the personnel whom he has trained and the organisation which he has perfected, have reacted in sudden strain and emergency in accordance with the highest traditions of His Majesty's Service.

22 I therefore desire to submit to your special notice the following:-
COMMANDER JAMES GREGSON ROPER, ROYAL NAVY.

I have the honour to be,
Sir,
Your obedient servant
(Signed)        G. A. SCOTT
CAPTAIN, ROYAL NAVY

THE VICE-ADMIRAL COMMANDING
SECOND CRUISER SQUADRON,
H.M.S. *SOUTHAMPTON*

## CHRISTMAS AT SEA, 1943

*(Impressions of Lieutenant W. P. BROOKE SMITH, R.N.V.R. which he wrote at the time)*

JANUARY 4th, 1944.

Christmas Eve, 1943, found H.M.S. *Belfast,* 10,000 ton cruiser, Flagship of Vice-Admiral R. L. Burnett at sea, covering a convoy from Murmansk. The convoy was then approaching the dangerous passage between Bear Island and the North Norwegian Coast, lair of U-Boats and the remnants of the German Battle Fleet. The Flagship had assumed a high degree of readiness which involved all personnel having Action meals of bully-beef and biscuits at their Action Stations and snatching what sleep they could on the decks. As usual in those waters, the weather was bitterly cold and the sea was rough.

These conditions could not dampen the spirits of my crew, perched in a director tower, exposed to the full force of the wind and the spray which was sweeping over the ship. Towards evening, they became sentimental and struck up carols and soon other positions joined in, echoing "Hark the Herald Angels Sing", "The First Nowel" and other old favourites out into the Arctic Sea.

I found a billet in which to get a few hours' rest that night, and rather optimistically hung my sea-boot stocking up. To my delight I found that Santa Claus had put a bar of "nutty" in it when I turned out for my watch, and at midnight some anonymous humorist made an unauthorised broadcast over the loudspeaker system, "I wish you all a Happy Christmas—and many more like it—Ha, Ha, Ha!"

Christmas Day dinner consisted of bully-beef and a boiled potato in jacket. We tried calling the bully-beef turkey, but it tasted the same. At 3 p.m. (by the time we were keeping) the King's Christmas speech was relayed over the ship's broadcast system, and although the wind drowned much of it, the homely words that we heard, as we sat huddled up in our "goon skins" and balaclavas, brought us closer to our families, especially as we knew that they too would be listening to that same voice at home.

**Sunday, December 26th, St. Stephen's Day,** began for me with the Middle Watch. I got in a couple of hours' sleep, had breakfast and then closed up in my director tower with my crew again at 7 a.m. We were destined to remain up there for the next 17 hours without relief.

For 12 months the *Belfast* had patrolled Northern Waters or covered Russian convoys, watching and waiting for the *Tirpitz* or *Scharnhorst* to come out. *Tirpitz* had been damaged by the brilliant and daring midget submarine attack in September, so now we awaited the 26,000 ton battleship *Scharnhorst.*

This was our Admiral's third winter in Northern Waters, and was to be his last trip in command of the Cruiser Squadron before taking up another appointment. I think he prayed very hard to meet the *Scharnhorst,* and, at 10 o'clock on the morning of St. Stephen's Day, we did.

It speaks well of the high pitch of training and anticipation we had achieved that when the first sighting report came through the reactions of my crew were casual and nonchalant. "So the bastard's turned up at last," was all they said. This is what we had been waiting for—the inevitable had arrived.

At least to us it appeared inevitable, but the inevitable doesn't always happen without assistance, and a most brilliant tactical move had been employed to bring us into the path of the *Scharnhorst.* At the first suspicion that she might be out (*Intelligence received on Christmas Eve— Author*), the Commander-in-Chief had diverted the convoy to the North and had ordered our Force, consisting of the two six-inch cruisers, *Belfast* and *Sheffield,* and the eight-inch cruiser, *Norfolk,* to take its place. *Scharnhorst,* lying in wait in the darkness of an Arctic morning like a wolf for its prey, found instead three cruisers to contend with.

The Commander took advantage of a respite to have Action dinner served out—"Mystery" pie, as the troops called it. It was on this occasion that the Gunnery Officer broadcast from his Control Tower to all his Quarters, facetiously perhaps, "There will now be a lull in the action while the Gunnery Officer eats his lunch". Half-an-hour later a plaintive voice came through the Multiphone from the Royal Marine's Turret "Ain't it about time the Gunnery Officer finished his dinner and we got on with the action?"

Dawn was now breaking, but there was no sun, and for two hours we enjoyed the light of Arctic day, light just sufficient to read a newspaper by, I suppose.

We contacted the enemy again, and then began a running battle through those dark wintry seas, that was to result in the destruction of Germany's last effective capital ship. It is difficult to describe the eeriness of that engagement, the slow descending flares of star-shells, the flash of the guns, their noise, and the sound of the wind screaming through the rigging and the seas breaking against the ship as we raced on in pursuit at 30 knots. Occasionally, from my tower I could see the *Scharnhorst,* but mostly it was the yellow flames from her guns and the pin-prick flashes denoting hits, that indicated her position.

Being a cruiser force was comforting as we always imagined that the enemy would be firing at the others. But suddenly my layer called out, "Look at that, sir!" and I saw great columns of water rising in our wake, a cable-length away. My crew's reaction was comical: "The ROTTEN swine! They're firing at US!" they said with great indignation.

Throughout the action, as the secondary armament which I controlled was not employed in engaging the enemy, I was a spectator and passed a running commentary through my 'phones to the men on the Gunnery Table below. One of the crew there took it down in short-hand and typed it out afterwards. "That last one landed astern," I passed, "all right for range but out for line. There! She's fired again." The Petty Officer in charge below took out his watch and counted off the seconds. "If she's made the right correction, the next salvo should hit— now!" But nothing happened. The German Gunnery Officer made a mistake in his drill, and we breathed again.

Everything had been so unreal until now that I hadn't given a thought to the possibilities of being hit. But now I must confess that I felt a twinge of fear—at least, if a tremor in the legs and a sinking feeling in my stomach meant fear. I never for a moment lost faith but I began to feel rather naked and exposed with eleven-inch bricks whistling about. I thought of my family and girl-friend. I offered up a silent prayer. It seems at moments like this as if the enemy is shooting at you personally. One feels that one could well dispense with the honour of being an Aunt Sally for the German Navy!

At this juncture, *Norfolk* received a hit which caused her to fall back temporarily to cope with the minor damage inflicted, and we had outstripped the *Sheffield.* The Admiral made a whimsical little signal "Am all alone," to the Commander-in-Chief, who was now racing up in his Flagship, *Duke of York,* to cut off the *Scharnhorst* from her base. We stopped firing and received her full attention, but the redoubted German gunnery had sadly fallen off, for, although we had several near misses, we received no damage.

Our Admiral now ordered a signal to be made to the Commander-in-Chief, "Dinner is now served," but then, thinking that Admiral Bruce Fraser in the *Duke of York,* being at that time on the point of engaging the enemy, might have too much to think about to appreciate its humour, our Admiral belayed the signal, a signal which might well have gone down in history.

We now illuminated the *Scharnhorst* with star-shell for the *Duke of York* and a great cheer went up from the upper deck when an orangy-red sheet of flame from *The Duke* announced that she had joined battle. "Whoa, Neddy," said my range-taker, "*Scharnhorst* should come up all standing now." We imagined her reining back hard, bewildered at this sudden unexpected development. There were in fact now two courses open to her, to double back and break through the cruisers, or to try to outstrip *The Duke*. The former course would have brought her to a close-range battle with us, but she chose the latter. As the Commander-in-Chief said to us afterwards—"She wasn't afraid of me in *The Duke*, but she ran away from the *Belfast!*" And so for the next hour the heavyweights pounded away at each other. Miraculously, *The Duke* escaped with no worse damage than a hole through each of her masts, but her superb gunnery must have made a shambles of *Scharnhorst*'s decks.

We watched this "ding-dong" battle with great enthusiasm from my tower, but after a time it seemed to get monotonous, so we trained the tower aft to get more shelter from the wind. I'm ashamed to say that we professed to be bored in the middle of one of the most decisive actions of the War!

But our interest quickly revived when we heard that the destroyers were going in. That they had reached their target was indicated by a terrific burst of firing from the *Scharnhorst*. She was firing everything she had on both sides, a last agonizing effort to stave off defeat, from her big guns to multiple Bofors, which made a rare spectacle with their stream of red tracers. The anti-aircraft guns were firing H.E. timed to explode fifty to a hundred feet above the water. "A regular Brock's benefit," as one of my crew said. It was certainly more impressive than any fire-work display I have ever seen. I'm sure we all offered up a silent prayer for the men in the "boats." It is by far and away the most gallant feat I have ever witnessed. The *Saumarez*, under fire for eight miles though damaged, closed in to 9 cables to fire her tin-fish. The Norwegian destroyer *Stord* went even closer—to 6 cables—to hit the *Scharnhorst* with at least one torpedo. It was very fitting that the Norwegians should have had the chance of avenging some of their Country's agony on a German Battleship within 60 miles of the occupied Norwegian Coast.

*Scharnhorst* now had a large fire raging amidships and was being heavily pummelled by the *Duke of York* when the Commander-in-Chief signalled the *Belfast* and *Jamaica* to go in and finish her off. We closed in to short range and fired our torpedoes. *Scharnhorst* was still firing her main armament. Then suddenly she ceased firing and the fires went out. There were no star-shells in the air to illuminate the scene at that moment. I passed down through my 'phones "Damn—they've managed to put the fires out." We fired a star-shell, but there was nothing to be seen. Nobody had actually seen her sunk. There had been no big flash of an explosion, although several underwater ones were heard. She had slid under in obscurity. It came as rather an anti-climax. It was all over. We could not realise it until we steamed into a mass of wreckage. Lights were shining on rafts with survivors clinging on to them. A pall of smoke hung over the scene. The sea, illuminated now by our searchlights, was strangely calm. The strong tarry smell of fuel oil was nauseating.

Despite the risk from U-Boats, our Admiral, reminding himself of Nelson's great prayer: "May humanity after victory be the predominant feature of the British fleet", ordered 2 destroyers to pick up survivors, of whom 36 out of a complement of over 1,400 were saved.

We hadn't very much room for sentiment for the foe when we thought what havoc she would have made of the helpless merchantmen in the convoy. The men, exhausted but exhilarated, were now fallen out to sleep, but first were issued with their tots of rum which it had been impossible for them to have at mid-day. Our only casualty was the Admiral's reindeer which was driven wild by the gunfire and had to be shot.

On return to harbour, many were the congratulations we received—but the best signal of the day was from the Commander-in-Chief, "Splice the Main Brace," which we did in truly Naval fashion.

In the Wardroom, after dinner that evening, a solemn toast was proposed, "To the *Scharnhorst*," and we gravely drank to our enemies who, though misled, had put up a gallant fight and had gone down with their guns firing, as we know we would have done had the fate of the battle been otherwise.

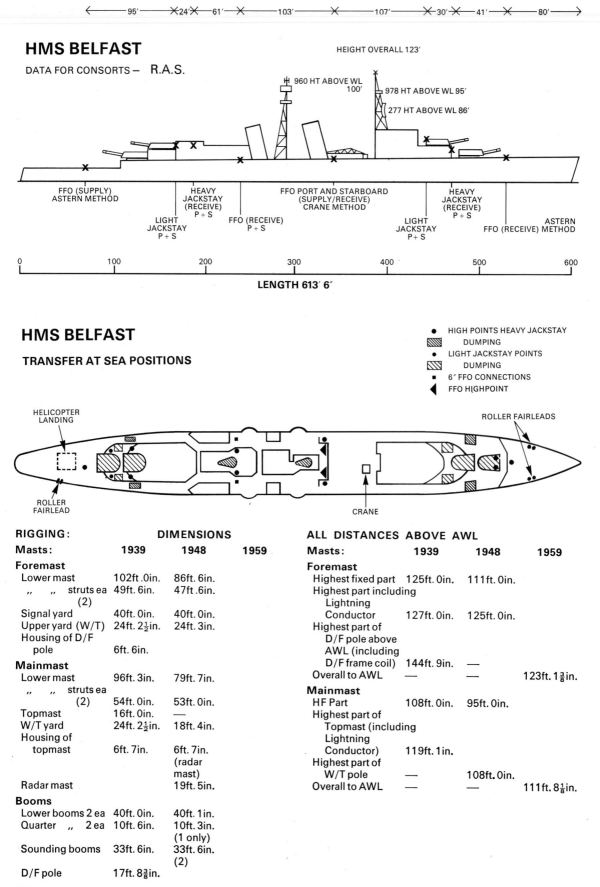

# HMS BELFAST

95' — 24' — 61' — 103' — 107' — 30' — 41' — 80'

DATA FOR CONSORTS – R.A.S.

HEIGHT OVERALL 123'

960 HT ABOVE WL 100'
978 HT ABOVE WL 95'
277 HT ABOVE WL 86'

FFO (SUPPLY) ASTERN METHOD — HEAVY JACKSTAY (RECEIVE) P + S — LIGHT JACKSTAY P + S — FFO (RECEIVE) P + S — FFO PORT AND STARBOARD (SUPPLY/RECEIVE) CRANE METHOD — LIGHT JACKSTAY P + S — HEAVY JACKSTAY (RECEIVE) P + S — FFO (RECEIVE) — ASTERN METHOD

0    100    200    300    400    500    600

LENGTH 613' 6"

# HMS BELFAST

## TRANSFER AT SEA POSITIONS

- ● HIGH POINTS HEAVY JACKSTAY
- ▨ DUMPING
- • LIGHT JACKSTAY POINTS
- ▨ DUMPING
- ■ 6" FFO CONNECTIONS
- ◀ FFO HIGHPOINT

HELICOPTER LANDING
ROLLER FAIRLEADS
ROLLER FAIRLEAD
CRANE

| RIGGING: | DIMENSIONS | | |
|---|---|---|---|
| Masts: | 1939 | 1948 | 1959 |
| **Foremast** | | | |
| Lower mast | 102ft .0in. | 86ft. 6in. | |
| „  „  struts ea (2) | 49ft. 6in. | 47ft .6in. | |
| Signal yard | 40ft. 0in. | 40ft. 0in. | |
| Upper yard (W/T) | 24ft. 2½in. | 24ft. 3in. | |
| Housing of D/F pole | 6ft. 6in. | | |
| **Mainmast** | | | |
| Lower mast | 96ft. 3in. | 79ft. 7in. | |
| „  „  struts ea (2) | 54ft. 0in. | 53ft. 0in. | |
| Topmast | 16ft. 0in. | — | |
| W/T yard | 24ft. 2½in. | 18ft. 4in. | |
| Housing of topmast | 6ft. 7in. | 6ft. 7in. (radar mast) | |
| Radar mast | | 19ft. 5in. | |
| **Booms** | | | |
| Lower booms 2 ea | 40ft. 0in. | 40ft. 1in. | |
| Quarter „ 2 ea | 10ft. 6in. | 10ft. 3in. (1 only) | |
| Sounding booms | 33ft. 6in. | 33ft. 6in. (2) | |
| D/F pole | 17ft. 8⅜in. | | |

| ALL DISTANCES ABOVE AWL | | | |
|---|---|---|---|
| Masts: | 1939 | 1948 | 1959 |
| **Foremast** | | | |
| Highest fixed part | 125ft. 0in. | 111ft. 0in. | |
| Highest part including Lightning Conductor | 127ft. 0in. | 125ft. 0in. | |
| Highest part of D/F pole above AWL (including D/F frame coil) | 144ft. 9in. | — | |
| Overall to AWL | — | — | 123ft. 1⅜in. |
| **Mainmast** | | | |
| HF Part | 108ft. 0in. | 95ft. 0in. | |
| Highest part of Topmast (including Lightning Conductor) | 119ft. 1in. | | |
| Highest part of W/T pole | — | 108ft. 0in. | |
| Overall to AWL | — | — | 111ft. 8⅛in. |

## Ship Handling Characteristics

1 The ship handles very well, but she is a heavy ship and takes some stopping.

2 When steadying on a new course, "Midships" 10° before, and opposite wheel 3-5° before for slow swing, and 5-7° before for a fast swing.

3 She has a fairly quick roll and is rather wet.

4 The following reductions in speed have been used:

| (a) Anchoring | 10 cables | 8 knots |
|---|---|---|
| | 3 cables | Stop |
| | 1 cable | Slow astern; increasing to half astern as necessary |
| (b) Mooring | 10 cables | 8 knots |
| | 2 cables | Stop |
| | Let go (First ⚓) | Slow astern |
| (c) Coming to a buoy | 10 cables | 8 knots |
| | 3 cables | Stop |
| | 1½ cables | Slow astern |
| (d) Going alongside | 8 cables | Slow ahead |
| | 2 cables | Stop |
| | 1 cable | Slow astern; increasing to half astern as necessary |

These distances have been used when steaming on 4 shafts with 4 boilers connected. Should only two boilers be connected it is necessary to start going astern about a quarter of a cable earlier.

5 There is quite a noticeable difference in the acceleration when four boilers are connected and when two are connected. Gain and loss of speed allowances under normal circumstances and in speeds range 8-20 knots have been:

(a) With normal rate of increase/decrease 55 yards per knot

(b) With E.R. using timed increase/decrease 80 yards per knot

In practice if the E.R. are given warning the 55 yard per knot figure is fairly good, but a good deal depends on the personalities in the engineroom.

When accelerating with four boilers connected use 55 yards per knot figure, and when accelerating with two boilers connected rather more should be allowed and 60 yards/knots is a fair estimate for an increase in speed.

6 If only two shafts are connected turning at rest becomes a very tedious affair, and should only be attempted if there is no leeway problem.

Otherwise for turning at rest 80 revs ahead and 90 revs astern with 20 wheel has been found satisfactory. The ship is slow to turn, though, when dead stopped and due allowance should be made when leaving harbour in formation, as *BELFAST* always seems to take longer than anyone else to get pointed.

7 Sternboards.

This has been tried with success in Grand Harbour. The ship turned in the entrance with a little headway on between St. Elmo breakwater and Ricasole point. Having pointed the stern down harbour, 120 revs astern were rung on and the ship having gathered sternway steered quite well. When 720 feet from the required stopped position engines were rung on to half ahead 150 revs, and the ship stopped in the required position.

This method of approaching the buoy was quicker than approaching the buoys direct and turning in the berth.

8 Weighing.

Caution is needed when weighing to avoid the cable getting jammed on the P.V. ram on the forefoot. Should the cable be growing around the bow it is advisable to point the ship to open the hawse or give the ship a kick astern to achieve the same effect. This should be particularly guarded against when weighing in company.

9 Suez Canal.

The ship was a little sluggish at 7½ knots (canal speed) but stable. At 106 revs (12 knots) in the southern part of the canal steering became a little erratic (tide was against). The most comfortable speed seemed to be between 86 and 96 revs on four shafts. Some opposite wheel was needed occasionally on the turns but the ship did not take a sheer. 19 knots were rung on through the Bitter Lakes with no adverse effect.

10 Approaching a buoy with two shafts only.

The following plan was used with success in calm conditions, with two boilers connected.

| 10 cables | 8 knots |
|---|---|
| 8 cables | Slow |
| 3 cables | Stop |
| 1½ cables | Slow astern |
| 1¼ cables | Half astern (80 revs) |

*Cut off distances*

| | |
|---|---|
| From G.D.P looking directly ahead | 32 yards from bow |
| From G.D.P looking directly astern | 35 yards from stern |
| From Compass platform looking ahead | 58 yards from bow |
| From Compass platform looking astern | 61 yards from stern |

## H.M.S. *BELFAST*, EXTRACT FROM REPORTS OF STEAM TRIALS (FORM D.408) (MAY–JUNE 1939)

| Nominal S.H.P. | Means of Measuring Mile Runs | | | Fuel Consumption Tons per hour | | | Steam Consumption Lbs. per H.P. Hour | | Water Loss | |
|---|---|---|---|---|---|---|---|---|---|---|
| | Mean Revs. | Mean Speed | Mean S.H.P. | By Tanks | By Sprayers | Main Engines | Auxiliaries | All Purposes | lbs./H.P. Hour | Tons/1,000 H.P. per 24 hrs. |
| 80,000 | 293·7 | 32·975 | 81,075 | 26·1 | 26·96 | 8·106 | 1·194 | 9·25 | 0·066 | 0·707 |
| 64,000 | 275·9 | 31·291 | 63,832 | 19·91 | 20·65 | 8·06 | 1·223 | 9·33 | 0·089 | 0·955 |
| 48,000 | 253·3 | 29·388 | 47,638 | 15·8 | 15·98 | 8·523 | 1·36 | 9·928 | 0·896 | 1·026 |
| 32,000 | 226·2 | 26·332 | 31,992 | 12·32 | 11·5 | 8·77 | 1·41 | 10·306 | 0·126 | 1·35 |
| 24,000 | 205 | — | — | 8·8 | 8·0 | 9·044 | 1·35 | 10·48 | 0·091 | 0·975 |
| *C*20,000 | 196·4 | 23·358 | 20,082 | 7·0 | 7·0 | 8·97 | 1·306 | 10·495 | 0·137 | 1·47 |
| *C*14,000 | 175·6 | — | — | 5·96 | 5·22 | 9·198 | 2·05 | 11·468 | 0·203 | 2·17 |
| 10,000 | 157·3 | 18·99 | 10,033 | 4·78 | 4·78 | 13·57 | 2·74 | 16·574 | 0·253 | 2·71 |
| *C* 8,000 | 146·6 | — | — | 3·6 | 3·4 | 10·24 | 1·683 | 12·185 | 0·363 | 0·389 |
| *C* 3,000 | 106·2 | — | — | 1·99 | 2·07 | 14·997 | 3·779 | 19·93 | 1·036 | 11·21 |
| 3,000 | 100·7 | 12·99 | 3,082 | 2·7 | 2·65 | 17·88 | 8·74 | 27·58 | 0·923 | 9·89 |

(*C* = With Cruising Turbines connected).

## Steaming arrangements

The following arrangements of engines and shafts were available:

| Turbines | Boilers | Shafts | Controlling Engineroom | Use |
|---|---|---|---|---|
| Main | Four | Four | Forward E.R.—outer shafts<br>After E.R.—inner shafts | Manoeuvring and pilotage |
| Main | Two | Two | Either Forward E.R.—outers<br>or after E.R.—inners | Passage speeds 15 to 22 kts. required |
| Cruising | Two | Two | Either Forward E.R.—outers<br>or after E.R.—inners | Economical steaming |
| Cruising | Two | Four | Forward E.R.—outer shafts<br>After E.R.—inner shafts | Passage speeds up to 20 kts |

## MACHINERY

### Boilers

Four Admiralty 3-drum with superheaters and air pre-heaters.

### Main engines

Four Parson's type geared turbines made by Harland and Wolff, designed to produce 80,000 s.h.p.

Gear ratios:  High pressure  11·2 to 1
Low pressure  8·03 to 1
Cruisers to high pressure  2·77 to 1

### Evaporators

Two twin shell evaporators by G. & J. Weir (6 tons/hour). One auxiliary single shell.

### Auxiliary machinery

Three Turbo generators by W. H. Allen (350 kW).
Two Diesel generators by Paxman (230 kW).
Four High Pressure air compressors.
Two Low Pressure air compressors.
One Vao air-conditioning plant.
One Diesel generator by G.C.E. (400 kW).

## FUEL EXPENDITURE AND RANGE

Six months out of dock, temperate waters

### Four boilers, four shafts

| Speed | Revs | Fuel expended tons/hour | Miles Range |
|---|---|---|---|
| 10 | 88 | 4·1 | 5,380 |
| 11 | 96 | 4·5 | 5,390 |
| 12 | 104 | 4·9 | 5,400 |
| 13 | 112 | 5·3 | 5,420 |
| 14 | 120 | 5·6 | 5,500 |
| 15 | 128 | 6·1 | 5,400 |
| 16 | 138 | 6·6 | 5,333 |
| 17 | 146 | 7·1 | 5,270 |
| 18 | 154 | 7·6 | 5,202 |
| 19 | 164 | 8·7 | 4,807 |
| 20 | 174 | 9·6 | 4,583 |
| 21 | 184 | 10·7 | 4,325 |
| 22 | 194 | 12·0 | 4,040 |
| 23 | 204 | 13·2 | 3,840 |
| 24 | 214 | 14·8 | 3,570 |
| 25 | 224 | 16·4 | 3,355 |
| 26 | 236 | 18·6 | 3,080 |

*Figures above dotted line are for cruising turbines.*

### H.M.S. *BELFAST*

Table showing particulars of steaming at *Standard Displacement* with *Clean Bottom*.

| Knots | Revs. | S.H.P. | No. of Boilers | Fuel Tons/hour |
|---|---|---|---|---|
| 5 | 47 | | 1 | |
| 6 | 53 | | | |
| 7 | 60 | | | |
| 8 | 67 | | | |
| 9 | 74 | | | |
| 10 | 82 | 2,000 | | 2·6 |
| 11 | 90 | 2,300 | | 2·66 |
| 12 | 98 | 2,600 | | 2·76 |
| 13* | 106 | 3,000 | | 2·89 |
| 14 | 115 | 3,600 | | 3·05 |
| 15† | 124 | 4,400 | | 3·25 |
| 16 | 132 | 5,400 | | 3·5 |
| 17 | 141 | 6,600 | | 3·8 |
| 18 | 150 | 8,000 | | 4·3 |
| 19 | 158 | 10,000 | 2 | 4·8 |
| 20 | 167 | 11,600 | | 5·5 |
| 21 | 176 | 13,800 | | 6·2 |
| 22 | 185 | 16,400 | | 7·0 |
| 23 | 194 | 19,400 | | 7·8 |
| 24 | 203 | 22,600 | | 8·7 |
| 25 | 212 | 26,300 | 3 | 9·7 |
| 26 | 221 | 30,700 | | 11·0 |
| 27 | 231 | 35,400 | | 12·2 |
| 28 | 241 | 41,000 | | 13·5 |
| 29 | 251 | 47,500 | 4 | 15·0 |
| 30 | 261 | 54,600 | | 16·8 |
| 31 | 271 | 62,800 | | 19·0 |
| 32 | 282 | 71,000 | | 21·7 |
| 33 | 293 | 81,000 | | 27·0 |

*Authorised Economical Speed.
†Actual Economical Speed for above conditions.

This table agrees with Steaming Curves from Contractor's Trials 1939

### Two boilers, two shafts

| Speed | Revs | Fuel expended tons/hour | Miles Range |
|---|---|---|---|
| 10 | 104 | 3·0 | 7,350 |
| 11 | 112 | 3·3 | 7,320 |
| 12 | 122 | 3·7 | 7,160 |
| 13 | 132 | 4·2 | 6,810 |
| 14 | 142 | 5·1 | 6,050 |
| 15 | 152 | 5·8 | 5,700 |
| 16 | 162 | 6·5 | 5,400 |
| 17 | 172 | 7·3 | 5,120 |
| 18 | 184 | 8·6 | 4,620 |

*Figures above dotted line are for cruising turbines.*

| | Speed | Revs | Tons/hour | Range |
|---|---|---|---|---|
| Authorised full power | 30 | 275 | 30 | 2,200 |
| With all despatch | 29 | 270 | 27·3 | 2,340 |
| With despatch | 26 | 256 | 18·6 | 3,080 |
| With all convenient despatch | 23 | 204 | 13·3 | 3,810 |
| With moderate despatch | 19 | 164 | 8·6 | 4,880 |
| Economical (2 shafts) | 10 | 104 | 3·0 | 7,350 |

## FIRST GROUP—*SOUTHAMPTON* (TOWN) CLASS: 9,100 tons

| | Built | Fate |
|---|---|---|
| *Newcastle* (ex-*Minotaur*) | 23.1.36 Vickers Armstrong (Tyne & Barrow) | Scrapped 1959 |
| *Southampton* (ex-*Polyphemus*) | 10.3.36 Clydebank | Sunk by bombing Med 11.1.41 |
| *Birmingham* | 1.9.36 Devonport | Scrapped 1960 |
| *Glasgow* | 29.6.36 Scotts | Scrapped 1960 |
| *Sheffield* | 23.7.36 Vickers Armstrong | Scrapped 1970 |

Dimensions: $591\frac{1}{2}$ (oa) $\times$ $61\frac{3}{4}$ $\times$ 17

Machinery: 4-shaft geared turbines, SHP 75,000 = 32kts.

Protection: Main belt 3-4in., Deck 2in., turrets 1-2in., DCT 4in.

Armament: 12-6in. (4 $\times$ 3), 8-4in. HA (4 $\times$2) 8-2pdr. AA (2 $\times$ 4) 8-0·5in. (2 $\times$ 4) 6-21in. (2 $\times$ 3) TT 3 Aircraft

Complement: 700

## SECOND GROUP—*SOUTHAMPTON* (TOWN) CLASS: 9,400 tons

| | Launched | Fate |
|---|---|---|
| *Liverpool* | 24.3.37 Fairfield | Scrapped 1958 |
| *Manchester* | 12.4.37 Hawthorn Leslie | Sunk by E-boat off Hammamet, Tunisia 13.8.42 |
| *Gloucester* | 19.10.37 Devonport, Scotts | Sunk by bombing Crete 22.5.41 |

Dimensions: $591\frac{1}{2}$ (oa) $\times$ $62\frac{1}{4}$ $\times$ $17\frac{1}{2}$

Machinery: 4-shaft geared turbines, SHP 82,500 = $32\frac{1}{2}$kts.

Protection: Main belt 3-4in., Deck 2in., turrets 1-2in., DCT 4in.

Armament: 12-6in. (4 $\times$ 3), 8-4in HA (4 $\times$ 2) 8-2pdr. AA (2 $\times$ 4) 8-0·5in. (2 $\times$ 4) 6-21in. (2 $\times$ 3) TT 3 Aircraft

Complement: 700

## THIRD GROUP—*EDINBURGH* CLASS: 11,550 tons

| | Launched | Fate |
|---|---|---|
| *Belfast* | 17.3.38 Harland & Wolff | Preserved by HMS *Belfast* Trust, Port of London, 1971 |
| *Edinburgh* | 31.3.38 Swan Hunter | Sunk by U-456 and destroyers, Russian convoy to QP 11: 2.5.42 |

Dimensions: $613\frac{1}{2}$ (oa) $\times$ 66 $\times$ 19

Machinery: 4-shaft geared turbines, SHP 80,000 = 32kts.

Protection: Main belt 3-4 in., Decks over magazine: 3in. Over machinery and upper and lower decks: 2in.

Armament: 12-6in. (4 $\times$ 3) 12-4in. HA (6 $\times$ 2) 16-2pdr. AA (2 $\times$ 8 ) pom-poms 8-0·5in. AA (2 $\times$ 4) 6-21in. (2 $\times$ 3) TT 3 Aircraft

Complement: 881 (Flagship) 781 (Private ship)

# Index

All matters relating to HMS *Belfast* are to be found under the heading *Belfast* in the main index.
Ship classes (e.g. *London*-class) are to be found in the main index. Individual ships (e.g. HMS *London*) are in the Index of Ships.